THE
CHARISMATIC
MOVEMENT

edited by
Michael P. Hamilton

William B. Eerdmans Publishing Company ● Grand Rapids

Reprinted, May 1977

Library of Congress Cataloging in Publication Data

Hamilton, Michael Pollock, 1927-
  The charismatic movement.

  Includes bibliographical references.
  1. Pentecostalism—Addresses, essays, lectures.
I. Title.
BX8764.Z6A2   270.8'2   74-14865
ISBN 0-8028-3453-1
ISBN 0-8028-1589-8 (pbk.)

Some paragraphs in the chapter by Dr. Nathan L. Gerrard have appeared in previous articles and are used with the permission of the University of Pennsylvania Press and the editors of Society.

Contents

Preface   Canon Michael Hamilton   7

THE CHARISMATIC MOVEMENT IN THE CHURCH
   1: The Gifts of the Holy Spirit   *The Rev. Dennis J. Bennett*   15
   2: Controversial Aspects of the Movement   *Dr. James C. Logan*
      33

THE BACKGROUND FOR UNDERSTANDING THE MOVEMENT
   3: The New Testament Evidence   *Dr. Krister Stendahl*   49
   4: A History of Speaking in Tongues and Related Gifts   *Dr.*
      George H. Williams and Edith Waldvogel   61
   5: The Charismatic Gifts in Worship   *Dr. Josephine Massyng-*
      berde Ford   114
   6: Psychological Observations   *Dr. John P. Kildahl*   124

TWO AMERICAN EXPRESSIONS
   7: The Black Pentecostal   *Dr. Lawrence N. Jones*   145
   8: The Holiness Movement in Southern Appalachia   *Dr. Nathan*
      L. Gerrard   159

THE IMPACT OF CHARISMATICS ON THE LOCAL CONGREGATION
   9: A Story of Integration   *The Rev. Raymond W. Davis*   175
  10: A Story of Division   *The Rev. Frank Benson*   185

Bibliography   195

Preface

In the last ten years there has been an extraordinary worldwide growth in Pentecostalism. Even more surprising, charismatic groups have emerged within non-Pentecostal denominations. Roman Catholics, Lutherans, Methodists, and Episcopalians all now have charismatics in their membership. The term *charismatic* applies to those who have experienced a "baptism of the Holy Spirit" that involves receiving certain spiritual gifts. This event, sometimes as important as conversion, usually leads to a new style of living for the recipient, and public witness to the benefits of baptism in the Spirit becomes a central and joyous aspect of his life. Tongue-speaking, technically known as glossolalia, is the distinctive, though not necessarily the most important, gift received at this baptism of the Spirit.

Other gifts sometimes received by adherents include the interpretation of tongues, prophecy, healing powers, and a desire for an active style of participatory worship in which these gifts are practiced. Through enthusiastic evangelism, the movement has found support not only in local congregations, but also on university campuses, in newly founded residential communities, and in various types of societies. Those involved include laity of all professions and trades who come from a variety of economic and educational levels. Clergy are also members, and in their number can be found bishops and ministers as well as newly ordained seminarians.

The movement has also brought confusion and fear to those who have not received these gifts and do not think they are necessary or even advantageous to their religious lives. Many congregations which have been faced with ardent charismatic evangelism have as a result fallen into strife and division. Members have left, and sometimes clergy have been expelled. The movement is accused of being narrow in its interests, biblically fundamentalist, and anti-intellectual. Tight-knit friendships in the worshiping groups of charismatics are criticized for being self-righteous and unwilling to take their share of the burden of long-term involvement in projects of social justice and other public concerns so necessary to maintain the political fabric of our national life. Some think that the movement is an irrational reaction to the complexity and dangers of modern technological life, an escape from the challenge of dealing with the serious and difficult problems of our age. Others point to its simplistic world-view and its internal authoritarianism as the explanation for the large number of mentally ill people who are attracted to it.

But those who have received the gifts interpret them as being of God. In a time of uncertainty and dissatisfaction with the cold, impersonal, formal worship of the "mainline" denominations, participating in an ecstatic worship is refreshing. For someone weary of academic discussion of theological questions, or impatient with the lukewarm commitment of many members of established churches, speaking in tongues satisfies a hunger for an authoritative, immediate, personal, and powerful religious experience.

How then shall we evaluate this contemporary expression of Pentecostalism? Is it a judgment of God upon the lackluster church? Is it an irresponsible movement born of emotional needs and doomed to subside as quickly as it has risen? Is it a genuine religious experience bringing a new love for God and his service or just an emotional catharsis for repressed individuals? What is its relationship to the New Testament record of charismatic experience? What was St. Paul's opinion of it in his day? Where down the centuries in the history of the church has it arisen before? What kinds of people are attracted to the movement and why? What effect, if any, does it have on the liturgical and social life of the churches?

This book is addressed to these and related questions and is written for noncharismatics who wish to understand the movement and for charismatics who want a perspective on their own involvement. Finally the book may aid those who are confronted with charismatics in their congregations and who wish to learn how best to live with them in a creative and peaceful manner.

Since as editor I have been responsible for the selection of the authors who contribute to this book (though I do not agree with all their judgments), the reader may legitimately be curious about my opinion of the movement and about any bias I might have. Hence a few personal comments are in order.

I am not a charismatic myself, though I have been friendly with a variety of charismatics during the last fifteen years of my ministry. It is my judgment that charismatic gifts are a rightful part of the full ministry of God's church. However, I do not believe that people who speak in tongues are spiritually more advanced than those who do not. It may be that it is only some people, those with a particular kind of spiritual need or those who are exposed to a hardship in their social environment, who receive and benefit from this gift. The great majority of Christians down the ages, those who have been mainly responsible for sustaining the life of the church and spreading the Gospel, have not been charismatics. Nor should speaking in tongues be confused with the much rarer mystical experience which, in its classical form, is a more profound and illuminating one in its reli-

gious antecedents, the experience itself, and its personal fruits. Finally, I believe it is important for charismatics to participate in the total
life of the church. All too often, because of the demand for frequent
charismatic worship, they segregate themselves within the Body of
Christ. The church needs their enthusiasm; they need to participate
in the fullness of the church's ministry.

My first acquaintance with glossolalia came when my wife and I
began our ministry working with Appalachian migrants in Cincinnati,
where we lived with them in a tenement slum for three years. They
were mostly members of the Holiness Church, and tongue-speaking
was a part of their normal social upbringing. It was for them a
God-given catharsis, a momentary relief from the very difficult lives
they led both in Appalachia and when they came to the city. The
religion they brought with them was harsh and demanding, their
culture was narrow and offered little of beauty to them. As long as
they felt themselves part of this native culture—and most of the
first-generation migrants never lost it—then tongue-speaking was a
religious and psychologically beneficial experience for them. I believe
their charismatic practice was appropriate and a healthy response to
their environment. Professor Nathan L. Gerrard, who knows Appalachia very well indeed, has contributed a chapter on this peculiarly
American expression of the charismatic movement. The Black rural
Pentecostal churches have also been an important part of American
religious life, and Professor Lawrence N. Jones, a scholar in this field,
has written about them.

The Reverend Dennis J. Bennett, who was rector of St. Mark's
Church in Los Angeles, created a sensation in 1960 by announcing
that he had received the baptism of the Holy Spirit and intended to
share these gifts with members of his parish and the church at large. I
happened then to be in Los Angeles working as a chaplain at the
University of Southern California and was able to observe the events
which followed his pronouncement. Perhaps because it was such a
new phenomenon for him and for the Episcopal Church, his witness
was not well given or received, and after protracted controversies
within the parish he resigned. Since then Dr. Bennett has become a
leader in the charismatic movement and a very able exponent of it.
He has contributed a chapter to the book which is an eloquent
expression of charismatic witness from his ethos. His enthusiasm is to
be weighed against Professor Logan's caution. Dr. James C. Logan is
a theologian who has been teaching a course on the charismatic
movement and was invited to contribute a chapter in which the
controversies and dangers surrounding the movement are explored.
His criticisms of the excesses in the movement are sobering.

Two clergymen have contributed contemporary accounts of the
development of the charismatic movement within their congrega-

tions. One account, by a Presbyterian pastor, the Reverend Frank Benson, carefully describes the divisions which almost destroyed his church and which resulted in the departure of his predecessor. To balance this story is one related by the Reverend Raymond W. Davis, rector of Truro Episcopal Church. Dr. Davis is himself a charismatic and for the past three years has ministered with distinction to a large congregation which has both charismatics and noncharismatics within it.

Finally, the book contains four chapters analyzing the charismatic movement from disciplinary perspectives. The contributors are all well-known scholars in their fields. Dr. Krister Stendahl, Dean of the Harvard Divinity School, writes on the crucial issue of the New Testament experience and interpretation of the phenomenon. Dr. George H. Williams, professor of history at the Harvard Divinity School, has provided a valuable and comprehensive history of the many expressions of the movement in the church's life. Dr. J. Massyngberde Ford, herself a charismatic and a member of the Department of Theology at Notre Dame, has written on the influence of the charismatic movement on liturgy. Dr. John Kildahl, an astute observer who has studied the movement for the past twelve years and has written about it extensively, provides an analysis of it on a psychological level.

The authors were chosen to include first-class scholarly analysis of the movement and first-hand experience with it. There are those who are sceptical about it and those who are charismatics themselves and understandably enthusiastic about it. My hope is that the book will provide sufficient information for a balanced understanding, which neither ignores the value of the charismatic gifts nor underestimates their dangers; an understanding which does not overrate the importance of the current revival of the phenomenon, but also does not deny its power and appeal.

In closing I wish to express my thanks to the trustees of the Marcia Brady Tucker Foundation, who have assisted the cathedral ministries in more than one project and have partially funded this book. The book, and the conference at which these essays were originally presented, also received substantial funds from the Washington Cathedral and the National Presbyterian Center, whose director at the time of the conference was Dr. Lowell R. Ditzen. Dr. Ditzen cooperated with the Reverend Merrill W. Drennan, pastor of the Metropolitan Memorial United Methodist Church, and Monsignor Robert Lewis, archdiocesan liaison to the Roman Catholic charismatic communities in the Washington area, in sponsoring the conference. Professor John P. Kildahl of New York Theological Seminary, Dr. James C. Logan of Wesley Seminary, and the Reverend Raymond

W. Davis, rector of Truro Episcopal Church, gave me valuable assistance in understanding differing aspects of the charismatic movement.

I am grateful to Peter Hackes of NBC who suggested to me that a small record of speaking in tongues would greatly enhance the ability of the reader to understand the phenomenon. With the technical aid of Geoffrey Dirksen, the sound technician at Washington Cathedral, and the kind cooperation of the Roman Catholic Mother of God community in Rockville, Maryland, we made such a record. You are now in possession of a multimedia exposition!

On the cathedral staff I'd like first to give my sincere thanks to the Very Reverend Francis B. Sayre, Jr., Dean of Washington Cathedral, whose winsome and broad vision of the cathedral's ministry enables his staff to venture on a wide range of educational and cultural projects. It was the Reverend Jeffrey Cave, Canon Precentor of the cathedral, who first thought of having a conference about the new Pentecostal movement, for which suggestion I am most grateful. Nancy Montgomery, editor of *The Cathedral Age*, gave generously of her expertise and provided major assistance in editing the texts. Nancy Vetterling, my hard-working and good-humored secretary, provided continual help which I much appreciated.

In spite of all this advice and assistance, I suspect the book will not please everyone, and for whatever failures and mistakes there are in it I am responsible. I will be pleased if it is recognized to have achieved a common intellectual and experiential base for charismatics and noncharismatics to talk with each other about the new Pentecostalism.

—Canon Michael Hamilton
Washington Cathedral

The Charismatic Movement
in the Church

1 THE GIFTS OF THE HOLY SPIRIT
DENNIS J. BENNETT

This chapter is more of a personal testimony than a scholarly treatise or research paper. Many earnest and capable scholars and researchers are studying the phenomenon in Christendom today called charismatic renewal. Many are examining the manifestations of spiritual gifts that come from it. In rightful keeping with scientific method, these investigators are trying to be as objective as possible and thus tend to avoid becoming personally involved themselves in the experiences they are seeking to describe, study, and understand. I have been personally involved in the charismatic renewal for fifteen years and am therefore unable to assume a position of complete objectivity. But I can perhaps bring a combination of objective analysis and subjective witness that may prove useful. This chapter hopes to combine "Come now, and let us reason together" with "That which we have seen and heard declare we unto you."[1]

I want first to discuss the general nature of the gifts of the Holy Spirit, and then to focus on the question of speaking in tongues— what it is and what it means. I am not going to spend a lot of time discussing the other gifts and manifestations in detail, as that has already been done quite adequately in a number of books.[2] However, so much discussion and research is taking place on the subject of speaking in tongues that it seems to warrant a more detailed treatment.

The Rev. Dennis J. Bennett, rector of St. Luke's Episcopal Church, Seattle, for the past thirteen years, has served as vicar of St. Paul's, Lancaster, California, and rector of St. Mark's, Van Nuys, California. In 1960, while at St. Mark's, Father Bennett received the baptism in the Holy Spirit, as did many of his congregation, and this marked an important beginning of the charismatic movement's emergence in the established non-Pentecostal denominations.

Father Bennett was born in London, England; he grew up in central California and took his undergraduate work at San Jose State College. He then entered the ministry of the Congregational Church in 1944. He received his graduate degree in divinity from the University of Chicago in 1949, and in 1951 he joined the ministry of the Episcopal Church. He is the author of the book *Nine O'Clock in the Morning* and co-author, with his wife, of *The Holy Spirit and You*. Father Bennett is widely known as a witness in behalf of the charismatic renewal in the church and has lectured both in the United States and Great Britain.

To talk intelligently about the gifts of the Holy Spirit, we must first review something of the Christian doctrine of the Holy Spirit. Briefly we may say that the Holy Spirit is that person of the Godhead who lives in the believer. The Christian faith does not hold the very common notion that there is a little spark of God in every man. God only lives in people because He has been invited to come through Jesus Christ.

When Jesus is received, the Holy Spirit is given. He joins himself to the human spirit, and a new creature comes into existence—the human spirit brought to new life by the Holy Spirit. This is the new birth Jesus spoke of. A Christian precisely is a person who has been "born again of the Spirit" and thus is indwelt by the Holy Spirit.

This means that the nature and power of God lives in the believer. The gifts of the Holy Spirit are simply the outward manifestation of that indwelling. It was Jesus' expressed intention that his followers would continue to do the things he did, and to say the things he said. He made it clear that this would be made possible because he was returning to the Father and was going to send the Holy Spirit. We may call the gifts of the Holy Spirit the power of Jesus being manifested through the believer, and we may call the fruit of the Holy Spirit the character of Jesus being shown through the believer. The Christian life is not so much an imitation of Christ as it is an expression of Jesus Christ.

The Apostle Paul categorizes the gifts of the Holy Spirit in the First Epistle to the Corinthians as follows: "A word of wisdom; a word of knowledge; faith; miracles; healings; prophecy; distinguishing of spirits; speaking in languages, interpretation of languages."[3] These are the *charismata*, meaning "gifts of love," or *pneumatikoi*, "spiritual things." Paul also speaks of them as the *phanerosis* or manifestation of the Spirit. These gifts are not to be thought of as awarded to particular believers as their permanent possession. The gifts are not received by those who administer them, but by those who are helped by them. They are to be used in helping others. Thus a gift of healing is not given to the person who is praying for the healing of another. He does not have the gift of healing—rather he is privileged to deliver a gift of healing to the one who needs it. The sick person who is healed is the one who receives the gift; and thus in the body of believers, the Holy Spirit moves, distributing to "each man severally as he will."[4] On one occasion a person might administer a gift of healing, but on another he might be given a needed word of knowledge for someone. Some will be used repeatedly in certain gifts, because they have the faith for them or because they have the opportunity. A pastor or doctor, for example, might expect to bring a gift of healing, while a Christian attorney, judge, or counsellor might expect to be permitted to deliver a gift of wisdom or knowledge.

These spiritual gifts are being manifested today with increased intensity and frequency, but they have always been in the church, implicit in the lives of believers. They can be subtle and easily overlooked. You may have had the experience, as many have, of finding yourself speaking or counselling with a wisdom that surprised you! Or of suddenly knowing something that you could not, in the ordinary course of things, have known. Or you may have received a sudden infusion of faith, so that even before a prayer was offered, you knew it would be answered. Miracles are usually small things— changes in circumstances brought about by God's intervention, answers to prayer. A parking place when needed is quite a common miracle, and can be a very significant one in a crowded city at rush hour! But of course the big miracles still happen too. I have myself seen sixteen people amply fed from food adequate for five, at my own dining table.[5] Healings have been taking place right along. The old quibble "I'd believe in healing if I could see some scientific evidence: x-rays, etc." is certainly a called bluff. There are fully attested healings on the files of doctors and hospitals; in fact, many doctors are quicker to acknowledge the reality of Christian healing than are some clergy. The Episcopal Church, of course, recognized the reality of this gift long ago, and incorporated it into the Prayer Book of 1928 in the section titled "Unction of the Sick."

Prophecy does not refer necessarily to foretelling the future. It means rather "speaking forth" (προφητεύειν) words from God. It has been variously and confusingly identified with preaching and witnessing, and certainly these activities may involve prophecy, but as it is being experienced again in the church it simply means that the indwelling Spirit of God can inspire the believer to deliver words from God to his people. "Thus saith the Lord" is still the key phrase to prophecy.

Discerning of spirits means sensing, by the Holy Spirit, what spiritual influences are at work in an individual or at a meeting. Interpretation is the Holy Spirit-inspired ability to explain the meaning of something that has been said in an unknown language. Thus we come to the interesting and sometimes trying question of speaking in tongues, a center of curiosity and also of much misunderstanding as people consider the charismatic renewal.

Much effort is being made to separate the movement of renewal in the Holy Spirit that is unquestionably taking place in Christendom today from the awkward issue of speaking in tongues. The other gifts and fruits of the Holy Spirit sound most desirable, but surely this is the least of the gifts, a bit of childishness left over from primitive days, an emotional outburst satisfying to the individual in a sensuous and selfish sort of way, but disturbing and divisive in the fellowship of believers; something that men like the Apostle Paul wanted to see minimized and ultimately eliminated in favor of more rational expressions. A more kindly view is expressed by some concerned psychologists. It is an activity, they tell us, that is often beneficial. It does not imply maladjustment, immaturity, or instability on the part of its practitioners. Nevertheless it is a learned psychological activity, purely natural in its source.

Yet persistently, and not only among the unsophisticated, but among intellectuals of the deepest dye—lawyers, physicists, psychiatrists and psychologists, physicians, college professors, clergymen—the phenomenon not only occurs and recurs, but is hailed as supernatural and very important, if not vital, to a life of freedom in the Holy Spirit. What is this speaking in tongues? Can it be defined rationally and objectively?

Speaking in tongues, or praying with the Spirit, is what happens when a Christian believer speaks and allows the indwelling Holy Spirit to guide the form of the words uttered. It is not ecstasy, suggestion, hysteria, or hypnosis. It has nothing to do with a working up of emotion—in fact excessive emotion can inhibit speaking in tongues. It is not an emotionally caused experience at all, although it may stir emotion, as any moving spiritual activity might do. Many think of speaking in tongues in terms of a meeting they may have attended, perhaps many years ago, in a "little holy-roller church across the tracks," where they heard and saw what certainly looked and sounded like emotional behavior; or they remember an experience in a church where someone suddenly broke into the proceedings with strange utterances. The emotional excitement in either of these cases, however, did not come from the speaking in tongues, or cause the tongue-speaking. It was simply the way the person chose to express himself, just as one might choose to speak English, or any other known tongue, in a highly emotional manner.

Speaking in tongues is initiated by a simple act of the will, just as speech in any language would be. There are two kinds or ways of speaking in tongues. When the Apostle Paul says, "I thank God I speak in tongues more than any of you, but in an assembly I would rather speak five words with my understanding in order to teach others by what I have to say, than ten thousand in some unknown tongue,"[6] he is making a distinction between speaking in tongues in private, which he says he does more than any of them, and speaking in tongues in an assembly of believers, which Paul says he doesn't feel led to do. He makes it clear elsewhere, however, that he is perfectly willing for others to engage in speaking in tongues at an assembly, provided they do it "decently and in order,"[7] without confusion, and that it is interpreted so that others can understand the meaning.

Private speaking to God and praising God accounts for 99.99 percent of all speaking in tongues. It is this that any believer can do

at any time: "I want you all to speak with tongues. . . ," says Paul.[8]
This kind of speaking in tongues does not require interpretation:
"Let him speak to himself, and to God. . . ."[9] It is for the edification
of the individual: he or she is speaking to God.[10] Jude says: "But ye,
beloved, building yourselves up on your most holy faith, *praying in
the Holy Ghost*, keep yourselves in the love of God. . . ."[11] It is a
powerful means of intercession: "We know not what we should pray
for as we ought, but the Spirit puts our desires into words which are
not in our power to say."[12] This private speaking is the most general
and the most important way in which tongues are used.

The other kind of speaking in tongues is rightly called the gift of
tongues. This gift of tongues, like the other gifts, is one of the ways
by which one person can minister to another or to many others. It is
by definition, like the other gifts, a community phenomenon, and
when it is interpreted in due order the community is inspired and
edified. It corresponds to prophecy—God is speaking to his people. [13]
The gift of tongues, like the other gifts, is not a permanent ability
given to the person, but is manifested as the Holy Spirit empowers
and decides. The person cannot expect to open his mouth at any
time he decides to and utter words which when interpreted will be
significant to others present. Any believer can speak in tongues at
any time, but if he simply prays out loud in tongues in a meeting
because he decides to, it will not necessarily have significance to the
others. He should speak to himself and to God, unless the Holy Spirit
specifically moves him to speak in tongues in the meeting.

The distinction shows up, interestingly enough, in the nature of
the language spoken. A person will characteristically have one or two
or maybe more languages that he uses in his private prayers "in the
spirit." Although he cannot understand these languages, he can
recognize them. When the Holy Spirit moves a person to speak in
tongues with others present, however, there is no telling what language may be given. Frequently, as we shall discuss later, it is a
language that is understood by someone else. This is also true in
other circumstances where a person feels led to use the gift of
tongues for something besides self-edification. Someone like myself,
who is regularly called upon to speak on the manifestation of
tongues, may feel free to speak out in the language the Holy Spirit
gives, letting the group, so-to-speak, listen in to a private prayer in the
unknown tongue. The Holy Spirit may and sometimes does take
advantage of this opportunity to provide a language that is unknown
to the speaker but understandable to someone present. At the
conclusion of a meeting in an Anglican Church in Calgary several
years ago, a woman said: "I have never heard anyone speak in
tongues. Would you speak in tongues for us?" I felt free to comply
and so very simply spoke out in the words the Holy Spirit supplied.

Immediately another woman said: "But you know that language?" "No, I don't," I replied. "But it's Nepali!" the woman went on. "How do you know?" "Why, my brother is a Jesuit missionary in Nepal, and he sends me tape recordings. You have just quoted the Epistle for Gaudete Sunday[14] in perfect Nepali, just as I have it on a recording at home!" I had correspondence later with this person, confirming what she had said.

Then there are those situations in which a person feels led to use the gift of tongues when there is great need to communicate with someone whose language he doesn't know, and the Holy Spirit honors the situation by giving the needed expression. Amy, a very faithful member of our parish, felt led to make a weekly visit to the General Hospital in our city, where there are many who have been forgotten by families and friends or who don't have any. One day she came across a little man sitting on the side of his bed looking very downcast. "Can I help you?" she asked. "I no spik. I no spik!" was his reply. Amy said, "I just knew that I was supposed to pray with that little man, so I began to speak and trust the Holy Spirit to give me words." As she spoke, guided by the Holy Spirit, the little man brightened and very excitedly pulled a little book from his bedside drawer. "Canary Island Spanish! Canary Island Spanish!" he exclaimed. The book was obviously a New Testament in his language. Amy gestured that she wanted to pray for him and then continued to speak as the Spirit gave the words. As she prayed, in a language her mind did not grasp at all, she said: "The little man prayed right along with me, and my words and his were just the same!"

This is the gift of tongues—praying in some kind of corporate or public situation—in the assembly, or elsewhere, perhaps with only one other person present. The person speaking in tongues does it because it is part of his or her practice to do so, and knows that it will bring refreshment and inspiration far deeper than any emotional excitement. He need not have any tremendous urge to speak. He may have just a quiet conviction that he is supposed to do so. In private, of course, there is no need even for that. In fact, a good time to speak in tongues in private is when you *don't* feel like it, because that's when you most need the benefits that it can bring! On the other hand, sometimes there is a very strong urge to speak, a deep joy and excitement that wants to be expressed.

It is important to note that none of this is compulsive behavior, nor is it especially conditioned by the presence of others. Far from being a product of some kind of mass psychology, speaking in tongues is, if anything, inhibited by the presence of others, just as regular speech tends to be. Those studies which claim to have discovered some kind of necessity for an authority figure to be present, or for some other kind of corporate situation to be necessary for people to speak in tongues, simply baffle me, as they would baffle anyone who has been in close contact with this phenomenon for any period of time. There is simply no accuracy to these claims, and they can only be adduced to insufficient research. The person who speaks in tongues does so as he would perform any other act of prayer or praise. He wishes to speak to God. He decides that he will allow the Holy Spirit to give him the form of the utterance, and so he opens his mouth and speaks, and the Spirit provides the words. Even where there is a strong inspiration from the Holy Spirit to speak, the speaking is no more compulsive than a person stirred to laughter by a humorous incident, or an artist stirred to write or paint because of inspiration. It is still a completely voluntary matter, under the control of the individual, and just as one would not give way to laughter if the time were not fitting no matter how funny the situation and how great the desire to laugh, so it is with speaking in tongues. The gift of interpretation provides further evidence of the nature of speaking in tongues. The number of persons speaking in tongues at a given meeting is to be limited to two or three, they are not all to speak at once, and interpretation should follow. He that speaks in a tongue in a corporate situation must "pray that he may interpret."[15] He should not speak in tongues unless he is prepared to pray for that interpretation, for he does not know whether anyone else will interpret or not and the tongue must not go uninterpreted.

Interpretation is not translation. Following a speaking in tongues, the Holy Spirit gives the gist of what has been spoken, but leaves it to the interpreter to clothe it in words as he or she wishes. There is nothing automatic about it, and again the free will of the person is respected.

The reality of interpretation is objectively shown by the fact that sometimes several people in a meeting may all have an interpretation of a given speaking in tongues, and the interpretations, while not exactly agreeing in the way they are worded, will agree in meaning. One interpreter may say, "Thus saith the Lord: I will be with you in the mountains and in the valleys." Another may put it: "God says this: I will not leave you alone, on the heights or in the depths." Yet another, "God will always be with you, whether you are high or low." I remember a meeting at St. Luke's in Seattle when about seventy-five were present and someone spoke in tongues. There was an interpretation, and afterwards another person put up his hand: "Father Bennett, I just wanted you to know that I had exactly the same interpretation." I thanked him, and then said: "How many are there here in the room who got the same interpretation?" Seven hands went up. Seven people had been inspired by the Spirit with the meaning of what had been said in the unknown language! I recall another occasion when about a hundred people were present. Fol-

lowing a speaking in tongues, a person in the back of the hall began
to interpret. He stopped short right in the middle of a sentence, but
without any noticeable pause at all another person in the front of the
hall continued the sentence and the interpretation. There was no
break, either grammatically or in the meaning or in the style. The
two persons were separated by about thirty feet. There was no
possibility of collaboration, and, so far as I know, the two speakers
did not know each other. In circumstances like these it seems
impossible to deny the fact that the gift of interpretation is objectively real.

I am writing these words while in Hawaii, and just recently in Hilo
something happened which beautifully illustrates several of the
things I have been writing about. There has been an extensive
ministry in Hawaii to the young people who came to the imagined
simplicity of the South Seas looking for escape from the pressures of
modern life. Many of these young people, after discovering the
illusory nature of their hopes, have come out of the jungles and come
to Christ, banding themselves together in a well-regulated group
calling itself the "Fellowship of Christian Pilgrims," under the leadership of Ken Smith. They have the support and cooperation of many
Christian people, including many laity and clergy of the Episcopal
Church.[16] Last night, at a meeting at St. Andrew's Cathedral in
Honolulu, I heard a good friend tell of an incident that had just
happened in Hilo. A young man who had recently come to Christ in
the Pilgrims group stood up in a meeting and began to speak in
tongues. My friend said, "I was pretty sure it was the Hawaiian
language, for I've lived here all my life." My friend does not understand Hawaiian, which is almost a dead language except in areas such
as the island of Niihau, but as soon as the young man had finished
speaking, the Holy Spirit gave my friend the interpretation of what
had been said. Before he could speak out, another person present
began to interpret. My friend said: "This other person was bringing
almost word for word the same interpretation that I had received! I
was about to get to my feet and say so, when a young Hawaiian who
was a graduate student at the University stood up. He was deeply
shaken and said in effect: "I need to repent and apologize to you and
to God. I thought this was all a lot of nonsense that you were
involved in, but this young fellow was speaking in the Hawaiian
language. I am a student specializing in this field. He was not
speaking in everyday Hawaiian, but in an ancient dialect which I
recognized because it has been a special study of mine. Not only
that, but the interpretation brought was an accurate translation of
most of what he was saying, and the rest of the time he was just
praising God!" My friends told me that the young man who spoke in

Hawaiian had just come from the mainland and was totally new to the Hawaiian Islands; moreover, he was so bashful and inhibited that he could scarcely be counted on to speak in a group in English![17]

Here is a typical example of what is happening in meetings and prayer groups all over the world. By the inspiration of the Holy Spirit, people are speaking in languages unknown to them. Others present receive interpretation through the Holy Spirit, and often these interpretations corroborate and complement one another. Occasionally someone testifies to recognizing and translating the language spoken.[18]

Why a language unknown to the speaker? Speaking in tongues enables a person to speak or pray to God without interference from any human source, including himself; without the mind or emotions or will intruding into the picture. The indwelling Spirit says in effect, "I know what you need to express to God the Father. Trust me to guide you as you speak." Thus confession can be made of sins that the mind does not even know about and would not acknowledge, or would soften and rephrase if it did. On the positive side, love for God can be expressed with a fullness and freedom otherwise impossible to the person because of inhibitions and fears of expression. Intercession can be made for others, expressing their deepest needs, without the intercessor knowing what those needs are.

"We know not what we should pray for as we ought," says Paul, "but the Spirit itself maketh intercession for us. . . ."[19] The Basic English New Testament Version of this quotation is "The Spirit puts our desires into words which are not in our power to say. . . ." The *Living Bible* paraphrases it thus: "The Holy Spirit prays for us with such feeling that it cannot be expressed in words, and the Father, who knows all hearts, knows of course what the Spirit is saying as he pleads." Surely these describe speaking in tongues.

The voice is our chief means of expression. No matter how artistic we may be or how creative in other areas, the voice is the most direct and understandable means by which we express ourselves. In Scripture the voice or tongue occupies a very special place. "I will sing and give praise with the best member I have," says the Psalmist.[20] In the King James Version this reads, "I will sing and give praise, even with my glory." The term "glory" is used several times in the Psalms as a metaphor for the voice: "Awake up, my glory; awake, psaltery and harp: I myself will awake early."[21] "Therefore my heart is glad, and my glory rejoiceth."[22]

The book of Proverbs echoes the same thing: "A man's belly shall be satisfied with the fruit of his mouth; and with the increase of his lips shall he be filled. Death and life are in the power of the tongue: and they that love it shall eat the fruit thereof."[23]

To be unable to speak or hear is perhaps the most crippling handicap a human being can suffer. It is not surprising then that the Holy Spirit should seek in some special way to inspire our chief means of expression and communication. On the other hand the voice is the means by which we commit the most evil. In James 3:3-12 the Apostle points out that the tongue, although very small, can control the whole of the human personality; that it is untameable; that it can be set on fire with the "fire of hell" and as a result set fire to the whole "course of nature." Neither is it surprising then that the Holy Spirit would regard it very important that the tongue be tamed.

But through all and beyond all this, speaking in tongues is a shatteringly simple and childlike evidence that God is really dwelling in his people, and that as Jesus said: "The kingdom of heaven is at hand."[24]

But what about those incidents of speaking in strange languages that reportedly take place under other conditions? The history of various cults, as well as of the classical pagan religions, shows many examples of strange powers of speech in which the devotee utters sounds in a presumed unknown language. In spiritist seances, it is reported, the medium may while in trance speak a language that he or she does not know. Another person present may, also while in trance, give a translation of what has been said. Then too, one of the symptoms of certain forms of schizophrenia is a speaking in strange noises. How do these manifestations relate to what we have been talking about? You will note that up to now in this discussion we have not used the word *glossolalia*.[25] This is because *glossolalia* is used in the dictionary and in medical parlance mainly to describe morbid and pathological symptoms or manifestations that take place when the subject is in an unusual state such as hypnosis! Webster's dictionary defines *glossolalia* as follows: "ability to speak in a foreign language when in a condition other than normal, such power being absent when the subject is not in hypnosis."

In the various cults and occult practices—spiritism, voodoo, etc.— the manifestation is indeed spiritual in origin, but it is from a possessing evil spirit that the strange language comes.[26] As far as schizophrenia is concerned, a growing number of psychologists point out its resemblance to demon-possession as described in the Bible. The difference between these glossolalic manifestations and Christian tongues-speaking is first of all in the nature of the source; the glossolalic, as we have defined this term, is possessed by spiritual sources other than God while the Christian speaking in tongues is inspired by the Holy Spirit. Further evidence of this is seen in the way in which the utterances are brought. Glossolalia comes when the subject is under hypnosis, in trance, or in some unusual state of consciousness amenable to being controlled automatically by the possessing entity. The Christian on the other hand speaks in tongues by his or her own volition, with no compulsion or strange state of consciousness.[27]

As with other questions of comparative religion there are superficial resemblances between the two classes of phenomena, especially if the Christian variety is not properly disciplined or conducted (in "decency and order," as Paul put it), but the difference is essential.

The utterances of the Christian speaking in tongues, when interpreted, will evidence the fruits of the Spirit—love, joy, peace, etc.— and will help to lead people to faith in Jesus Christ. The expressions from the other direction will be random, confusing, frightening, or calculated to mislead the persons listening. The prince of darkness seeks to counterfeit the gifts of the Holy Spirit, and speaking in tongues is not excluded.

I want to say a little more about the recent conclusions drawn by clinical psychologists that speaking in tongues is a learned activity, that it requires the presence of an authority figure, that the so-called languages are simply strings of meaningless, although perhaps pleasant-sounding, syllables not constituting any real language, that there is no real evidence of anyone speaking in tongues in a known or intelligible language that he did not know. It is quite baffling for anyone who has been in contact with the manifestations of the gifts of the Holy Spirit, including speaking in tongues, for a period of years to encounter these hypotheses. One is simply overcome with amazement at how they could be put forward as the result of serious research. Anyone in the field knows that many begin to speak in tongues in their private prayers without ever having heard anyone else speak in tongues, and sometimes without even knowing such a thing is possible.

Many people begin to speak in tongues in a totally private situation with no one else present, authoritative or otherwise! And for those who do not, there is virtually no tendency, in any normal circumstances, to become dependent upon the one who prayed with them when they first began to speak in tongues. To say that an authority figure has to be present in order for the person to be able to speak is simply ludicrous. I myself see the people who first prayed with me about every four or five years, and rarely have any other contact with them. Yet I speak in tongues many times a day every day. An authority figure is indeed present—our Lord the Holy Spirit! He is all that is needed. It is not unusual to find a person who has been speaking in tongues ever since childhood but who did not know the significance of what he or she was doing. Recently, while I was conducting a mission to Anglican churches in Canada, one priest said in effect, "When I was a child I used to have a language that I spoke when I felt especially happy and close to God. I can remember running over the grass, laughing, and speaking in this way! Could this be what you are talking about?" Another clergyman present began to chuckle: "I like to sing sometimes when I am by myself. I don't sing in English but just in syllables that come to me, and the tune comes too! This couldn't be what you are talking about, could it?"

In Seattle a woman came up after a meeting and said, "I'd like to speak in tongues!" "Why don't you?" I inquired. "I did once, but I wouldn't want to try again, because you see I have this little 'play language' that I speak for my children. They like it, and think it funny. We have a good time together when I speak this language for them, but I'm afraid that if I tried to speak in tongues, I'd get that 'play language.' "

"But my dear friend," I expostulated, "that is undoubtedly your 'tongue'—you just aren't using it in the right way. Although I am sure God has no objection to your having fun with your children, why don't you use this 'play language,' as you call it, and address it to God?" It was not easy to persuade her, but when she consented and began to speak, she dissolved in tears of joy: "That's it! That's it!"

None of these examples could have been learned languages, for the people had no idea that anyone else did such things, nor had they ever heard anyone else speak in tongues.

Another proof that these are not learned languages is that when one person is praying for another person to speak in tongues, the person who begins to speak rarely speaks in a language that is similar to the language of the person praying with him. Not only that, but it is not uncommon for the person to speak in two or three different languages before settling down to one. An example of this, which also illustrates an answer to the question, "Are these ever real languages?" is that of an Episcopal vestryman in Springfield, Illinois, who came to me after a meeting there at a small Episcopal church:

"I've been prayed for to receive the Holy Spirit," he said, "but I haven't spoken in tongues." "Why haven't you?" said I. He looked a little surprised: "I don't know how to do it." "Neither do I," I replied, "but I do it all the time." Then I challenged him simply to open his mouth and begin to speak, trusting the Holy Spirit dwelling in him to give him expression. There was absolutely no emotion in the situation—we were sitting on folding chairs following the meeting, people were standing around in groups, the young man was looking at me in a very serious and cool manner, he was not at all convinced that anything had happened to him. There was no sense of excitement and certainly no high pressure. After a moment's hesitation, he opened his mouth and accepted the first sounds that came to him. He spoke out a long sentence. I am not fluent in Spanish, but I recognized several of the words. His accent was a beautiful Castilian.

When he stopped I said, "Do you know any Spanish?" "No," he answered, "I took it in high school, but I didn't learn anything!"

"Say something else," I continued, and again after a moment's hesitation, he began. This time it was a different language and one that I was able to understand with no difficulty, because although my knowledge of that language is also limited, the Holy Spirit was nice enough to give me phrases that I knew very well! "C'est bon! C'est bon! Tres bon est le bon Dieu!" he said in the most perfect French imaginable. His expression was slow and definite, and there was no mistaking the words. "Do you know any French?" I asked. He shook his head, "I can say parlez-vous Francais!" "You don't know what you just said?" "No," he shook his head again. "You just said: 'It's good, it's good, very good is the good God!' " "I did?" he replied in amazement. "Say something else," I continued, and again he began to speak. This time the language was not understandable to either of us. It sounded like an oriental tongue, perhaps a dialect of Chinese. I don't know what it was, but my friend began to enjoy it! I could tell he was sensing now that the language was coming from God, and that he was talking to God, so I left him praying. He must have continued for twenty minutes or so talking to God in this language, obviously very uplifted by it. Significantly, the very next day the young man led his business associate to Jesus Christ!

I have encountered many examples of someone speaking in known languages, but unknown to himself. At our Thursday communion service not long ago, an elderly lady presented herself at the altar rail for healing prayer. I had never seen her before and I have not seen her since. I didn't know her needs. Laying my hands on her head, I said the liturgical prayers for healing, and then added some of my own. Then realizing that although I did not know her needs the Holy Spirit did, I prayed quietly in words the Holy Spirit gave me to utter. I did not recognize the language that came to me, and I'm sure the woman did not either. Soon, feeling that my prayer had been completed, I moved along to pray for others. The next day a friend called: "Did you realize that Gloria S. was kneeling next to that woman yesterday, and she says you prayed in Japanese?"

Gloria S. is an old acquaintance, the daughter of a well-known family in the diocese who were occasional attendants at St. Luke's. She and her husband had just returned from four years in Japan, where he had been with the State Department. I called Gloria: "Oh, yes," she said, "You prayed in Japanese." She proceeded to tell me some of the phrases of the prayer in Japanese and then in English. She had not heard the whole prayer but had picked up phrases. "Your conclusion was, 'Because you have asked this thing,' " she said, giving it to me in Japanese and English. "By the way, your accent is perfect!"

What was this all about? The Holy Spirit knew that there were things this elderly woman needed that were not my business, and that it would probably have upset her if she had heard me express them. Therefore he allowed me to pray for the woman in a language unknown to her and to me, in order that the prayer might be said freely, without interference and in confidence. Secondly, knowing that Gloria understood the Japanese language, the Spirit decided to allow me to pray in Japanese thereby building both Gloria's faith and mine, as she was able to pick up a few sentences.

Several years ago in Seattle a friend, an Evangelist with the Assemblies of God, told me that while he was conducting services in an Assembly of God Church in Oregon a young man had come to the altar with his Japanese bride, a young lady he had married while on military duty in Japan. The man was an earnest Christian, the girl was a Buddhist. She had seen no reason to alter her religion, although her husband, of course, was eager for her to do so. This particular evening, my friend told me, she had come with her husband to the altar. As they knelt, he prayed to God in the name of Jesus while she presumably was saying Buddhist prayers. A woman kneeling next to the Japanese girl, whom the pastor of the church described later as his "most weary-willie housewife," began to speak in tongues. Undoubtedly she thought that she was just expressing herself to the Lord and telling of her needs and offering him praise. But as soon as she began to speak the Japanese girl grasped her husband's arm and said, "Listen! This woman is speaking to *me*! She has just addressed me by my entire Japanese name, and she says to me: 'You've tried Buddha and he hasn't helped you; why don't you try Jesus Christ?' " The Japanese wife received Jesus that night.

I wondered if I had the record straight, so about two years after hearing of this incident I called the pastor of the church in Oregon and asked him if I had it correct. The pastor corroborated the incident in every detail and added: "Not only that, but the couple now live next door to me, and the wife is always looking for a chance to meet other Japanese people so that she can tell them of her experience."[28]

Anyone who has been involved in the charismatic renewal for any length of time could add similar testimonies. My wife has spoken in the Portuguese language. We know of a physician who spoke Hebrew, a language he did not know, to a Jewish woman and led her to Christ.[29] Another physician in New Orleans, a good friend of ours, prayed for an Episcopal priest in Latin. The doctor knows no Latin. And so it goes.

It does seem strange that in the face of well-documented evidence to the contrary, some investigators are still insisting that no one ever speaks in a tongue in a real language. Surely such a statement is unscientific! Even if they could investigate every tongue-speaking

Christian in the wide world and found no real languages spoken in their presence, they would still only be able to say, "It seems *probable* that people do not speak in tongues in real languages." The nature of their conclusions suggests that they have gone into the study with prejudgment.

Our friends will not accept documentation from those who have heard these real languages spoken, or who have spoken them themselves. They insist on tape recordings in order to satisfy "objectivity." So they attend meetings with recorders ready, or ask people to come and speak in tongues for the recording machine, searching vainly for a speaking that is recognizable by an objective group of listeners. Perhaps, they are overlooking one very important question: If speaking in tongues is indeed the result of the direct guidance of the Holy Spirit, who is very much aware and present in the whole process, is he interested in providing them with the proof they are seeking?

One of those who received the Holy Spirit shortly after my coming to St. Luke's Episcopal Church in Seattle was a very intelligent man of limited education. His background was Swiss-German. When he began to speak in tongues it sounded much like Chinese. This man promptly went to a business acquaintance of his who was Chinese and spoke the language for him. The other, in amazement, identified it as the Mandarin dialect. A little later at a prayer meeting at the church, Bob prayed in his Holy Spirit language. There happened to be present a woman from China whose husband, a physician, was an exchange fellow at the University of Washington. She said, in effect, "How can this man speak Chinese so well? He is praising and glorifying God in perfect Mandarin. Caucasians cannot usually speak Mandarin so well. Where did he learn it?"

One of our parishioners was a student at the University of Washington. He heard of Bob speaking in Chinese and came to me, saying, "May I make a recording of Bob praying in his "tongue" and take it over to the University to the Department of Eastern Languages and see what they make of it?" I said, "It's all right with me if it's all right with Bob." Then I added, "However, I don't think the Lord will allow himself to be put into a test tube. I believe you will get an untranslatable dialect!" I don't know exactly why I said this. The student went to Bob and made a recording of him speaking in tongues. He took it over to the University, but the Professor of Chinese happened to be away and there was no one else there who understood the Chinese language. The young man next went to the Buddhist Temple in Seattle, but all the priests there were Japanese and none of them understood Chinese. They did say, however, "We don't speak Chinese but we believe the language you are playing on the tape is a dialect of Chinese." Next the young man went to the home of a Chinese clergyman of our diocese. The priest was not home, but his wife was. She listened to the tape and said, "I believe this is a Chinese dialect, but I don't understand it." When the Chinese priest came home, he said essentially the same thing, and they forthwith proceeded to call up various members of the Chinese community in Seattle and play them the tape. All of them said the same thing, "It sounds like Chinese, but it is a dialect we don't understand!" It seems very much as though my words had been true—that the Lord was not going to allow himself to be analyzed this way. Yet, was it not a sizeable miracle that this man could speak a language which, while not being a translatable dialect of Chinese to these people, nevertheless sounded so much like Chinese that they all believed that it was a form of the Chinese language?

After all, if we who are involved in this charismatic renewal are right, we are not dealing with some interesting psychological phenomenon when we are dealing with speaking in tongues, but with the very work of God himself. It is our continuing hope that those who seriously investigate the matter will come to realize this, and receive a share of these wonderful things God is doing in the world today. After all, objective investigation of a subjective experience has its limitations. Man, like God, is not an object but a subject and ultimately can be understood only by self-revelation, his willingness to tell what he is experiencing from within. To hypothesize that it is possible to investigate human experience with complete objectivity is simply to dehumanize man. If a scientist desires to know what apple pie tastes like—what is the subjective experience of human beings eating apple pie—he or she can set up any number of experiments in which persons are observed eating pie and their reactions clocked and chronicled. Ultimately, however, the scientist might be well advised to taste a piece of pie. He might learn more from that than from years of investigation of others.

It is our hope that those who desire to know why so many Christian leaders today are convinced of the validity and importance of the baptism in the Holy Spirit and of spiritual gifts and who desire to understand the importance of speaking in tongues will ask God for these experiences in their own lives. We hope they will accept Christ as Savior and Lord, if they have not already done so, and allow the Spirit to manifest himself in their lives in his fullness to their joy. So many who came to scoff remained to pray, and we pray that many more will do so.

Notes

1. Isaiah 1:18 and John 1:3. (Unless otherwise noted, all subsequent references to the Bible will be to the King James Version.)
2. See, e.g., Dennis and Rita Bennett, *The Holy Spirit and You* (Plainfield, N.J., 1971).
3. I Corinthians 12:8-11 (my translation from Westcott and Hort's text).

4. I Corinthians 12:11.
5. Dennis J. Bennett, *Nine O'Clock in the Morning* (Plainfield, N.J., 1970), p. 95.
6. I Corinthians 14:19 (my own paraphrase from Westcott and Hort).
7. I Corinthians 14:40.
8. I Corinthians 14:5 (Revised Standard version).
9. I Corinthians 14:28.
10. I Corinthians 14:2.
11. Jude 20-21 (italics mine).
12. Romans 8:26, *The New Testament in Basic English*.
13. I Corinthians 14:5.
14. Philippians 4:4, the Epistle for the Fourth Sunday in Advent, which in the Roman Missal begins: "Gaudete in Domino semper. . . ."
15. I Corinthians 14:13.
16. Ken Smith is currently seeking ordination to the ministry of the Episcopal Church.
17. The author would be happy to put the reader in touch with the persons bringing these reports so that further documentation can be secured if desired.
18. Several books have been published recently giving copious illustration and documentation of speaking in tongues in known languages. Two such titles are: *Spoken by the Spirit*, by Ralph W. Harris (Springfield, Mo., 1973); and *The Miracle of Tongues*, by Don Basham (Old Tappan, N.J., 1973).
19. Romans 8:26.
20. Psalm 108:1; *Book of Common Prayer*.
21. Psalm 57:8.
22. Psalm 16:9.
23. Proverbs 18:20-21.
24. Matthew 3:2.
25. We are quite aware that the word *glossolalia* is being used widely as an equivalent term for speaking in tongues. We know that it is thus used by respected leaders and spokesmen for the charismatic renewal; but we do feel that this definition needs to be given and the distinction made, and we wish that the term *glossolalia* could be dropped from the vocabulary when speaking of the scriptural phenomenon.
26. It is not within the scope of this paper to discuss the nature of these cultic and occult practices so popular today, which are counterfeits of the gifts of the Holy Spirit. The reader will find many books on this subject. We recommend *The Holy Spirit and You* (Plainfield, N.J., 1971), Chapter Four; Raphael Gasson, *The Challenging Counterfeit* (Plainfield, N.J., 1966); Michael Harper, *Spiritual Warfare* (London, 1970). Suffice it to note here that the so-called psychic manifestations, occult practices, ESP, telepathy, precognition, clairvoyance, etc., although they may seem to resemble the gifts of the Holy Spirit in some ways, differ from them in this essential point: They do not come from God, but from random and rebellious spiritual sources, which the Bible calls demonic. They are forbidden in the strongest language throughout Scripture, as is the practice of necromancy or spiritism. The person practicing the occult or psychic usually claims to have received these powers from God (e.g., Edgar Cayce, Jeanne Dixon, et al.), but the Christian knows that God does not confer the gifts of the Spirit in this way. Each gift and each individual manifestation is given directly by the Holy Spirit to meet the situation. The person bringing the manifestation is not "gifted" but simply faithful. A very small child can, and sometimes does, manifest the most striking of spiritual gifts, and often a gift will be brought by an adult under extremely unlikely circumstances. The occult manifestations require careful preparation—fasting, abstinence from certain food, from sex, long meditations, trances, ascetic practices, dim lights, seance rooms—and it is claimed that the psychics or occultists are adept, highly trained people who have developed these powers. All this is totally different from

the simplicity of the gifts of the Holy Spirit. Perhaps the greatest spiritual danger to our culture is the tremendous outpouring of the occult, and Christians need to be alerted to the diametric difference between these practices and the work of the Holy Spirit.

27. The New English Bible confuses the issue by introducing the terms *ecstasy*, *ecstatic tongues*, or *tongues of ecstasy;* but there is no such word in the Greek. Certainly, persons can and do become ecstatic under the influence of the Holy Spirit, and various physical results can ensue, but this never happens without the subject's consent and cooperation. The glossolalic expressions are compulsive, usually taking place when the subject is in some kind of hypnotic, hysterical, or trance state, whereas Christian speaking in tongues is done as objectively as any other speaking, while the person is in full possession and control of his wits and volition, and in no strange state of mind whatever. The Holy Spirit's inspiration does not have to be obeyed; it is not compulsive or automatic.

28. This happened in Garibaldi, Oregon, in 1955. The couple, Mr. and Mrs. Alan Thomas, are still living there. For further reference see *Spoken by the Spirit*, note 18 above.

29. Basham, *The Miracle of Tongues*, pp. 37-38.

2 CONTROVERSIAL ASPECTS OF THE MOVEMENT

JAMES C. LOGAN

History takes strange and unpredictable routes. Who could have predicted in 1906 that what was happening in that abandoned stable on Azusa Street in Los Angeles would by 1974 send currents sweeping through the "denominational establishment," Protestant and Catholic alike? The phenomenon is the same and yet not quite the same. The Azusa Street revival called for baptism in the Holy Spirit confirmed by outward signs of which the most notable was speaking in tongues. The Pentecost of a Jerusalem upper room became the Pentecost of a California stable. Today we see a sectarian Pentecostal movement translated into a Pentecostal movement within the structures of established denominational life. It is the same, and yet it has a new face.

Like the older Pentecostal movement, the newer charismatic movement mourns the loss of spiritual vitality in the church and celebrates the baptism in the Holy Spirit as the means of new life. The newer movement, like the older, expects that such a baptism will be confirmed by extraordinary evidences such as new tongues, healing, and exorcisms. Unlike the older Pentecostal movement, however, the newer charismatic movement does not withdraw from—but remains within—the framework of the numerically larger and historically older denominations. Also unlike the older Pentecostal movement, which originated principally in the lower socio-economic strata, the new charismatic movement flows on the tides of rising social and economic mobility and finds its home in the middle class. With these differences come certain modifications which tend to

Dr. James C. Logan, a native of Abingdon, Virginia, is Professor of Systematic Theology at Wesley Theological Seminary in Washington, D.C. Dr. Logan completed his undergraduate work at Florida Southern College in 1953. He received his S.T.B. at Boston University School of Theology in 1956 and his Ph.D. from Boston University Graduate School in 1966. He has done additional study at Harvard University; St. Mary's College, University of St. Andrews, Scotland; and the University of Basel, Switzerland. He has also pursued postdoctoral studies at Cambridge University. Before coming to Washington he was an assistant professor of religion and philosophy at Emory and Henry College until 1966, when he joined the faculty of Wesley Seminary. Professor Logan is a frequent contributor to religious journals and has published a book entitled *Theology in the Shape of Christian Education* (1974).

hone down the sharp edges of the earlier sectarian emphases of Pentecostalism. Some modern charismatics hold that the baptism in the Spirit is not necessarily accompanied with speaking in tongues, though tongue-speaking nevertheless remains a desirable objective. Modern charismatics tend to emphasize the rational, linguistic character of glossolalia and play down the ecstatic or irrational dimensions of the phenomenon. Where the earlier Pentecostalism occasionally found historical antecedents in such so-called heretical movements as Montanism, the modern charismatic sprinkles his writings with appeals to church fathers and reformers. Ecumenism is no longer eschewed but is gloried in. As one charismatic Christian remarked recently, "You should have been with me last night. Catholics, Presbyterians, Baptists, and even Methodists praised God in the Spirit!"

The new charismatics are, nevertheless, one with the older forms of Pentecostalism in appealing to Holy Scripture as their authority, particularly emphasizing the Acts of the Apostles as the normative pattern for the church. With their historical antecedents, the new charismatics insist on the necessity of a new baptism in the Spirit different from and usually subsequent to water baptism. The latter witnesses to salvation and initiation into the church; the former is a necessary second step toward fullness of the Spirit. Likewise, they continue to speak of the Holy Spirit in terms of a force and power given through the laying on of hands. And so Azusa Street comes to the historic denominations.

My particular concern here is to point to some of the controversial aspects of the charismatic revival. No Christian, particularly one who stands within the Wesleyan tradition and who takes that tradition seriously, can minimize the life-giving activity of the Holy Spirit. No one whose eyes are open can conclude otherwise than that the Christian establishment needs enlivening and renewing. Anyone who reads the New Testament knows that what is to be desired above all else is love. What follows is expressive of a deep personal concern for the Spirit of God in the life of the church working to bring both Pentecostal and non-Pentecostal Christians to a fuller knowledge of the love of God through Jesus Christ.

THE CHARISMATIC REVIVAL AND THE BIBLE

Charismatic Christians are people of the book. They see their experience as a revival of biblical Christianity. The prime distinguishing mark of charismatic believers is their insistence that the baptism in the Holy Spirit, accompanied by external signs of confirmation, usually glossolalia, is necessary for empowerment to witness, and that the normative pattern for such is found in Scripture. They therefore speak of two baptisms. One baptism is *with water*, whereby salvation through Jesus Christ is affirmed. The second baptism is *with the Spirit*, which with signs confirms one's new life. A statement of the charismatic movement explains it this way:

> Once we have accepted the Lord Jesus Christ, there is a further step which is necessary to receive the full promise of God, and that is the acceptance of the gift of the Holy Spirit.
> We might say, regarding the speaking with other tongues, that "it comes with the package."
> . . . The sign of the infilling of the Holy Spirit is still the speaking with tongues.[1]

Charismatic Christians emphasize the nine gifts of the Spirit (I Cor. 12), placing special stress upon speaking with other tongues. The gifts are of great importance, for they confirm the Spirit-baptism and empower new life.

Most charismatic Christians claim to take the Bible literally. All charismatic Christians certainly claim to take it fully and seriously. On these scriptural grounds they seek to justify their experience of the baptism in the Spirit. While their religion is highly experiential, it is held to be equally biblical.

No student of the Bible can for a moment ignore the fact that mind-boggling and wondrous happenings through the working of the Holy Spirit permeated the early church. St. Paul both experienced and witnessed such activity by the Spirit. Luke in the Acts of the Apostles chronicles the earliest such events. Twentieth-century skeptics can be scandalized by these reports and seek through rationalistic maneuvers to explain them away. But such reductive biblical interpretation is not my concern here.

There are Christians who take the Bible just as seriously as do neo-Pentecostals but who come to somewhat different conclusions. They do not doubt that the original Pentecost was a word-miracle as well as a hearing-miracle. They are not skeptical of the Pentecostal experience itself. Rather, they question the accuracy of the biblical interpretation given to that experience. To illustrate:

(1) Charismatics lay particular emphasis upon the nine gifts of the Spirit. Actually, if one were to compile a list of the gifts as recorded in the New Testament epistles, the number is not nine but at least seventeen such gifts (Rom. 12:6-8; I Cor. 12:9-10, 28-30; Eph. 4:11-16).

(2) The insistence upon a second baptism subsequent to the sacramental baptism is difficult if not impossible to substantiate on the basis of Paul's writings. For Paul there is one decisive baptism into Christ which is itself the external mark of the new life given by the Spirit to the believer. To be baptized into the death of Jesus Christ is to receive the Holy Spirit.

(3) Regarding the gifts of the Spirit, and in particular the gift of tongues, Paul is concerned in the Corinthian correspondence to establish these in some kind of order for the sake of the well-being of the Corinthian church. He does not wish to rule out the experience, but he clearly values the gift of prophecy above glossolalia (I Cor. 14:1, 3, 6). Above all the various gifts of the Spirit there stands the "agape which never ends" (I Cor. 13:8), and which is the "more excellent way" to Christian maturity.

(4) The crucial texts for charismatic believers are, however, not Pauline but those found in the Acts of the Apostles. Aside from the account of Pentecost itself (Acts 2), the manifestation of tongues appears in two accounts: the baptism of Cornelius and others (Acts 10), and the baptism of the Ephesians (Acts 19:1-7). In the first case, the gift of tongues preceded the sacramental baptism. In the second case, the Ephesians had received the baptism of John the Baptist but not the Christian baptism. Upon receiving Christian baptism from Paul, they spoke in tongues. Neither of these accounts will support a doctrine of two baptisms. The most crucial text for Pentecostals is Acts 8:1-24. A careful reading of this passage casts doubt upon the baptism of the Samaritans by Philip. No disrespect to Philip, but the Samaritans went on living their old life until Peter and John arrived and corrected the situation by bringing them to the point of a baptism of repentance and conversion. In fairness it should be noted that this text can be interpreted in several ways, but it is the only text in Acts which will support a doctrine of two baptisms.

Charismatic Christians seem to be highly selective in their approach to Scripture. Having experienced a compelling encounter with the Holy Spirit, they come to Scripture and interpret it in the light of that experience, instead of interpreting the experience in the light of Scripture. This, no doubt, explains why the Acts of the Apostles is lifted above other New Testament documents as a kind of "canon within a canon." This is, indeed, a strange move for those charismatics who insist upon a doctrine of plenary inspiration of Scripture.

Nowhere in Paul nor in Acts do I find the gifts of the Spirit spoken of as signs confirming that the Spirit has been received. Only once does Paul speak of tongues as a sign, and there tongues are a strange sign for unbelievers, not for believers (I Cor. 14:22-23). Only in the concluding verses of the Gospel of Mark (16:14-20) are tongues (along with the handling of snakes and the drinking of poison) spoken of as signs of faith. Here the Spirit is not mentioned, and these signs are the consequences of faith demonstrating the power of faith to an unbelieving world.[2]

The controversy can be stated tersely: Taking seriously the New Testament scriptures as a whole, one discovers a multiplicity of gifts of the Spirit given as means of producing the fruits of the Spirit.

While the experience of tongues is one of the gifts, it is one among many. And for St. Paul, it is not a primary one. The overwhelming evidence of Scripture is that all Christians have the Spirit as a consequence of their baptism into the death and resurrection of Jesus Christ. But there is a strange reluctance to claim for the gifts of the Spirit the status of signs confirming externally to the believer the authenticity of his experience. No doubt this is due to two factors: The Spirit is known through faith, and signs would transform faith into proof. To major upon signs is tantamount to putting God on the stand and requiring that he justify himself.

To be certain, there are many Christians who experience a dramatic or quiet life-renewing encounter with the Holy Spirit after their Christian baptism. Not rejection but rejoicing is here in order. That experience is a part of the process of going on to the fuller life of "walking in the Spirit," or what my confessional father in the faith, John Wesley, called perfect love. But such an experience does not require a doctrine of two baptisms the case for which rests on tenuous scriptural grounds.[3]

Neo-Pentecostals claim with evangelical fervor to be biblical Christians. Being biblical involves us in reckoning with the whole sweep of biblical thought, not banking on isolated texts. The controversy with charismatic Christians is not that they are unbiblical, but they are not biblical enough.

THE CHARISMATIC REVIVAL AND EXPERIENCE

At the heart of Pentecostalism is an intense experience of being filled with the Spirit or of awakening to a new life through the transforming power of the baptism in the Spirit. Charismatic Christians enthusiastically witness to their new experience. John Sherrill, in a book read by almost every neo-Pentecostal, puts it this way:

> The Baptism in the Holy Spirit is the gift of love such as we have never known it. The natural aftermath is to be propelled forward by the power of this overflowing love into the world, seeking opportunity to share the thing that has come to us.[4]

The experience of mystery has always been a potent factor in Christian experience. Father Kilian McDonnell sees this experience of mystery inescapably tied to the dialectic of transcendence/immanence. Where this dialectic is broken, with radical emphasis upon either transcendence or immanence, the mystery is destroyed. The Pentecostal experience is an attempt to reestablish this dialectic and thereby to restore the sense of mystery lacking in so much of contemporary experience.[5]

For this reason Pentecostals have resisted any attempt to deny the autonomy of this experience. Try to explain it as you will, it is still the

experience of the Holy Spirit. To insist upon the autonomy and integrity of the experience is one matter. The *uses* to which such an experience can be put is another matter. The controversy with the charismatic revival should be joined at the latter and not the former. Critical questions regarding the uses of the experience can and must be
raised for the benefit of both Pentecostal and non-Pentecostal alike.

With such strong emphasis on subjective experience, charismatic
Christians are vulnerable to what one Catholic Pentecostal calls
charismania.[6] *Charismania* is a preoccupation or fixation with *charismata*—the gifts of the Spirit. The power of the subjective experience
can become an end in itself. The consuming desire can be for *feeling.*
Having the Spirit is having the experience. This propensity for feeling
is understandable given the conditions of the times. Much in modern
culture tempts us to reduce reality to neat, manageable formulas.
The church itself so rationalizes its worship and even its broader life
that many are compelled to complain of its sterility. The charismatic
senses this loss of mystery and of the personal and the experiential in
both church and society. In the wider society he is not alone, for
others are also acutely aware of this loss and have gone the route of
some new experientialism—Eastern meditation, encounter groups,
the Jesus "trip," or psychedelic drugs. The charismatic is to be
commended for not going the route of the exotic, and the charismatic ministry of David Wilkerson to the drug culture is one model
of mission for the contemporary church.[7]

But *charismania* persists. The quality of the Christian life comes to
be gauged in terms of the number and spectacular intensity of
experiences one can recite.[8] A church's spirituality is judged in terms
of the liveliness of its experiential life. Some charismatics even judge
the value of their group meetings according to the barometric readings on an experience scale.

With *charismania* comes the tendency to play down the rational
and intellective capacities of man. "Head trips" get played off against
"heart trips." The rational faculties are sometimes viewed as of a
lower order than the affective faculties. To be sure, the human
intellect can be perverted into an idolatrous exercise. The power of
discernment was, however, extolled by St. Paul as a charism also.
Any deeply experiential movement is always confronted with the
danger of anti-intellectualism in the name of a deepened experientialism. This is especially true in the American context, where anti-intellectualism has been a common factor in our religious heritage. I have
known theologically trained pastors who having received an experience of the Holy Spirit feel it necessary to repudiate the historical
and theological learning of their previous education. That education
may have been lacking in the experiential conviction which they have

now received. But without sound historical and theological understanding, the experience is left to the danger of extravagant and
distorted interpretation. What has happened to Jesus' summary of
the law, where he calls us to love God with our minds as well as with
our hearts?

This is not a criticism of the experience itself. It is rather a
criticism of uses of that experience. *Charismania* fails to appreciate
the full power of God to inspire the complete person, who is rational
mind and ethical will as well as feeling heart. St. Paul's response to
charismania in Corinth was not to reject the experience, but to hold
before that church the objective content of faith itself: "I determined not to know anything among you, save Jesus Christ, and him
crucified" (I Cor. 2:2).

Recent psychological studies of the Pentecostal experience rid us
of one of the old mythical bugaboos which has long plagued the
Pentecostal movement. Pentecostals are not any less healthy mentally than are other Christians. These same psychological studies do
point to certain psychological dangers which frequently accompany
the experience. One such danger is the development and encouragement of what psychologists call "the dependency syndrome." Speakers in tongues exhibit a strong compulsion to submit themselves to
the charism of a leader, placing unqualified trust in him. John
Kildahl, after his careful study,[9] concludes, "We never met a deeply
involved tongue-speaker who did not have some leader to whom he
looked for guidance." Charismatics employ such terms as "reverence" and "awe" to describe their relationship to their leader. From
such a relationship they derive feelings of acceptance, contentment,
and well-being.

Heavy dependence upon a leader is fraught with dangers both for
the follower and the leader. For the charismatic follower the experience itself and the strong attachment to the leader become so
integrally mixed that a fracture or crisis in the relationship with the
leader produces a concomitant crisis in the experience. Enthusiasm
for the experience wanes when the relationship with the leader begins
to deteriorate or when the leader is no longer available. On the other
side, such power of charismatic leadership presents the danger of
manipulation, of playing with people's feelings, which is to play with
their very lives. Unwittingly, both leader and followers can become
engaged in a psychologically detrimental game of "spiritual elitism."
Susan L. Bergquist observes in one recent report:

> ... Certain individuals would at one time point out to me the dangers of
> "spiritual elitism" only to follow this warning with reference to a particular
> person with great respect, admiration and perhaps even adoration. The
> respect and admiration seems fitting, but in a few cases I felt as though

certain individuals are being "sacralized" to the point where they are elevated above human fallibility.[10]

The strong egalitarian dynamics of what is commonly called the "renewal of the laity" can be mitigated by the development of such a dependency. Such can move in the direction of a *paraclericalism*, which will make a renewed lay movement into simply a church within a church. Psychologically, such a strong dependency prevents the charismatic Christian from becoming himself a mature center of regenerative power in the lives of other people.

Psychological studies also indicate that in the majority of cases the Pentecostal experience is preceded by a clearly defined anxiety crisis. These crises may be of many kinds—marital or financial, crises in health, a conflict in values, or a deep religious sense of guilt. This in itself does not argue against the experience. The disciples in the upper room had gone through a crisis experience also. Personal crises of a psychological nature do not exclude a person from receiving the gifts of the Spirit. In fact, such personal crises may heighten the sense of need of the divine. The heightened awareness of God and the supportive fellowship of the charismatic group can be aids toward resolving these crises and steps on the way to fuller health. There are ample testimonies to this effect.

On the other hand, there are cases, though rarely described in charismatic literature, in which because of the emotional condition of the person the results of the charismatic experience have not been salutary. The stress on the conditions for receiving the Spirit, such as seasons of prayer and deep earnest longing for the Spirit, can fortify and intensify the compulsive dynamics at work in the stress situation. At this point the charismatic need not fear psychology as a secular attempt to explain away his experience. That very psychology is needed to develop keener and more informed awareness of the psychological dynamics at work in the human personality. There are persons whose emotional states attract them to deeply experiential religion and who in their present condition cannot appropriate the experience without severe distortions involving illusion, hallucinations, and a deep disjuncture from reality. Certainly these persons need the ministry of the Spirit of God as much as anyone. But do they need this particular experience at this particular time? Real Christian sanity is found in the remarks of one neo-Pentecostal:

> It is better for the prayer meeting, and for such persons themselves, that they not be admitted to it. And if they are excluded (or counseled not to come), one need not fear that they are being cut off from the Holy Spirit. He does not need the prayer meeting as the medium for his communication.[11]

One wonders, however, how clearly this concerned Christian warning gets through. Experience is both a tender and powerful force in personality. It is both vulnerable and positively creative. Since religious experience is always this mixture, it cannot stand alone. It requires an alliance, never to be broken, with the gifts of rational discernment. Otherwise, what is authentic can, in its use, become destructive.

THE CHARISMATIC REVIVAL AND CONTEMPORARY CULTURE

Religious movements cannot be properly understood and assessed without attention to the cultural or societal context within which a given movement functions. The contemporary charismatic movement is no exception. To take note of the formative nature of the sociological context for the charismatic movement is particularly important, for today that movement is not just the continuation of the earlier Pentecostal movement. While that older movement is in many respects the father to the new, the child is nevertheless in many appearances different from the father. This is particularly evident when we recognize that the current charismatic movement rides on the tides of upward social and economic mobility. The chief proponents of the charismatic movement are no longer manual laborers but stalwart figures of the business community. In this respect the movement is strikingly different from its parent, and sharply different from the Pentecostalism in Africa and South America.

Now resident within the American denominational "establishment," the charismatic movement confronts some of the same problems and dangers that have long plagued the so-called "main-line" denominations. Beginning in the 1950's and extending into the early 1960's, some voices on the American scene called attention to the cultural capitulation of the churches. The churches seemed anemic and lacking in the requisite power to supply moral force in molding the national life. Rather than mold the national life, the churches simply reflected or legitimated certain key national values.

These observers referred to this phenomenon as a further development of American cultural religion. Such cultural religion was no respecter of denominational or confessional line. It was pervasively ecumenical! Such features as these can be delineated: (1) an emphasis on private virtue and an accompanying social acquiescence; (2) the subservience of institutional religion to the role of a means to achieve goals not defined by the religion itself, goals such as patriotism, business success, and an inner sense of well-being; (3) a pragmatic spirit which affirms the valuable and true to be what gets results. Enshrining these values, the American church became comfortable and contented in its social environment. It did not test or pester the larger society. It drew upon and enjoyed those cultural values and called them Christian.

Despite its desire to renew the institutional church, the charismatic revival is in danger of insidiously falling victim to the same trap of accommodation which grips the larger parent church. As illustration, charismatic literature frequently reflects the typical American success story. A dispirited man joins a local charismatic group, receives the charismatic experience, and quickly rises to business success. The implication seems to be, in keeping with American advertising philosophy, that this product "brings results."

The charismatic revival is the inheritor of a tradition which placed almost exclusive emphasis on individual morality. When that tradition attacked the social vices, it was always in terms of the effects which these vices had upon the individual. "Demon rum" was evil because it wrecked individual and family life. To that extent the analysis was correct. Rarely did that tradition, however, attack the greed nurtured in the profit motive itself, or the state of economic servitude which many times created the conditions for alcoholism in the first place. The charismatic revival continues to reflect this same myopic vision of the range of evil and the demonic in our society.

Charismatic literature propagates a theology of Satan and demonic powers. These demons are most usually depicted in highly individualistic guise. Appropriately, charismatics advocate the exorcism of demons. But is this demonology radical enough to do justice to the biblical understanding or to engage with the rampant evil of our society today? One searches in vain in American charismatic materials for references to the "principalities and powers" of racism which hold the Black man in the ghetto, the ravages of war pouring devastation upon a foreign people, the business imperialism which "develops" a third world and keeps its peoples deprived of the basic necessities of life and liberty, and the blatant corruption and abuse of political power in high places of government. The cultural captivity of the churches can easily captivate the charismatic revival within those churches. A renewal of individuals without the redemption of the society in which they must live is hardly sufficient for the renewal of the church which is Christ's body broken and given for the life of the world.

If we turn our eyes to other forms of Pentecostalism in other parts of the world we discover something there which could correct the American religious experience of domesticating and tranquilizing the Christian Gospel. Pentecostalism in Brazil and Chile has a very different social character. Here the baptism in the Spirit brings with it a vision of the whole person, soul and body, and a resolute commitment to transform the society through the power of the Spirit. Black Pentecostalism on the American scene possesses that same vision of the wholeness of human life and a sense of urgency for mission in society as well as to the inner life of the individual. Principally for this reason, Black Pentecostalism has kept its distance from the new charismatic movement. Until a wider vision of the realm of redemption is captured, the charismatic movement will continue to look strangely white and middle class.[12]

THE CHARISMATIC REVIVAL AND THE CHURCH

The most frequently articulated criticism of the charismatic movement is a quite practical one—that it causes dissension and divisiveness in the church. While there are enthusiastic reports in charismatic literature of renewed vitality and increased participation in the life of the church where charismatic rebirth has taken place, there is also another picture. There are churches, and today the number is on the increase, where the emergence of a charismatic group has been the occasion for hostile division, censoriousness, and the ugliness of charge and countercharge.

To be fair, it should be said that it takes two to tango. The institutional church by its conservative defensiveness toward something new can create a climate of distrust encouraging the new charismatic to expect alienation and martyrdom. On the other side, however, the charismatic Christian often displays an attitude of spiritual aristocracy. The intensity of the experience can easily lead one to conclude that such experience is of a higher order than a spirituality not so demonstrative. Then the characteristically sectarian distinction between those baptized with water and those baptized in the Spirit becomes explicit. Divisive comparisons are made—some have received a symbolic baptism while others have gone on to a deeper spiritual baptism; some have made affirmations of faith in Jesus Christ, but still others have gone on to encounter God in the Spirit; some are "lukewarm" and others "on fire" Christians. These distinctions are usually made on the basis of external behavioral manifestations.

I have heard the ministries of deeply committed and passionately spiritual pastors denigrated because they have not had a particular type of experience which the charismatic has enjoyed and deems essential. With some amusement, I have read in charismatic literature claims that such figures in the history of the church as Martin Luther and John Wesley had received such baptism and had spoken in tongues. These claims are put forward to lend support to the superior status of the experience. There is no documentary evidence to support these assertions. Quite frankly, an authentic experience of the Spirit deserves something better than historical deceit for substantiation!

When such methods are employed, many honest Christians are

made to feel needlessly guilty or anxious about their Christian experience. Or on the other hand, they are placed in a position of defensiveness which can give rise to anger and frustration. Divisiveness is the consequence.

The clear indication of Scripture and the history of the church is that the Holy Spirit pours himself out upon all kinds of persons and in all kinds of situations. There is no one normative gift unless one speaks of *agape*, love, as the supreme gift. There is no warrant in the New Testament for assuming that because one has not had a particular identifiable experience with external signs one is somehow less Christian than others who have had such experiences. While the Christian is always engaged in the process of going on to maturity, there are not two grades of the Christian life. To many different people and under many different circumstances the same Holy Spirit witnesses to the human spirit that we are the sons of God.

The criticism of divisiveness and concomitant spiritual self-righteousness is not new to the Pentecostal movement. Today many neo-Pentecostals are alert to the dangers of a spiritual aristocracy. In fact, these neo-Pentecostals can be more pointed in their denunciation of the censorious spirit of dissension than I have been. But is the message really getting through? There is statistical evidence and personal experience that it is not. Why?

One fundamental reason is that the Pentecostal experience has been wedded to a theological explanation which in social operation spells divisiveness. When such heavy theological weight is placed upon the necessity of two baptisms, whether these occur simultaneously or subsequently to each other, the seeds of invidious comparison have already been sown. The observation of a Roman Catholic, appreciative of the Pentecostal experience but nevertheless critical of some of its uses, is instructive:

> By taking the theological weight off the central experience of Pentecostalism, what they call the "baptism in the Spirit," we can accept their spiritual practice with considerably less reserve. Neo-Pentecostals have tended to play down the Pentecostal insistence on tongues, while keeping to their doctrine of "baptism in the Spirit." It seems to me preferable to keep their insistence on tongues, but to take the theological weight off.[13]

This is but another variation on the repeated theme of this paper: the experience is not under question, but the *uses* of that experience are ambiguous in many instances. When the theological weight is taken off, the experience is then set free to play its way on the field of a wide variety of rich experiences of the Spirit. The church would be the richer and its shared life together deepened if such were to be the case.

CONCLUSION

The controversial aspects of the charismatic revival, as these have been enumerated, have been stated cogently by some neo-Pentecostals themselves. The fact that there can be such self-criticism indicates health.

In the meantime the institutional church cannot afford simply to go its own way and leave the charismatics to go their way. What the charismatic is seeking, the whole church should be seeking. If the church is itself charismatic, i.e., the gift of grace, then no Christian should turn aside. In the wilderness of our modern civilization we need to see again a burning bush and to hear again a voice, "Take off your shoes; the ground on which you stand is holy ground."

We need an unapologetic praise to the God who has brought us thus far and will see us on our way. We need the deepened prayer life that will bring us to encounter with this God. We need the Spirit-driven power that will invigorate a renewed sense of mission to the world which God so loved. Somewhere in his lectures the late Rabbi Abraham Heschel remarked that we of the Western world have been through two generations of theological reconstruction and yet do not have a reconstructed spirituality. Such a spirituality must be deeply personal without being individualistic, intensely communal without a blindness to the wider human community—a spirituality of the gifts which forges them into the fruits of a new humanity under the Lordship of Christ. This task is too great for any gift to be despised or for any to be hoarded. All the gifts must be used for the edification of the body of Christ. The charismatic needs the institutional church or else the spiritual fires burn out in the coldness of our cultural night. The institutional church needs the charismatic or else the institution may miss an appointment with the life-giving Spirit.

Notes

1. *Why Tongues?* (Blessed Trinity Society, Van Nuys, California), pp. 1-2.
2. Recent exegetical studies in dialogue with the charismatic movement are instructive. A non-Pentecostal critique of Pentecostal theology from a New Testament perspective is offered in Frederick Dale Bruner, *A Theology of the Holy Spirit* (Grand Rapids, 1970), while James D. G. Dunn, *Baptism in the Holy Spirit* (Naperville, Ill., 1970) is a non-Pentecostal but somewhat more sympathetic treatment. Arnold Bittlinger, *Gifts and Graces: A Commentary on I Corinthians 12-14* (Grand Rapids, 1967) is illustrative of charismatic scholarship from a German Lutheran.
3. For a fuller theological analysis, see Donald G. Bloesch, "The Charismatic Revival: A Theological Critique," *Religion in Life*, XXXV (Summer, 1966), 364-80.
4. John L. Sherrill, *They Speak with Other Tongues* (New York, 1965), p. 133.
5. Kilian McDonnell, OSB, "The Ideology of Pentecostal Conversion," *Journal of Ecumenical Studies*, V (Winter, 1968), 105-26.

6. Edward D. O'Connor, CSC, *The Pentecostal Movement in the Catholic Church* (South Bend, Ind., 1971), pp. 225-28.
7. Wilkerson, John and Elizabeth Sherrill, *The Cross and the Switch-blade* (New York, 1963).
8. Sherrill, *They Speak with Other Tongues*, p. 138. Sherrill is aware of this danger when he correctly warns, "I'm not talking about witnessing to the experience of Pentecost. Christ did not say, ' . . . ye shall be witnesses to the Baptism in the Holy Spirit.' It is never the function of the Spirit to call attention to himself. The Baptism is nothing more than a means to an end, and the end is always Christ."
9. John P. Kildahl, *The Psychology of Speaking in Tongues* (New York, 1972).
10. Susan L. Bergquist, "The Revival of Glossolalic Practices in the Catholic Church: Its Sociological Implications," *Perkins Journal*, XXX, 3 (October, 1973), 256-65.
11. O'Connor, p. 225.
12. See the perceptive analysis by Walter Hollenweger, "Pentecostalism and Black Power," *Theology Today*, XXX, 3 (October, 1973), 256-65.
13. Simon Tugwell, OP, "Catholics and Pentecostals," *New Blackfriars* (May, 1971), 214.

The Background for
Understanding the Movement

3 THE NEW TESTAMENT EVIDENCE
KRISTER STENDAHL

The word *glossolalia* comes into our language from a couple of New Testament references where the Greek expression *glossais lalein* occurs. The traditional translation "to speak in tongues" is a good one if it is remembered that the English word *tongue*, like the Greek word *glossa*, can mean both "tongue" and "language." Paul seems to play on this double meaning in the poetic 1 Corinthians 13, where he has the practice of glossalalia in mind when he opens with the sentence, "If I speak human language or even angelic language, but I do not have love. . . ."[1]

I

It is in his grappling with the problems that faced the Corinthian church that Paul happens to give us clear and significant insight into the phenomenon of glossolalia as part of the Christian experience. We should perhaps first check our language in one more respect. Scholars and modern readers are quick to put the label "problem" on the topic of glossolalia. And it is obvious that Paul does see problems in the Corinthian church. One of them is the tension created in the congregation by the practices of glossolalia. But it is significant that he does not use that term "problem" when he discusses the glossolalia. To him it is rather the question of gifts, *charismata*, graciously given divine gifts. The genius of his discussion is perhaps exactly in that initial perspective. (As an administrator I have learned that once I have labeled something a problem, then I have already lost the first round.) So we must remind ourselves that we are not dealing with

Dr. Krister Stendahl, a New Testament scholar, is Dean of Harvard Divinity School. Born in Stockholm, Sweden, in 1921, Dean Stendahl received his Th.D. degree from Uppsala University in 1954. He has also studied in Paris and in England at Cambridge University. Ordained a priest of the Church of Sweden in 1944, Dean Stendahl was an assistant pastor in the diocese of Stockholm from 1944 to 1946 and chaplain at Uppsala University from 1948 to 1950. Since 1968 he has been a pastor in the Lutheran Church in America.
    Dean Stendahl is the author of *The School of St. Matthew and Its Use of the Old Testament* (1954) and *The Bible and the Role of Women* (1966), and the editor and co-author of *The Scrolls and the New Testament* (1957). He has published articles and essays in Swedish, German, and American journals and encyclopedias.

the "problem" of glossolalia, but that we are approaching the subject in a Pauline manner: What about the gift of glossolalia?

We do not get much of a description of glossolalia from Paul or from any other New Testament writer. To Paul it is just an obvious part of the Christian experience, and one with which he is quite familiar from his own practice thereof. We know that Paul has a tendency—an annoying one at that—to claim that he is the greatest in everything. He had been the greatest of sinners, and the hardest of workers for the Gospel, and he had suffered more than all others, etc., etc. So it does not surprise us that when it comes to glossolalia he says, "I thank God that I speak in tongues more than you all" (1 Cor. 14:18). But even if we allow for the arrogant exuberance of Paul, we have reasons to believe him to be a mighty speaker in tongues.

There is other evidence that Paul considered glossolalia to be part of the common Christian experience. I have in mind a passage in his epistle to the Romans, in which he is not dealing with specific congregational problems that have been brought to his attention. Thus his reference here to glossolalia is not triggered by questions raised about this phenomenon. Paul brings up the subject himself because he thinks it important to remind his readers of this wonderful gift of the Spirit. He says:

> Likewise the Spirit helps us in our weakness; for we do not know how to pray as we ought, but the Spirit itself intercedes with unspeakable groanings; and he who searches the hearts knows what is the mind of the Spirit, for the Spirit intercedes for the saints in a divine manner (or: "according to God's will"). (Rom. 8:26-27)

It is fascinating to notice how Paul comes to think about the role of glossolalia in the context of his argument in Romans 8. He has spoken of how in the cultic cry of "Abba! Father!" the Spirit bears "witness with our spirit that we are children of God" (8:16). He then, in typically Pauline fashion, interrupts the flow of triumphant language and takes great pains to stress how such glories are yet in the future. He speaks of how we groan with the whole of creation as we wait for the redemption to take place. Faith is hope rather than possession. "For who hopes for what he sees?" (8:24). This groaning and beleaguered existence places us in a position of weakness. But now the groaning takes on another connotation. There is an unspeakable sound in the church that is not of human pain and longing but of the Spirit. The unspeakable groan of glossolalia is that of the Spirit interceding for the saints.[2]

Thus, in Paul's mind, the gift of glossolalia is not a sign of spiritual accomplishment, it is not the graduation with high honors into the category of the truly spiritual. To him glossolalia is the gift that fits into his experience of weakness. All this is quite in keeping with

Paul's consistent argument against any piety or theology marked by triumphalism, i.e., by an overstatement of spiritual superiority and gnostic flight from the powers of sin and death. It is important to have this perspective in mind as we turn to his handling of the situation in Corinth.[3]

And so we turn to the Corinthian scene. The church of Corinth had many problems. It had almost all the problems that churches have had through the ages, except the chief problem of our churches today: it was never dull.

It appears that in Corinth the phenomenon of glossolalia had fired the imaginations of the Corinthian Christians. Paul's argument about this and the polarization it created in the congregation is a simple one, built on the image of the body that needs different members (1 Cor. 12). He observes that there are many gifts, all of which are needed, and that it can only be considered silly to play the one gift against the other or to organize them in a hierarchy of value. All these gifts belong to the church and should not be valued or sought on the basis of spectacular appearances.

It is at this point that Paul enters the hymnic plea for love (1 Cor. 13). This familiar passage—often read at weddings for some reason—is not a general praise of love. It is shaped and created for the very specific purpose of demonstrating the solution to the tensions in the Corinthian congregation. The references to glossolalia (13:1, 8), prophecy (13:2, 8), *gnosis* (i.e., the claim to revealed special knowledge—13:2, 8), the power of miracles (13:2), and the capacity for "helpful deeds" (13:3; cf. 12:28) all point toward the gifts that manifest themselves in the church there. And Paul's point is made obvious when he shows how all these gifts can become divisive unless they are controlled by what he calls love, *agape*. To him this love is not a feeling in the heart. Love is rather the criterion by which one can distinguish between those on an ego-trip and those who exercise these gifts toward "the building up" (*oikodome*) of the community (1 Cor. 14:4 etc.). In 1 Corinthians 8:1 Paul has given his catchword for this attitude: "*Gnosis* puffs up, but love builds up." And in I Corinthians 14 he then proceeds to apply this principle that he has expanded in poetic style in I Corinthians 13. It is very clear and simple. The exercise of the gifts of the Spirit should be governed by what best builds up the community. Love means concern for the community and is the check on the exercise of the gifts for personal gratification or the gratification of some rather than all.

From this perspective it makes much sense when Paul, the mighty practitioner of glossolalia, says: "I thank God that I speak in tongues more than you all. Nevertheless, in church I would rather speak five words with my mind, in order to instruct others, than ten thousand words in a tongue" (14:18-19). And if tongues, then there should also be interpretation (14:27). For "he who speaks in a tongue edifies [builds up] himself, but he who prophesies edifies [builds up] the church" (14:4).

The import of this line of argument could best be expressed by our concluding that to Paul glossolalia is a communication between the believer and God. As such it is a wonderful and treasured gift, part of the complete spectrum of Christian experience. But it is not suited for evangelism or for publicity. It can become divisive when used for any other purpose than the edification of the person who has that gift. It is a family affair, and we may rejoice in the family with those who practice the gift. But with humor and irony he describes at length how singularly nonproductive glossolalia is for those who come into the church as strangers. He says that they will just think you are crazy (14:23).

Now, we know that Paul is not afraid of being a fool for Christ's sake (1 Cor. 4:10). But at this point he is afraid of wrong foolishness. I guess he knew that some Christians love to feel encouraged in their witness by the world's accusing them of being crazy. The more they are labeled crazy the more they feel sure that their witness is strong and courageous.

But did not Paul say that the Greeks seek wisdom and the Jews demand signs, but we preach Christ crucified, a stumbling block to Jews and a folly to Gentiles (1 Cor. 1:22-23)? I think Paul knew how such fearless witness could send him on what we have called ego-trips. At least he sees the risk when others do it, and therefore he brings in his principle of "love," of the building up of the whole community. That "building up" is done better by understandable speaking than by glossolalia. There is a passage in Scripture (Isa. 28:10-11)[4] which uses strange language, words that have no meaning understandable to human beings: sav lasav, sav lasav—kav lakav, kav lakav—zeer sham, zeer sham.[5] Paul quotes God's comment on this to Isaiah: "By strange speakers (*heteroglossoi*) and by the lips of foreigners shall I speak to this people and even so they will not listen to me" (1 Cor. 14:21).[6]

Interpreters have been thrown by the unexpected shift in Paul's argument at this point. He seems to have been saying that glossolalia is for insiders but that the outsider is lost and cannot say his Amen to a thanksgiving uttered in tongues (1 Cor. 14:16). But now we are told, on the basis of the quote from Isaiah, that glossolalia is for a sign not to believers, but to unbelievers, while prophecy is not for unbelievers but for believers (14:22). After which Paul returns to his plea for the use of prophecy rather than glossolalia in the assemblies, and this for the specific reason that prophecy has the power of leading to the conviction and conversion of the outsider.

A resolution of this apparent inconsistency is important for our understanding that according to Paul glossolalia has no function as a means toward impressing the outsiders, that it belongs to the warmth of individual thanksgiving, not to the public realm.

The key to the problem is what Paul means by "sign."[7] I suggest that the word "sign" had a negative connotation for Paul.[8] It refers to a "mere sign," a sign that does not lead to faith but to non-hearing, to the hardening of unbelief. To the believers the glossolalia is not a sign, it is part of their experience. And Paul's point is that the church owes the outsiders and unbelievers who come to the assemblies more than a mere negative sign toward their judgment. It owes them the full opportunity of repentance and the chance to recognize fully that God is truly in the midst of the assembly. This can be accomplished by prophecy, by the plain and clear speaking of the word of God.[9] It cannot be achieved by glossolalia, which for the outsider simply enforces his alienation, causing him to stumble over the mere sign, as Isaiah had predicted it in that passage.

II

Within the New Testament there is another, and totally different, way of speaking about tongues and about the phenomenon of glossolalia. In Acts 2 we find an account of the first Christian Pentecost. It may surprise you that I did not begin there, rather than in Corinth, especially since in this century we have come to use the term *Pentecostals* for groups and churches that give special emphasis to glossolalia. My reasons for the order I have chosen will soon appear.

In Acts 2 the tongues are tongues as of fire,[10] distributing themselves over the apostles and hovering over them as they, full of the Spirit, begin to speak in "other tongues" (*heterai glossai*). This happens in Jerusalem, accompanied by the sound of a mighty wind from heaven. It appears that here the situation is the opposite of that in Corinth: This glossolalia is not in need of interpreters. The speaking with tongues is a miraculous and marvelous means of communication so that a large number of people from diverse countries hear in their own tongues the disciples proclaim "the mighty works of God" (2:11). It seems that the tragic breakdown in communication at the Tower of Babel (Gen. 11:6-9) has been overcome. This contrast to the understanding of glossolalia that emerges from Paul's discussion in 1 Corinthians is striking, and it is not obviated or softened by the various discussions about whether the miracle in Acts 2 is one of speaking (the apostles speaking different languages or dialects), or one of hearing (the listeners recognizing a "heavenly" language as their own true language).[11] In either case the difference remains between intelligible (Acts) and unintelligible (Paul) glossolalia.[12] I am, however, inclined to think that little is to be gained by this line of reasoning. We must rather begin by considering the nature of the Pentecost account and its function within that work called the Acts of the Apostles.

The account of Pentecost is unique in the sense that nowhere else in the New Testament or in the early extra-canonical literature is there ever a reference to such an event. While we have practically no Christian literature that does not hail the event of Easter, there is no reference to Pentecost as an event except in Acts. All Christian literature is aware of the Spirit being around. But the account of a specific event rests solely on the author of the Book of Acts. It may well be that he, the author, is the one who has stylized and put into story form a theological interpretation of the phenomenon of speaking with tongues. Furthermore, nowhere else in early Christian literature is there any understanding of glossolalia as the speaking of a language known in some other part of the world. The very point of glossolalia elsewhere in early Christian tradition is that it needs an interpreter, that it is unintelligible; i.e., that it is just as described in the Corinthian correspondence. But in Acts it sounds as if there were a divine shortcut to the Berlitz school. It is also questionable whether the places from which the hearers come (Acts 2:9-11) really represent distinct languages.

It must be recognized that the very structure of the Book of Acts is one of "theological geography." Just as in the Gospel of Luke Jesus moves from Galilee to Jerusalem—and much of the narrative and teaching is comprised in the so-called Lukan Travel Narrative (Lk. 9:51-18:14); this in complete variance with the other gospels— so in Acts the Gospel is brought from Jerusalem (ch. 1) to Rome (ch. 28), and the scheme is announced in the parting words of the Risen Lord prior to his ascension, when he promises the coming of the Spirit as the starting point for such a mission out of Jerusalem "to the end of the earth" (Acts 1:8).

Thus it is tempting to follow the rather common suggestion that Luke has translated his awareness of how the Spirit is abroad in the church and his acquaintance with the phenomenon of glossolalia into a historic event, of which we have no other evidence. The global outreach is symbolized by the phenomenon of glossolalia.[13] If this is true, then it becomes rather precarious—to say the least—to base our understanding of the actual phenomenon of glossolalia on the account in Acts 2.[14]

III

In our discussion of the Pauline attitude toward glossolalia and the spectacular gifts of the Spirit we had reason to stress quite strongly how such gifts were not to operate in the public domain. Actually, it is worth asking how the early Christians thought of their relation to the public world, and, more especially, how and where they saw the point of intersection between the church and the world. The reason for my raising that question within a study of glossolalia is perhaps less obvious. Yet the connection is an important one.

We have said that the spectacular gifts of the Spirit are for the edification of the individual and not for public relations. But a special gift of the Spirit *is* promised for the most public of relations in which a Christian could be involved: "And when they bring you to trial and deliver you up [to the authorities], do not be anxious beforehand what you are to say; but say whatever is given to you in that hour, for it is not you who speak, but the Holy Spirit" (Mk. 13:11; see also Mt. 10:19-20, Lk. 12:11-12). As a matter of fact, the Christian before the courts is the only one to whom the Scriptures promise the gift of the Spirit. No one individual is otherwise promised a special gift of the Spirit. This is not so strange, for it was in the courts that the Christian church had the opportunity to witness to the powers of this world. Out of this view and conviction comes the elaborate account of how Paul appealed to Caesar although he presumably could have been freed (Acts 25:11; 26:32), and also the passage in Ephesians (3:10-13) in which appearing before Caesar and confronting the heavenly principalities and powers blend into one, and in which Paul's sufferings are the glory of the church, since the judicial process occasions the confrontation between the Gospel and the world, between Christ and Caesar. To be a witness (the Greek word is "martyr") is to be a witness before the authorities. Thus there should be no surprise when we find that the Spirit is especially promised for such a situation.

This line of biblical thinking strikes me as significant at this time. The concern for the gifts of the Spirit in the charismatic movement has sometimes been seen as being at the opposite end of the spectrum from the exposed place where we find the Berrigans and the conscientious resisters in our land. If that feeling and interpretation were correct (and it is often enforced by the press and the other media), then we are seriously removed from a biblical understanding of the gifts of the Spirit. Then we have distorted deep Christian insight. There are those who identify the public impact of the Spirit with spectacular religious exhibitions on TV and maximum publicity for evangelistic campaigns, while casting suspicion over those who challenge the authorities by their courageous witness to Christ's justice in the courts. It seems that the biblical model is the opposite one. In the courts is *the* confrontation that has the promise of the Spirit.

IV

It seems to me that the witness of the New Testament texts as to the phenomenon called glossolalia is quite clear and quite simple—and quite up to date. The various texts carry with them a certain critique of the situation today. The history of our main traditions is one of fragmentation and impoverishment within the Christian community. As I read Paul it seems to me crystal clear that if the Presbyterians and the Episcopalians, the Lutherans, and all the "proper" Christians, including the Catholics, did not consciously or unconsciously suppress such phenomena as glossolalia, and if other denominations did not especially encourage them, then the gifts of the Spirit— including glossolalia— would belong to the common register of Christian experience.

The Pauline recipe is sound. The fullness of the church cannot be better ridiculed than by the habit, long established, according to which every denomination or sect takes its gift of the Spirit and builds a special little chapel around it. The fullness of the church is, in the image of Paul, the body of Christ with many and diverse members, i.e., gifts.

There are signs at this time in the charismatic movement that we may have the chance to restore that fullness. And that is what fascinates me and gives me much hope in the charismatic movement. Could it be that we have come to a time when the main-line churches have enough Pauline love so as to be ready to accept within them the manifestations of the Spirit, including glossolalia? Could it be that those blessed with this experience could have enough love and patience as they speak to the Lord in the Spirit so as to recognize that they were given that gift in order to add to the fullness of the church, not in order to make others feel less Christian in their faith? Perhaps we are at that point. I hope we are, and that for the benefit of us all.

Glossolalia is a facet of what I like to see as high-voltage religion. It is obvious to me that to some people, and in some situations, the experience of God is so overwhelming that charismatic phenomena are the "natural" expression. In the history of religions and of the church there is an honorable place for ecstasy. Who said that only rational words or silence would be proper? As a preacher and lecturer, I even wonder if it is not wise to let glossolalia gush forth in the church so that those who are not professional in the shaping of words are free to express fully their overwhelmed praise to the Lord. Actually, in the history of the church the practice of glossolalia has often had a democratizing effect. It has been one of the expressions through which in a certain sense "the last have become the first."

Opening up the full spectrum of religious experience and expression is badly needed in those churches that have suppressed the charismatic dimension. Flashlight-battery-voltage Christianity is certainly not strong enough for fighting the drug habit. And no religious tradition can renew itself without the infusion of raw and fresh primary religious experience. It could well be that the charismatic movement is given to the churches as one such infusion. We noncharismatics need not become charismatics—glossolalia is a gift, not a goal or an ideal—but we need to have charismatics among us in the church if the church is to receive and express the fullness of the Christian life. Thus *we* need *them*.

Those churches that have suppressed charismatic manifestations often argue that the biblical phenomenon of glossolalia was given to the early church for its breakthrough period, that once the church was established, such "primitive" things were no longer needed. Such reasoning has a defensive ring. The defensiveness is one of embarrassment, either for the absence of what the Bible describes as part of the full Christian experience, or for what "enlightened" Christians perceive as unsavory and primitive in the annals of their tradition.

When used in such a setting, the idea of a breakthrough period does not commend itself. But there is another sense in which it has meaning and contains wisdom born out of experience. For it seems to me that few human beings can live healthily with high-voltage religious experience over a long period of time. While I reject the breakthrough argument on the plane of institutional history, I am very sympathetic to it when applied to individual history. I am concerned about what happens to charismatics after five or ten or twenty years. From my observations it seems that *they* need *us;* they need to know that their home is the larger church in which their status as children of God does not depend on the intensity of their experiences. There are times and seasons in the long life of a Christian. There are times of spectacular breakthroughs and there are times of slow growth. Understandably, those who have had strong and beautiful experiences like to have them continue. If that experience eventually does not come quite as freshly and as strongly as it once did, then comes the temptation to "help the Spirit" a little— that is, to cheat. Which creates feelings of guilt. To be sure, the established churches need the refreshing influx of new and wider ranges of charismatic experience, but in the long perspective of spiritual growth the individual charismatic needs the home of the full church in which he or she matures in faith and learns the most important lesson of faith: to love God who gave the gift rather than to love the gift that God gave. That lesson can be learned only in a church where we rejoice with the charismatics in the gifts given to them—they are the precious seasoning of our common life—and where those who are given such gifts can grow in faith without feeling threatened if their experiences change during a long and honest life.

These reflections grow out of Paul's insights into the fullness of the church and the building up of our common life. They are born out of the conviction that the question of glossolalia in the churches is a pastoral one. It is not a question of whether glossolalia is a theologically proper phenomenon—of course it is. It is rather a question of how this phenomenon can be a force to the benefit of the whole church. It is in that sense that Paul's vision and perspective strike me as unsurpassed both in wisdom and validity.

It may prove important to pursue further how glossolalia is an integral part of what all religions know as mysticism, and how it relates to the practices and experiences of Christian mystics. I am inclined to think that such an analysis would reinforce the criterion mentioned above: not the gift that God gave, but God who gave the gift. The charismatics are in danger of becoming fascinated by the gift. The mystics are the pioneers in transcending all gifts so as never to rest until God is All in All. Which is another reason for saying that we need to stay together in that love which allows a maximum of diversification in gifts as God gives them differently and at different times.

Notes

1. See below (pp. 53f.) for the differences between Paul's understanding of glossolalia and that found in the Pentecost story (Acts 2:4, 11). The difference is not, however, one between "mere tongues" or "mere sounds" and "languages." The difference is between unintelligible speaking (Paul) and a miraculous communication understood by those who listen (Acts 2). For a dependable introduction to the exegetical questions in the New Testament, see J. Behm, article on *glossa* in *Theological Dictionary of the New Testament*, ed. Gerhard Kittel (Grand Rapids, 1964), I, 719-27. Behm's article also gives the relevant material about similar phenomena in surrounding cultures. For a discussion of the "language of angels" in Jewish and early Christian tradition, see Russell P. Spittler, Jr., "The Testament of Job," doctoral thesis, Harvard University, 1971.

2. For a more extensive interpretation of Romans 8:26-27 along these lines, see E. Käsemann, "The Cry for Liberty in the Worship of the Church," *Perspectives on Paul* (Philadelphia, 1971), pp. 122-37. In his *An die Roemer* (Handb. z. NT 8a, 1973), pp. 229-32, this interpretation is carefully compared with and defended against other interpretations.

3. It should be noted that when Paul refers to his having listened to words spoken in Paradise ("and he heard unspeakable words, which are not permissible for humans to speak," 2 Cor. 12:4), he does so as a stress on his own weakness manifested in his "thorn in the flesh," presumably the illness that taught him not to glory in his visions and revelations but in the grace of God (2 Cor. 12:6-10). Compare also 2 Corinthians 4:7 against the preceding words of glorious revelations.

4. Paul here uses the term *Law* for a quotation from the prophet Isaiah. This does not indicate that he quotes from memory and remembers wrongly. Jewish practice was to use *Law* for *Scripture*. Cf. Romans 3:19; John 10:34.

5. These words have no meaning. They were meant to be a mimicking either of child talk or of drunken talk or dialect peculiarities of the prophet. But the Septuagint interpreted them as meaning "affliction upon affliction, hope upon hope, yet a little, yet a little"; and the KJV and RSV gave the meaning "precept upon precept, line upon line, here a little there a little." However, Paul was familiar with these words in the Hebrew and untranslatable form.

They came to his mind when thinking of glossolalia. Perhaps his reference to childishness and adulthood in 1 Corinthians 14:20 is another indication that he has in mind not only Isaiah 28:11 but the whole passage, since in 28:9 there is a reference to little children.

6. Paul's quotation differs both from the Hebrew text and the Septuagint (although Origen reports that this wording comes close to Aquila). In any case, it is an adapted quotation, serving the point Paul wants to make.

7. The Greek of 1 Corinthians 14:22 should be translated carefully. The RSV translation, "tongues are a sign not for believers but for unbelievers," overlooks the expression *eis semeion* (for a sign). I would translate: "Thus [according to the quotation from Isaiah 28:11] glossolalia becomes [*einai eis*] a (mere) sign not for believers but for unbelievers."

8. In various contexts Paul refers to "signs" where he speaks of matters which for him are wrong (1 Cor. 1:22) or obsolete (circumcision, Rom. 4:11). In 2 Corinthians 12:12 Paul refers to the signs of the true apostle performed among the Corinthians, but it should be noted that this is part of an ironic, tongue-in-cheek exchange about his credentials as compared to other traveling missionaries: "For I am not at all inferior to these super-apostles, even though I am nothing" (12:11). The same expression is echoed in Romans 15:19, where again there is the note of reticence: "For I will not venture to speak . . ." (15:18). In 2 Thessalonians 2:9 the signs are of Satan, and false. In 2 Thessalonians 3:17 Paul's signature is the sign indicating that it is his letter. These (together with 1 Cor. 14:22) are all the references to "signs" in Paul's epistles. None of them refers to signs in a sense or context in which Paul glories unambiguously in them. It is well known that the synoptic Gospels have a similar negative attitude toward signs. In Mark we hear that "no sign will be given" (Mk. 8:12); in Luke the sign is Jonah's preaching (Lk. 11:29); and in Matthew 12:40, possibly by later addition (see K. Stendahl, *The School of St. Matthew* [Philadelphia, 1968], pp. 132f.), the death and resurrection is that sign of Jonah. The miracles of Jesus are never called signs, except in the Gospel of John, where seven chosen miracles are proclaimed and elaborated as "the Signs." Otherwise, signs are celestial and apocalyptic in the cosmic realm. And Jesus' fear of publicity from his miracles is a well-known gospel theme (e.g., Mk. 5:43).

9. With this interpretation, prophecy is of course not a "sign." C.K. Barrett, *The First Epistle to the Corinthians* (New York, 1968), pp. 313, 323f., translates "prophecy as a sign not for the unbelieving. . . ." He admits that "as a sign" is not in the Greek text but must be understood from the preceding sentence. I submit that there lies the key to the alleged problem with our text. Thus, I would paraphrase 1 Corinthians 14:21-25 as follows: From the Scriptures we learn that when God speaks through glossolalia, it will not lead to faith [*eisakousontai:* they will not hear, a prophetic future used by Paul to refer to the situation now at hand in the church]. Thus it is clear, according to this prophetic word, that glossolalia is a mere sign, incapable of leading the unbeliever to faith. Of course, to the believer glossolalia is not such a sign, for he has listened to the word of God and come to faith. Prophecy, on the other hand, is toward faith and not toward the hardening of unbelief. Thus, if in the assembly all speak with tongues, and outsiders and nonbelievers come in, will they not just say that you are mad? The sign of glossolalia will work on them as Isaiah has predicted. But if all speak in understandable prophecy, then the nonbeliever or the outsider will be brought to repentance, convicted and judged as the secrets of his heart are laid open and he falls down, worshipping God and declaring that God is really among you.

10. Note Mark 1:8, Matthew 3:11, and Luke 3:16, where John the Baptist makes the distinction between his baptism (by water) and that of the Greater One to come, who will baptize in the Holy Spirit (Mark) or in the Holy Spirit and fire (Matthew and Luke).

11. For extensive discussion of these and other exegetical questions, see Kirsopp

Lake, "The Gift of the Spirit and the Day of Pentecost," *The Beginnings of Christianity*, eds. F.J. Foakes-Jackson and Kirsopp Lake (New York, 1933), V, 111-21; see also E. Haenchen, *The Acts of the Apostles* (Philadelphia, 1971), pp. 166-75.

12. I fail to see the validity of C. S. C. Williams' assertion in *A Commentary on the Acts of the Apostles* (New York, 1957), p. 63, that "those who adopt the ordinary critical view tend to overlook that even to Paul glossolalia may well have meant or included speaking in foreign tongues, as well as unintelligible speech, not the latter alone." He refers to J.G. Davies, "Pentecost and Glossolalia," *Journal of Theological Studies*, III (1952), 228-31. Davies argues that the term *hermeneia/hermeneuein*, which Paul uses for the interpretation of glossolalia (1 Cor. 12:10, 30; 14:5, 13, 26, 27) has the primary meaning of "translate" rather than "interpret." That is correct, and obviously Paul thought about glossolalia as a language, even as the language of angels (1 Cor. 13:1). But that does not mean that he understood it as the acquisition of knowledge of an earthly foreign language. Tongues are unintelligible, since they express "mysteries in the Spirit" (1 Cor. 14:2). And Paul urges the speaker of tongues to "pray that he be able also to interpret" (14:13). It is not by knowing other languages, but by the special gift of interpretation/translation, that these mysteries can be made intelligible to others.

13. Such a suggestion is partly confirmed by the observation that when glossolalia is mentioned at other points in Acts (10:44; 19:6; cf. 4:31), the phenomenon appears much more similar to the picture we receive in 1 Corinthians 12-14. In Acts 10, for example, there is no reference to language difficulties. Rather, the point is that God has to overcome Peter's hesitations concerning Gentile membership in the church by having Cornelius and his people show the spectacular evidence of the Spirit, all of which led Peter to declare that there could be no reason not to baptize those who had received the Holy Spirit "just as we have" (Acts 10:47). Here the Spirit—manifested by glossolalia—does not cross linguistic or geographical barriers, but the barrier between Jews and Gentiles.

14. Our traditional Bibles include one further passage in which the Christian mission is pictured as including the speaking of "new tongues" (Mark 16:17). As can now be seen in the RSV, NEB, and other modern editions of the Bible, verses 9-20 of Mark 16 were not part of the original text and are missing in the most dependable of the ancient manuscripts. Nevertheless, the text in "Mark 16:17" could be taken as evidence for how the understanding expressed in Acts 2 caught the imagination of the church, especially when the topic was the missionary outreach, i.e., the very topic of "Mark 16:9-20." Note, however, that some manuscripts do not read "new tongues" but "tongues," thus referring rather to the general phenomenon of glossolalia.

4 A HISTORY OF SPEAKING IN TONGUES AND RELATED GIFTS

GEORGE H. WILLIAMS and EDITH WALDVOGEL

The phenomenon of speaking in tongues, firmly established in Acts 2:4[1] and referred to several times by Paul,[2] has a range of meanings in nearly two thousand years of Christian history in all lands and among all classes of believers. It is a phenomenon that has not attracted extensive notice in the usual sources and narratives of church history, and a full account, of the kind possible for example of Pentecostalism in America, is impossible at the present time because of the vastness of universal Christian history.

Generally, glossolalia embraces every ecstatic oral-auditory phenomenon from speaking in a language not generally known by the group present (sometimes a half-remembered childhood speech, sometimes a wholly unlearned but authentic language or dialect), to speaking in forceful declamations, incantations, and other verbal effusions that are more likely to be psychological-spiritual projections of an inner speech than some authentic language or dialect.[3]

It has been pointed out that the New Testament itself varies in its references to the phenomenon: "kinds of tongues" (I Cor. 12:10, 28); "tongues" or "tongue" (Acts 10:46; 19:6; I Cor. 14); "other tongues" (Acts 2:4); and "new tongues" (Mark 16:17).[4]

Dr. George H. Williams was born in Huntsburg, Ohio. He was a student at the University of Munich, received his A.B. from St. Lawrence University, and his B.D. from Meadville Theological School, affiliated with the University of Chicago. He did graduate work at the University of Strasbourg and the University of California, and received his Th.D. at Union Theological Seminary. Ordained to the ministry of the Unitarian and Congregationalist churches in 1940, he was a member of the faculty at Starr King School for the Ministry, Pacific School of Religion in Berkeley, California. Since 1947 he has been at Harvard, from 1963 as Hollis Professor of Divinity.

Dr. Williams is a frequent contributor to many journals, and was the Fulbright lecturer at the University of Strasbourg in 1960-61, a Protestant observer at Vatican Council II, and a Guggenheim Fellow in Poland and England, 1972-73. He has also published *Norman Anonymous of 1100 A.D.* (1951); *Spiritual and Anabaptist Writers* (1957); *Anselm and Communion* (1960); *Wilderness and Paradise in Christian Thought* (1962); and *The Radical Reformation* (1962); and he was co-editor of *The Writings of Thomas Hooker* (1974).

Edith Waldvogel is a candidate for the Ph.D. in American Church History at Harvard University.

When in the long history of Christianity, infant baptism (pedobaptism) had come to prevail, the charismatic movement seized upon the phrase "baptism with the Holy Spirit," or a comparable phrase, to describe a special experience independent of baptism by water. Although in this essay the standard phrase for the phenomenon besides "the gift of tongues" will be "baptism with the Holy Spirit" (Matt. 3:11), in the sources we find a variety of additional expressions: "baptism of the Holy Spirit," "in the Holy Spirit," etc. We are, of course, aware that in the New Testament itself certain converts who had been baptized by John received the baptism of the Holy Spirit with the laying on of hands by Paul: "And when Paul had laid his hands upon them, the Holy Ghost came on them; and they spake with tongues, and prophesied" (Acts 19:6). Moreover, there was in the ancient church the quite distinctive form of baptism—that of the martyrs—called "baptism in blood"; and it was often referred to as "baptism by fire," with possible allusion to the original pentecostal flames.[5]

Since the New Testament texts stand there for all to comment on and make some meaning of, even if tongue-speaking has not fallen within their own personal experience, we shall also occasionally note the various ways in which theologians sought to bypass the original literal meaning of the scriptural accounts and to reinterpret the gift as that of facility in many languages, the better to propagate the gospel among all peoples. Since the gift of tongues was scripturally associated with a second act, that of interpretation of what had been uttered in ecstasy (I Cor. 14:27, 28), we shall give some attention to this aspect of charismatic history as well as to such other charismatic phenomena recounted in Acts and elsewhere and associated with glossolalia—ecstatic bodily motions, prostrations, groaning in the Spirit,[6] benign helplessness in the unexpected presence of a spiritual power. But we shall, for the sake of keeping to the main theme, concentrate on the speaking and interpreting of tongues in all senses.

The quite contemporary Pentecostalist doctrine of tongues as the initial evidence of Spirit baptism, ideally signifying that a special intensity of Christian witness has been attained, has theological as well as experiential consequences.[7] As Pentecostals came to be organized in the early twentieth century in a congeries of denominations, each with its doctrinally refined statements, the distinction they drew between tongues as *evidence* (Acts 2) and tongues as *gift* (I Cor. 12) became denominationally decisive.

From the beginning glossolalia, both as evidence and as gift, was miraculous in nature and regarded as prophetically foreseen and, indeed, closely associated with the Old Testament phenomenon of inspired rhythmic and oracular declamation as well as with the more frequently preserved foretelling and forthtelling of the greater and lesser prophets. Not only in Acts 2, but also in Acts 10 and 19, glossolalia demonstrated the reception of the Holy Spirit. Peter, for example, had declared that the outpouring was the fulfillment of Joel's prophecy of the Holy Spirit (Joel 2:28, 29). At the home of Cornelius, as at Ephesus, speaking in tongues was likewise clear evidence of Spirit baptism and may well have been connected with the foreign origin of the Roman legionary stationed in Palestine. In I Corinthians 12, in contrast, tongues were no more associated with an initial infilling with the Holy Spirit than were any of the other spiritual gifts catalogued by Paul. Indeed, there the gift of tongues was said to edify only the glossolalist himself and others only when followed by the glossologist with his special gift of interpretation. The gift of tongues, in any case, was not expected to be possessed by all who were baptized with the Holy Spirit, for the Spirit "divid[ed] to every man severally as he will[ed]" (I Cor. 12:11) the gifts through which he revealed his presence in the church.[8]

In the course of charismatic history, this scriptural distinction between evidence and special gift, particularly important among contemporary Pentecostals, was only infrequently noted. For the most part, therefore, in our comprehensive survey, we shall be referring to glossolalia and related phenomena generically without reference to the contemporary Pentecostalist denominational and doctrinal distinction.

It is also useful to observe at the outset that commentators on and experiencers of the phenomenon of tongues differ quite often in the degree to which they variously tend to stress Joel with its eschatological implications,[9] Acts with its evidential character, or Corinthians with its clear implication that glossolalia, while a gift, is definitely on a lower rung and in need of supplementation. Furthermore, we shall be observing that both commentators on and experiencers of tongues are at times very much concerned as to whether the gift is primarily to the individual recipient or a benediction and benefaction for the group and even society as a whole.

It is, finally, to be recognized that as a spiritual phenomenon, glossolalia will not have been continuously experienced, as, say, ordinary water baptism, and that, accordingly, some periods and some groups will more richly abound in the evidence of this phenomenon than others. Surely, as we acknowledge, it will in any case be difficult to determine to what extent (1) the spiritual power (the Holy Spirit) operating in the charismatic movement, (2) the sense of continuity with groups so visited and blessed, and (3) the quite independently and recurrently operating influence of the glossolalic texts of the New Testament itself are to be weighted in determining the history of the phenomenon. Our task is all the more difficult because glossolalia must be reckoned as one of the most fugitive and one of the least easily recordable aspects of Christian experience.[10]

Pentecostalism as an organized movement is a phenomenon of the twentieth century, but as a force in Christianity it derives from many centuries of Christian tradition. The common religious experiences of individuals and groups throughout history demonstrate a shared and similar working of one Spirit. Such recurrent phenomena as speaking in tongues help provide a unity where one would expect to find only diversity. Speaking in tongues is today one of the distinctive practices of a growing and already immense global Pentecostal community. The controversy inspired by uses of this gift commenced with church history and has continued to inspire and also perplex Christians since that time.

GLOSSOLALIA IN CHRISTIAN ANTIQUITY
AND THE EARLY MIDDLE AGES

It has been noted that beyond the New Testament our earliest writings, such as those of the Apostolic Fathers (with the possible exception of Ignatius,[11] *The Shepherd* of Hermas of Rome, and the *Didache*) and those of the Apologists, preserve for us almost no evidence of ongoing glossolalia.[12]

During the middle of the second century, however, two movements arose alongside or within the main body of Christians, presenting a major crisis in polity, theology, and the interpretation of the Old Testament, which did have glossolalia. The older movement was Gnosticism, of which there are clear adumbrations in the New Testament. The other, a somewhat later reaction to the structural hardening of main-line Christianity, was Montanism.

The Gnostics generally adhered to a tripartite view of mankind, dividing human beings into pneumatics (the true Gnostics, capable of understanding the esoteric *gnosis* allegedly handed down secretly by the apostles), the psychics, who were at best capable of salvation by mere faith, and the hylics (the wooden ones), who would always remain inaccessible to the saving Spirit, having in them nothing of the primal light or power to be redeemed through the Gnostic Christ. Among some Gnostics there was an appeal to I Corinthians 2:15: "the spiritual man judges all things and is judged by none."

Among Gnostic groups, glossolalia of the type requiring interpretation was common, and there exist several transcribed Gnostic prayers in the Coptic tongue in which are included several lines of ejaculated glossolalic syllables or single vowels and consonants. There are also instances of nearly unintelligible utterances in some Gnostic texts in which Aramaic words or other *nomina barbara* can be recognized in somewhat distorted form. In the second *Book of Jeu*, a glossolalic prayer of Jesus of some six lines is preserved in garbled Greek within a Coptic text. The Gnostic sect of Marcosians apparently preserved Greek glossolalic phrases which, however, may have merely a formulaic or routinized character. In the recently discovered Nag Hammadi Gnostic library in *The Three Stelaes of Seph*, unintelligible syllables seem to be merely *nomina barbara;* but in *The Gospel of the Egyptians*, though there are many *nomina barbara*, there are some passages that look more like glossolalia, i.e., distorted Greek formulations in Coptic context.[13]

It is also of interest that against Gnosticism and particularly against Montanism, the early Church Fathers claimed that bishops collectively in local synod (the first was in Asia Minor against Montanism) or ecumenical council, since they were themselves *preeminently* "spiritual men," judging all things (I Cor. 2:15)[14] and dealing with heretics, possessed the Holy Spirit (*Pneuma Hagion*) which they expressly invoked.

As for Montanism, the more important movement for our survey, it was a rigorist challenge, beginning in Phrygia, to an increasingly organized and structured church.

Expansion had wrought significant changes as the churches had been forced to defend their faith against the subtle infusions of Gnosticism. Montanus and his Phrygian followers probably challenged the institutionalizing of their religion but undoubtedly contributed as well to that institutionalization by way of reaction. It is not certain whether the *Didache*, which refers to the ecstatic utterances of wandering prophets, though it does not expressly mention glossolalia, might not be a Montanist document, idealizing the relative informality in preaching and prayer (and possibly the use of tongues) of an earlier age. The response of the main body of the Christian community to the rigorism of the Montanists became crucial for the development of the patristic concept of the well-ordered hierarchical church.

Eusebius of Caesarea introduced Montanus in his *Ecclesiastical History* as follows:

> There [Phrygia] first, they say, when Gratus was proconsul of Asia, a recent convert, Montanus by name, through his unquenchable desire for leadership, gave the adversary opportunity against him. And he became beside himself, and being suddenly in a sort of frenzy and ecstasy, he raved, and began to babble and utter strange things, prophesying in a manner contrary to the constant custom of the Church handed down by tradition from the beginning.[15]

Montanus had once been a priest of the Asian cult of the Magna Mater, and his enemies accused him of combining the ecstatic elements of his former religion with his allegiance to Christianity. Associated with him were two prophetesses, Priscilla and Maximilla. Their essential message included the following: The ministry of

Montanus marked the initiation of the dispensation of the Paraclete; the Holy Spirit should work in individual believers, stirring up charismatic gifts; the millennial rule of Christ was imminent.

Montanus and his followers provoked immediate reaction. Some "rebuked him as one that was possessed" and "distracting the multitude." Others, "imagining themselves possessed of the Holy Spirit and of a prophetic gift, were elated and not a little puffed up."[16] His committed followers relied heavily on the prophetic utterances in Scripture which gave them instruction and warning, believing that biblical teaching (as yet not a fully defined canon) could be supplemented by new revelations.

The most illustrious follower of Montanus was Tertullian of Carthage (d. c. 220). The first major theologian to write in Latin, Tertullian shaped the vocabulary of Western theology. His defense of orthodoxy was immense. He claimed, however, against the main body of North African Christians, that spiritual gifts constituted the plenary Christian experience because they had been "foretold" by the apostles; and he challenged his skeptical contemporaries by citing Paul.[17]

When he wrote his defense of orthodoxy with respect to the Godhead and Christology against Marcion (after c. 207), Tertullian had himself become a Montanist. He challenged Marcion to produce from among his followers any "such as have not spoken by human sense, but with the Spirit of God, such as have both predicted things to come, and have made manifest the secrets of the heart."[18] Utterances, inspired "by the Spirit, in an ecstasy, that is in a rapture, whenever an interpretation of tongues has occurred," were "forthcoming" from his side "without any difficulty" and, according to him, attested to the orthodoxy of his experience and his theological dicta.[19]

Irenaeus (d. c. 200) served his age as Bishop of Lyons. A student of Polycarp (who, in turn, had been a disciple of the Apostle John), he had spent his youth in Smyrna and later represented a significant link between the East and the West. His major work, *Against Heresies*, was an attack on Gnosticism with a defense of the Christian faith drawn from those theological and canonical traditions at his disposal.

Irenaeus conspicuously associated tongues with the Last Days. Referring to the latter-day outpouring promised in Joel 2:28, 29, he wrote: "For God who did promise by the prophet that He would send His Spirit upon the whole human race, was He who did send."[20] Irenaeus went on to relate the events of Pentecost to his own experience: "In like manner, we do hear many brethren in the Church, who possess prophetic gifts, and who through the Spirit speak all kinds of languages. . . ." Those who exercised this gift of tongues were spiritual people who through their gift revealed "for the general benefit the hidden things of men" and declared "the mysteries of God" in the diverse, living languages of mankind.[21]

A pagan philosopher, Celsus, well acquainted with Christianity and its heretical aberrations, unwittingly provides us with significant observations among the Christians as seen from the outside. It was toward the end of the second century that he wrote his *True Discourse*, which survives in the pages of Origen's *Contra Celsum*. Origen (d. c. 254), an Alexandrian biblical scholar and a prolific writer, quotes Celsus as testifying that people spoke in tongues in his day: "To these promises are added strange, fanatical, and quite unintelligible words, of which no rational person can find the meaning: for so dark are they, as to have no meaning at all; but they give occasion to every fool or impostor to apply them to suit his own purpose."[22]

Origen, for his part, suggested with regard to tongues that the promise recorded in Joel 2:28 and fulfilled on the day of Pentecost was similar to the statement in Psalm 72:11: "All nations shall serve Him." As a result, then, of this outpouring of the Holy Spirit, the nations would know the Lord.[23] Origen may have been aware of the rabbinical tradition that at the Jewish Pentecost, which recalled the proclamation of the law at Mount Sinai, the Law was conveyed in seventy languages to the ends of the world.

In Rome the Presbyter Novatian (d. c. 257) in his *De Trinitate* referred to the gift of tongues in the literal sense. Novatian had an eventful career as leader of a faction opposed to the concessions that Cornelius, Bishop of Rome, offered to those who had "lapsed" during the Decian persecution of the mid-third century. He was eventually chosen as rival Bishop of Rome. His followers remained orthodox in doctrine, but their continued emphasis on severe discipline gave them reason for separate existence after peace had been restored. Novatian wrote concerning the Holy Spirit:

> This is He who places prophets in the Church, instructs teachers, directs tongues, gives powers and healings, does wonderful works, offers discrimination of spirits, affords powers of government, suggests counsels, and orders and arranges whatever other gifts there are of *charismata;* and thus makes the Lord's Church everywhere, and in all, perfected and completed.[24]

In Gaul Bishop Hilary of Poitiers (d. 367) was an important Western challenger to Arianism. In his *On the Trinity*, although he made no direct claim to firsthand knowledge of the gift of tongues and did not develop a doctrine of the gifts, he implied acceptance of their place in ordinary Christian life. After quoting the list of gifts in I Corinthians 12, he commented: "Here we have a statement of the purpose and results of the Gift; and I cannot conceive what doubt can remain, after so clear a definition of His Origin, His action, and

His powers."[25] In a subsequent chapter, he mentioned among other things the "gifts of either speaking or interpreting divers kinds of tongues" and concluded: "Clearly these are the Church's agents of ministry and work of whom the body of Christ consists; and God has ordained them."[26]

Bishop Ambrose of Milan (d. 397), famous preacher and champion of orthodoxy, and prophetic exponent of the superior authority of the church with respect to the state, commented briefly about the gift of tongues in *Of the Holy Spirit*. Although he made no explicit claim to experiential familiarity with the gift, he dealt with it as presumptive evidence of the unified operation of the Trinity in normal Christian experience. Each believer, in accordance with his capacity, received from the gifts listed in I Corinthians 12 those which he desired or deserved.[27]

The Eastern counterpart of Ambrose in religio-political and homiletical fervor, John Chrysostom (d. 407) of Antioch and then bishop of Constantinople, knew of glossolalia only as a scriptural happening that had in the meantime ceased, although in his *Homily XXIX*, dealing with I Corinthians 12:1-11, Chrysostom had no doubt that at their adult believers' baptism Christians of an earlier age "began to speak, one in the tongue of the Persians, another in that of the Romans, another in that of the Indians, or in some other language. And this disclosed to outsiders that it was the Spirit in the speaker." Chrysostom goes on to conjecture on the basis of texts from Paul in Romans 12 that while the gifts of prophecy, glossolalia, and interpretation were indeed impressive testimony to the living Spirit, they could easily be confused with intrusion of a spirit from below and had to be discouraged by the official church.[28]

St. Augustine of Hippo (d. 430) offered a new interpretation of the significance of speaking in tongues. First, he contended that the speaking in tongues of the day of Pentecost had been a sign "adapted to the time" which had vanished. This reason for its initial appearance at Pentecost became the basis of his second proposal. The tongues had been given "to show that the Gospel of God was to run through all tongues over the whole earth." The accounts in Acts had symbolical significance for church history: Now the church, not individuals, spoke in tongues, for Christian communities existed throughout the known world, and the church spoke in the tongues of its diverse members.[29]

Pope Leo I the Great (440-461) adhered to Augustine's view, exerting vast influence in the development of the papal office and the concept of the church. In a Pentecostal sermon, Leo expressed an Augustinian understanding of the relationship of the events of Pentecost to the institutional church. Reflecting on Luke's account in Acts, he wrote:

Oh! how swift are the words of wisdom, and where God is the Master, how quickly is what is taught, learnt. No interpretation is required for understanding, no practice for using, no time for studying, but the Spirit of Truth blowing where He wills, the languages peculiar to each nation become common property in the mouth of the Church.[30]

On that day in the upper room, the church had begun its preaching mission to the nations of the world, endowed with a "fervent eloquence" which made her message at once provocative and powerful.

A number of saints possessed the gift of tongues, which was usually manifested as the ability to speak in a foreign language without formal instruction. For example, Pachomius (d. 346), the founder of coenobitic monasticism in Egypt, never learned Latin. But once, after three hours of earnest prayer, he was enabled to converse in Latin with a visitor from the West.[31]

There is little evidence of any form of glossolalia during the Middle Ages in either East or West. In the East, Byzantine Hesychasm, with its preoccupation with the manifestations of the Uncreated Light, concentrated on mystical vision rather than mystical audition. However, out of Hesychasm came the famous "Jesus prayer," which, when mastered by the saint in faithfulness to the injunction to pray without ceasing (I Thess. 5:17), meant a continuous ejaculation of certain formulas even during sleep and during conversation—thus a kind of subliminal speaking in a familiar tongue but in the midst of other tongues.[32]

In the West in the early medieval period we have occasional references to the texts in Acts and Joel. It is uncertain whether the Celtic monks in any way connected their renowned ejaculations, incantational exultations, and protracted recitations of the Psalms in circumstances of extreme personal hardship or pain with the apostolic gift of tongues in the primitive church.

The Venerable Bede (d. 735) considered the event of Acts 2 as preeminently the phenomenon of heteroglossolalia, the miraculous understanding of a foreign tongue. This could indeed have been an observed phenomenon on the borders between Celtic and Saxon cultures overlaid with ecclesiastical Latin. He associated the gift of tongues with the facilitation of Christian missionary expansion.[33]

Bede's *Historia Ecclesiastica Gentis Anglorum* (completed in 731) contains many references to experiences of healing. Bede also recounts the experiences of the monk Caedmon, who received gifts of poetry and song. When passages of Scripture were interpreted for him, Caedmon could express them in English poetry. This gift, however, was limited in scope. It functioned only as he devoted himself to spiritual pursuits and themes to the absolute exclusion of all secular usage.[34]

For the most part, the spread of Christianity among the new barbarians meant the acquisition of Latin, the once universal language of the Roman Empire and now that of the universal church, ever more centered in Rome. One can well conjecture that under the severe tutelage of the Latin Church any reversion to one's mother tongue, even in personal prayer, would have been frowned upon in the monasteries, and for all the more reason the texts of Acts and Joel would have been readily passed over in silence or allegorized by the church as *mater et magistra gentium*.

CHARISMATIC SPIRITUALISM FROM JOACHIM OF FLORA (d. 1202) TO THE FINAL PHASES OF TERRITORIAL REFORMATION AND COUNTER-REFORMATION 1648/1689

Joachim of Flora, a Cistercian abbot, devised a view of history which anticipated the imminent commencement of the *Ecclesia Spiritualis* and which exerted widespread influence in Western thought. All of human experience, he contended, could be divided into three overlapping dispensations which corresponded to the persons of the Trinity. The first was the age of the Father (the *ordo conjugatorum*), the second the age of the Son (the *ordo clericorum*), and the third that of the Spirit (the *ordo monachorum*), to begin c. 1260.[35]

In the twelfth century, the Benedictine abbess, Hildegard of Bingen (1098-1179) sang in unknown words with such facility and winsomeness that her utterances were called "concerts in the Spirit." Although the strange language of her songs seemed to be a peculiar combination of local German dialect and Latin, both of which languages she of course knew well, she herself felt so strongly that the words that insisted on forming themselves in her mind in song and perhaps other powers of communication to the nuns under her were of such inspired and revealing significance that she prepared a glossary codex providing the translation. Elsewhere she speaks of her anointment with the Holy Spirit (*Salbung des Heiligen Geistes*).[36] Because her experiences were not understood, some of her contemporaries denounced her as demon-possessed, and she has not yet been officially beatified.

Spanish-born St. Dominic (d. 1221), after prayer, was enabled to speak German to an amazed audience. Angelus Clarenus (d. 1337), a Franciscan, spoke Greek, and an Augustinian Italian, St. Clare of Montefalco, spoke ecstatically in French.[37]

St. Anthony of Padua (d. 1231) was a leading Franciscan figure. Among his miracles and spiritual gifts recounted in the earliest sources was the gift of tongues. At times, "his tongue became the pen of the Holy Ghost," and on occasion his hearers were reminded of the day of Pentecost when they heard him preaching in their native tongues.[38] The Dominican mission preacher Vincent Ferrer (d. 1419), known for many miracles, while preaching in Latin was often said to have been understood by "Greeks, Germans, Sardinians, Hungarians, and people of other nations," as if speaking their languages.[39] The gift of tongues was not recognized as a normal outgrowth of Christian experience, however, but rather as an evidence of extreme piety. During the High Middle Ages, it did not function in isolation from other gifts of the Holy Spirit. Healings and other miracles accompanied the ministries of those who spoke in tongues.[40]

Thomas Aquinas (d. 1247) expressed his thoughts on the gift of tongues in his *Summa Theologica*. According to him the original purpose of this gift had been to enable the apostles "to teach all nations." It did not follow, however, that they had received a "gift of the knowledge of all languages." The gift of tongues was appropriate to the New Testament in the same way that prophecy had been proper to the Old. It directed men to God, remained "like a habit" in the person who possessed it, and could be used at will. Thomas suggested that men of his day could gain the same gift of tongues as appeared at Pentecost by assiduous linguistic study.[41]

The Protestant Reformation created a new context in which fresh attention was given to every text of Scripture. The new versions of the original Greek and Hebrew in vernacular, for the common people, made it inevitable that new attention be drawn to the various passages in the New Testament which we have considered.

The opinions of the great sixteenth-century reformers Martin Luther (1483-1546) and John Calvin (1509-1564) on the gift of tongues differed significantly.

Luther did not have direct contact with the more unusual gifts of the Spirit catalogued by Paul in I Corinthians 12, notably glossolalia, interpretation thereof, and healing. However, as an exegete and preacher using the lectionary, he occasionally had to advert to our charismatic passages. He was also familiar with the Zwickau Prophets, who derived something of their charism from the Hussite tradition.

Luther believed that in apostolic times, people had spoken "new tongues" as a sign and "witness to the Jews." In his own day, however, Christianity no longer required the confirmation of such signs.[42] Although they had ceased, each justified believer might expect to receive one or several other gifts of the Holy Spirit.[43] There would always be a diversity of gifts in the true church, and these would operate in harmony, whereas among "fanatical spirits and sectarians," everyone "want[ed] to be everything."[44]

Luther's clearest exposition of the meaning of the Corinthian texts for his day was in a treatise he published in 1525 against Andreas Bodenstein von Carlstadt. Drawing on Paul's first letter of advice to the troubled Corinthian church, Luther accused Carlstadt of misunderstanding the expression "speaking with tongues." Paul, he declared, had been concerned primarily with the office of preaching and the listening and learning of the congregation. With this as his premise, he used the passage on tongues to develop his case for preaching in the vernacular:

> Whoever comes forward, and wants to read, teach, or preach, and yet speaks with tongues, that is, speaks Latin instead of German, or some unknown language, he is to be silent and preach to himself alone. For no one can hear it or understand it, and no one can get any benefit from it. Or if he should speak with tongues, he ought, in addition, to put what he says into German, or interpret it in one way or another, so that the congregation may understand it.[45]

Carlstadt had used Paul's directives to the Corinthians to prove that all speaking in tongues (i.e., preaching in Latin) was wrong. Luther, on the other hand, demanded only that the "tongues" be interpreted into the appropriate vernacular, and used Paul's writings to defend his position: "St. Paul is not as stubborn in forbidding speaking with tongues as this 'sin-spirit' [Carlstadt] is, but says it is not to be forbidden when along with it interpretation takes place."[46]

Carlstadt also rejected Luther's contention that physicians were "our Lord God's menders of the body," with a mission analogous to that of theologians—the restoration of "what the devil has damaged." To Carlstadt's opposition to the use of medicine, Luther responded: "Do you eat when you're hungry?"[47]

Luther believed that the outpouring of the Holy Spirit on the day of Pentecost had wrought a fundamental change in the meaning of prayer. A "Spirit of supplication" had been "outpoured,"[48] and it was possible, in a new and more significant way, "to call upon God from the heart in My [Christ's] name."[49] The Spirit was not restricted in his activity, but had been promised to "all flesh"[50] accompanied by prophecy, visions, and dreams. In a sermon in 1531 on the Pentecostal text of Acts 2:4, Luther expressly affirms the ministry of "ordinary" people, called to preach by the Spirit, over against the official preachers of the Apostles' days, like those of the Sadducean or Pharisaic classes and the comparably highborn and highly educated Catholic preachers of his own day. Yet haughtily he even used the word *fanatic (Schwärmer)*, his special term for Anabaptists and other simple evangelists: it never occurred to him to carry the logic of his thought further. In any case, such New Testament phenomena anticipated by Joel, such as prophecy (or inspiration), typified for Luther his new doctrine; the "sacraments as

sing, or speak.[64] "The Lord's power" was frequently "so mighty upon" George Fox that he "could not hold, but was made to cry out."[65] The severity of the persecution against such groups could not deter them, and despite the tendency to fanaticism which constantly threatened, they remained committed throughout the century to similar notions of an inner light.

THE GIFT OF TONGUES IN LATER PROTESTANTISM AND CATHOLICISM UP TO THE BEGINNINGS OF PENTECOSTALISM

During the long reign of Louis XIV (1643-1715), French Protestants gradually lost the concessions they had been granted, and a steady stream of cultured and industrious emigrants found refuge abroad. The revocation of the Edict of Nantes in 1685 split the Huguenots into two factions over the lawfulness of resistance to civil authority. The rapid growth of an enthusiastic group among those who endorsed resistance, largely confined to the Cevennes mountains, further complicated the divisions. These Camisards, or Prophets of the Cevennes mountains, claimed that they were directly inspired by the Holy Spirit. Their religious "enthusiasm" as well as their political resistance made them special targets of the king's wrath. In the course of prolonged armed conflict, thousands on both sides were killed. Under divine inspiration, their prophets encouraged the Camisards to wage war against Louis' dragoons from 1701 until 1710. They fought for religious reasons, but the intensity of their political opposition was reflected in the increasing enthusiasm of their spiritual experiences.[66]

The Camisards maintained that "God has no where in the Scriptures concluded himself from dispensing again the extraordinary Gifts of His Spirit unto Men." Indeed, a "more full Accomplishment" of Joel's prophecy than that of Acts could be awaited.[67] They found historical roots by developing an interesting view of church history:

> [T]he Christian Truth survived the Deluge of the Grand Apostacy, and rested upon the Mountains of Piemont, Dauphine, and Languedocq, as the Ark once upon Mount Ararat; the Waldenses and Albigenses could never be quite rooted out by the Legions of Hell in Croisade; and when the great Tribulations of the modern Pharaoh had extinguish'd in appearance the other Churches of France, out of the Ashes of those of Languedocq there arose within a few Years last past, a powerful Testimony of Jesus, animated by immediate Inspiration. . . .[68]

This "inspiration" had startling results. Those so moved "struck themselves with the Hand, they fell on their Backs, they shut their Eyes, they heaved with the Breast, they remained a while in Trances, and coming out of them with Twitchings, they utter'd all that came into their Mouths."[69] Children as well as adults were so affected, and illiterates of the "Dregs of Mankind" amazed their hearers by quoting Scripture texts at length.[70]

John Vernett, who escaped from Bois-Chastel to England, recalled that when under this power of the Holy Spirit his mother spoke only French. This "surprized [him] exceedingly, because she never before attempted to speak a Word in that Language, nor has since to my Knowledge, and I am certain she could not do it."[71] This testimony was given in London on January 14, 1706. His mother had first experienced this linguistic ability in 1693 and had been imprisoned because of her spiritual gifts since 1695. Similar phenomena occurred repeatedly, and often when the operation had ceased the inspired had no memory of what he had uttered.

Another strange phenomenon which occurred quite frequently among the Camisards was the sudden ability of infants who could not yet speak to deliver discourses in perfect, fluent French. In 1701, for example, a child about fourteen months old "which had never of itself spoken a Word, nor could it go alone," in a loud, childish voice began exhorting "to the Works of Repentance."[72]

The Camisards also spoke sometimes in languages that were unknown: "Several persons of both Sexes," James Du Bois of Montpellier recalled, "I have heard in their Extasies pronounce certain words, which seem'd to the Standers-by, to be some Foreign Language." These utterances were sometimes accompanied by the gift of interpretation exercised, in Du Bois' experience, by the same person who had spoken in tongues.[73]

Twenty years after the dispersion of the Camisards in 1710, glossolalia appeared in the Jansenist community. Between 1730 and 1733, prophetic utterances became increasingly frequent among them. When seized by convulsions, some reportedly spoke in an unknown tongue and understood any language in which they were addressed. Much of the glossolalia was, however, not understood.[74] Although the Jansenists and the Camisards had similar physical reactions to inspiration, the Jansenists in self-defense against the charge of crypto-Calvinism were outspoken in their criticism of all Protestant enthusiasts.

During the same period another group, less dramatic but nonetheless inspired, was growing in Saxony. The Moravian Brethren of the eighteenth century had roots in the Bohemian Hussite tradition. Reorganized in 1722 at Herrnhut under the leadership of Count Nicholas von Zinzendorf (1700-60), they had close affinities with German Pietism and Lutheranism. Their emotionally expressive worship, particularly after the remarkable revival of 1727,[75] was marked by fervent prayer and much singing, and their religious zeal was channeled into ambitious missionary enterprises. Outsiders were apt to be puzzled by their simple confidence in God. Their enemies faithfully exposed the peculiarities and "delusions" of the sect, drawing analogies between the Moravians and the schismatics and heretics of Christian history to prove their arguments. In Britain, they were taken to task for, among other things, reviving a "ridiculous Piece of Nonsense" first advanced by "a mad enthusiastic Sect of the second Century called Montanists"—speaking in tongues. Said one John Roche:

> [Montanus] and his Followers were great Dealers in the Spirit; and affected strange convulsive Heavings, and unnatural Postures. And in one of these Fits they commonly broke into some disconnected Jargon, which they often passed upon the vulgar, "As the exuberant and resistless Evacuations of the Spirit," and many other such like enthusiastic Stuff.
>   That this is the frequent Behaviour, Speeches and Assertions of those deluded and deluding People, I refer to the public Voice, to all that are but even slightly acquainted with their Customs and Preachings; and to such cursory Proofs of it as shall appear through this Work: For a stated Proof of it would be an idle Attempt.[76]

Although speaking in tongues was not endorsed by the Moravian leadership, it occurred sporadically in their gatherings. Zinzendorf, like many others, believed that the gift of tongues had originally been given in order to facilitate missionary expansion.

This is, perhaps, the place to mention in passing the Swedish seer Emmanuel Swedenborg (d. 1772), who, though he was essentially a visionary and clairvoyant, cited the glossolalic texts of Scripture and in "The Speech of Angels" and "The Speech of Angels with Man" in *Heaven and its Wonders and Hell* (Latin: London, 1758) speaks of "things seen and heard."

The contribution of John Wesley (1703-91) to his century has been widely recognized. Recent Pentecostal scholarship has acknowledged his special significance among the antecedents of Pentecostalism and claimed him as the "father" of the Pentecostal movement.[77] His emphasis on a second crisis experience subsequent to conversion was only one of many innovations which shaped the context out of which organized Pentecostalism later emerged. Little attention has been directed to his attitude toward glossolalia, however. His opinion on the gift of tongues was undoubtedly influenced by what he knew of the operation of that gift in his world, as well as by his reading of Scripture.

The transformation of Wesley's religious experience which resulted from his contact with the Moravians is common knowledge. The individualistic experiential piety which informed their daily lives enriched his own after 1738. His attention was specifically drawn to speaking in tongues by the publication in 1748 of Conyers Middleton's *A Free Inquiry* and by the increasing activity of the French Prophets in England.

Middleton was a Fellow of Trinity College, Cambridge, whose work was based on *Traité de l'emploi des saints pères*, published by Jean Daillé (1594-1670), a learned French Reformed theologian, in 1632. Daillé had written to discourage "undue reverence" for the Church Fathers. The thrust of Middleton's book was probably best expressed by its full title: "A Free Inquiry into the Miraculous Powers, Which are supposed to have subsisted in the Christian Church, From the Earliest Ages through several successive Centuries. By which it is shewn, that we have no sufficient Reason to believe upon the authority of the Primitive Fathers, That any such Powers were continued to the Church, after the Days of the Apostles."

Middleton maintained that of all the gifts of the Holy Spirit the gift of tongues was "the most evidently and confessedly withdrawn."[78] He further contended that neither a "single instance" of tongues nor "the least pretension" to the gift had ever been made "by any writer whatsoever."[79] Middleton's attitude was undoubtedly strongly colored by his anti-Catholicism. Basing his arguments on Daillé's proofs of the unreliability of the Fathers, Middleton attacked such claims as were commonly established by reference to the Fathers. Because he felt that the Roman Catholic tradition had tolerated and validated much that was mere superstition, and because he saw it as an organization in which the self-centered quest for salvation predominated, he rejected Catholic pretenses to possessing the gifts of the Holy Spirit, including glossolalia. He used the gift of tongues, in fact, as a criterion for rejecting "the miraculous pretensions of all Churches, which derive their descent from the Apostles," and since the gift of tongues had been falsely claimed, the sectaries possessed no others which were "real and genuine."[80]

In the *Free Inquiry*, he claimed that the extant writings of those second-generation Christians who had known the Apostles made no mention of tongues. During the Patristic period, a revival of the gift had been "pretended" until it could no longer be supported. Middleton was so certain of himself that he made John Wesley's self-imposed task of refutation simple:

And I [Middleton] might risk the merit of my argument on this single point; that, after the Apostolic times, there is not in all history one instance, either well attested, or even so much as mentioned, of any particular person, who had ever exercised this gift, or pretended to exercise it, in any age or country whatsoever.[81]

In answer to this claim, Wesley reminded him:

It has undoubtedly been pretended to, and that at no great distance either from our time or country. It has been heard of more than once no farther off than the valleys of Dauphiny. Nor is it yet fifty years ago since the Protestant inhabitants of those valleys so loudly pretended to this and other miraculous powers as to give much disturbance to Paris itself. And how did the King of

France confute that pretence and prevent its being heard any more? Not by the pen of his scholars, but by (a truly heathen way) the swords and bayonets of his dragoons.[82]

It is understandable that the dispersion of people whose convictions had not yielded to the severe persecutions of Louis XIV and whose norms of religious experience included such dramatic expressions as those of the Camisards would arouse at least a curious interest and considerable hostility.

When Louis XIV had launched his attack on the French prophets, some had already fled to England. Fanning out from London, they called public attention to themselves by their convulsions and strange utterances; and they attempted to gain a foothold in the revivalistic gatherings of "the people called Methodists." Wesley's early preaching had often evoked a variety of pronounced physical manifestations. During his first visit to Bristol, emotional reactions similar to the convulsions of the Camisards had been particularly evident: "To our no small surprise," he recorded, some were "constrained to roar for the disquietness of their heart."[83] One hearer was "seized with a violent trembling all over." In response to a sermon at Newgate on the text "He that believeth hath everlasting life" (John 3:15), "one, and another, and another sunk to the earth; they dropped on every side as thunderstruck. . . . All Newgate rang with the cries of those whom the word of God cut to the heart."[84] Wesley, whose sermons had been rather dryly systematic, typical of the Oxford don he in part still was, could not understand "the unusual manner" of his Bristol ministry, but for the moment contented himself with laying it "before the Lord."[85]

In England, what was to turn out to be the notorious reputation of these French Prophets and their English adherents was the prophecy circulating among them that one of their deceased members, Dr. Thomas Emes, would be resurrected. A date was set for this event, and the appropriate "prophecies" were well publicized, in accordance with inspired instructions. All England was to observe God's vindication of his prophets. The scheduled day came and went, and the prophetic claim of a "spiritual resurrection" of the deceased naturally failed to satisfy skeptics of the divine credentials of the French Prophets.[86] They became targets for mockery and anathema among respectable Christians. Examples of both these attitudes are readily available.

One cynic who apparently derived a certain pleasure from destructive criticisms wrote of a "pretended prophet of the Camisar" whose English lacked perfection: "If he had the Gift of Tongues, English must necessarily have been one of them. And not having this in any perfection, it is natural to conclude that he has none other; and by consequence, that the Promise of this Gift to him could never have

been from God."[87] The same repulsion and disgust was expressed by
Charles Wesley, who inadvertently shared a room with a French
Prophet during one of his journeys. The man "gobbled like a turkey-
cock," and Charles "began exorcising him with 'Thou deaf and dumb
devil!' " He rested poorly that night—or as he put it, "nor did I sleep
very sound with Satan so near me."[88]

The founder of Methodism, despite his brother's protest, knew
that the gift of tongues was frequently dispensed in his day; and he,
for his part, believed that it had had authentic existence in other
post-Apostolic centuries. In fact, he regarded Montanists as "real,
scriptural Christians" and Montanus himself as "one of the best men
then upon the earth." The reason for the early withdrawal of the
charismatic gifts was that "dry, formal, orthodox men" had begun to
"ridicule" those gifts they did not themselves possess and to "decry
them all as either madness or imposture."[89]

Wesley once explained that God imparted his gifts as he chose, and
that in his wisdom he had not deemed it best to bestow on Wesley
himself this gift which he had granted to some of his contemporaries.
In a certain sense, he had received a tongue of fire similar to that of
Acts 2:3; for, as he once wrote, the cloven tongues of fire that had
descended at Pentecost had given "eloquence and utterance in
preaching the gospel," engendered "a burning zeal towards God's
Word," and endowed each Spirit-baptized disciple with "a fiery
tongue."[90]

For the spiritual edification of his contemporaries, Wesley published accounts of the religious experiences of some members of
Methodist societies as well as instructive passages from prominent
writers of other generations. In the surviving extracts from diaries,
there is a persistent longing for fuller Christian experience and a
conviction of the inadequacy of efforts to worship Christ in human
language: "Friday in the morning I rose with these words strongly
and sweetly impressed on my mind, 'Insatiate to the spring I fly, I
drink and still am ever dry.' O my dear Lord what angel tongue can
speak thy praise," wrote one Elizabeth Johnson. Her soul, she
declared, "burn[ed] with desire to praise thee; words I find fail,
there is no language known among mortals to express it; a glimmer-
ing expectation I have to be ere long, where I shall have new
language."[91]

In 1771, Wesley translated extracts from a French author and
published them as *The Manners of the Ancient Christians*. The
French author, in discussing intercession, noted a "sublime kind of
prayer" in which the soul "darteth itself towards God in sighs and
groans, and thoughts too big for expression." This was the mode of
prayer to which Paul had referred in Romans 8:26 and was "one of
the most powerful instruments of the divine life."[92]

Among the most esteemed of Wesley's colleagues was John Fletcher (d. 1785), Vicar of Madeley in Shropshire. Fletcher believed that his was the dispensation of the Holy Spirit, in which "every faithful servant of the Lord is enabled to prophesy out of the fulness of his heart; and to speak the wonderful works of God." The "extraordinary gifts" of the Spirit bestowed at Pentecost had been "peculiarly necessary" to the apostles and were entirely "distinct" from the Holy Spirit. Fletcher pointed out that in the Bible speaking in tongues had not always accompanied an outpouring of the Holy Spirit, nor had those in whom the gifts of the Spirit were manifested necessarily displayed more holiness than others. If the "edification of the Church" required it, the Holy Spirit, in taking full possession of an individual, might bestow on him an "extraordinary gift." In general, however, the presence of the fruits of the Spirit (Gal. 5:22, 23) would demonstrate that an individual had become a temple of the Holy Spirit. Fletcher's theology demanded recognition of the need for personal experiences with the Spirit of Pentecost.[93]

The kind of piety and devotion which characterized John Fletcher found expression in the diary of his wife Mary. Mrs. Fletcher's attitude was at once desirous and expectant. She prayed for an infilling with the Spirit, "that [her] tongue, being touched with the fire of heavenly love, might be enabled to plead the cause of truth"; she expected that "an outpouring of [God's] Spirit will soon be given, and 'times of refreshing shall come from the presence of the Lord'" (Acts 3:19); she declared: "We must look for the baptism with the Holy Ghost." What one called that baptism was inconsequential: it remained available for all Christians. Mrs. Fletcher's active faith, stimulated by persistent and increasing longing, was characteristic of many of her Methodist contemporaries. "I've tasted," she proclaimed, "but I want the fulness."[94]

Wesley later discouraged the more violent physical manifestations which had accompanied his early ministry and tried to maintain the delicate balance between formality and freedom. Despite their detrimental influence in Methodist societies (particularly among women, he noticed), he did not condemn the French Prophets unheard, and tried to preserve a judicious attitude when meeting their challenge.[95]

Wesley's life spanned his century. When he died, the "Great Century" was at hand, and a group related to the Camisards, fully accepting the gift of tongues as part of Christian experience, had left England to give expression to its distinctives on American shores. Speaking in tongues was an important part of Shaker worship. With roots in the Quaker and Camisard traditions, the Shakers were the followers of Ann Lee Stanley (d. 1784). They were more formally styled the United Society of Believers in Christ's Second Coming. Mother Ann Lee migrated from England to America in 1774, and in

1776 convened her few followers into a community near Watervliet, New York. The central emphasis of Shaker teaching was millennial: It was time for Christ's Second Advent, he would come as a woman, and Mother Ann Lee was that personage. A concomitant interest in the restitution of the gifts of the Holy Spirit to the church was the result of careful study of Scriptures. The operation of spiritual gifts was a sign of the Last Days. As the community gathered around Mother Lee prepared itself for the "marriage of the Lamb," the fulness of the Holy Spirit would again be its portion.

The first few years in upstate New York were devoted primarily to internal organization and stabilization. Then, in 1779, a revival upset the complacent Christianity of the surrounding main-line Protestant community; and the newly awakened regarded with a fresh interest the maligned religious community at Watervliet. Popular rumor claimed that Mother Ann Lee was a witch, and that her followers were traitors to the American revolutionary cause. Some had heard reports of people "exercised with very singular and apparently wild operations" who frequently engaged in drunken orgies. On the other hand, some were attracted by reports that all the gifts of the Holy Spirit were again operating in a Christian community.[96] While opposition was widespread, there were nonetheless those among the revived who realized that "there must be something of God there, else Satan would not bark so."[97] And so some went to see, and increasing numbers returned convinced. Among the reasons they recounted for their persuasion was the operation in Shaker worship of the gift of tongues.

For some, tongues served to "confirm the reality of Christ's second appearing." Others noticed the gifts in the services but found the personal dealings of Mother Ann Lee even more compellingly persuasive. One Jethro Turner recalled the first meeting he attended: "There were several young people present who had already confessed their sins, and had received the power of God, which was manifested in various and marvellous operations, in signs and visions, in speaking with tongues and prophesyings."[98]

Samuel Johnson, Presbyterian minister in neighboring New Lebanon, had been thoroughly trained in Connecticut Presbyterianism since his boyhood. A graduate of Yale, he participated in the revival of 1779 and became convinced by the gifts of the Holy Spirit he observed during the awakening that the second coming of Christ was imminent. Hearing of the Shakers, he went to observe their ways, "received the precious 'unction of the Holy One,' " which is the baptism of the Spirit," and "was confirmed beyond a doubt" of the validity of Shaker practices. Johnson reflected at considerable length on the gift of tongues, the signs, and the visions "by which the spiritual world was brought, as it were, into open view to my spiritual sight." With regard to them, Johnson wrote:

... I well know that a spirit of scepticism prevails almost universally, both among professors and profane, and especially among the learned priesthood. They are taught to believe that there can be no such gifts in this day, nor any divine or supernatural inspiration; because they all ceased with the primitive Church. It is true that when the primitive Church lost the life and spirit of Christ, and fell back into the spirit of the world, these gifts actually died away. But a restoration was promised, which was to take place when the true Church should rise in the spirit and life of Christ: for these gifts are the life of the soul, and a seal to the testimony of the true gospel.[99]

Among the Shakers, the gift of tongues was not restricted to a few. Although converts initially encountered it as a sign of the operation of the Holy Spirit, it soon became part of their normal religious experience. The gift of healing was present on a more limited basis.

The gift of tongues was not only claimed and defended by Shakers, but also became a favorite target for the ridicule of their critics, and thus its character must be determined by taking into account the charges of contemporaries as well as the accounts of adherents. In *Shakerism Unmasked* (1828), William Haskett provides the observations of a skeptic. In a chapter with the mildly ironic title "Quick Meeting, or Shaker High," he preserves, against his own basic intention, a rather impressive description of the worship which the Shakers' own more stylized statements often fail to convey.

The "Quick Meetings" were traditionally held just before or after Christmas and provided the setting in which the faithful professed to receive "all the divine gifts given to the apostle on the day of Pentecost, besides numerous others given in the 'gospel of mother.' "[100] Usually conducted in the evening in the "families," these meetings were ordinarily closed to spectators. Haskett, however, was able to observe one; and his literate description, though no doubt tendentious, paints a vivid picture of the frenzied commotion attending the Shaker experience of the gift of tongues. After a scene of stamping,

> [T]he sisters began to talk in "unknown tongues." Then commenced a scene of awful riot. Now was heard the loud shouts of the brethren, then the soft, but hurried note of the sisters, whose gifts were the apostolic gift of tongues. These gently gestured their language, waved themselves backward and forward like a ship on the billows of a ceased storm, shook their heads, seized their garments, and then violently stamped on the floor. The exercise had lost its violence, and exertion grew faint; yet a continued din of frightful yells rendered the scene a scene of confusion, a scene of blasphemy, an awful scene. After, probably, three quarters of an hour had transpired, the members were called to order, and the meeting adjourned.[101]

Haskett dismissed the gift of tongues as mere "enthusiasm" and went so far as to suggest that it was indicative of an inherent tendency in the individual and was no more than a spiritualizing of one's native inclination to garrulity.[102] His theological and psychological frame of reference was, however, inadequate for such generalizations; for elsewhere, as among the Shakers themselves, were those whose conviction that the "end of all things was at hand" (I Pet. 4:7) led them to pray earnestly for the promised restitution of spiritual gifts to the church.

In the United States, the first several years of the nineteenth century were years of revival. In the frontier areas, the Second Great Awakening was accompanied by unusual demonstrations of religious fervor in increasingly informal services of worship. Shouting, singing, and exhorting, interspersed with laughing, jerking, and barking "exercises" became characteristic of camp meetings. Some contemporary observers and chroniclers recognized a depth behind these superficial expressions which later historical analyses often fail to convey. Such "supernatural and extraordinary gifts of the Spirit" accompanied the revival in Kentucky that a restitution of the "apostolic faith" was believed to have occurred.[103]   Writing of the Cane Ridge meeting of 1801 a year later, Aeneas McCallister claimed that "the like wonders have not been seen, except the KENTUCKY REVIVAL last summer, since the Apostle's (sic) days. I suppose the exercises of our congregation this last winter, surpassed anything ever seen or heard of." [104] Stimulated by the revival spirit, people appropriated for their own experiences "the full and perfect accomplishment" of Joel's prophecy.[105]

In the summer of 1801, a North Carolina Presbyterian congregation held a series of special meetings, anticipating a revival. Despite their prayers and efforts, nothing remarkable occurred. The pastor rose to conclude the scheduled services a sorely disappointed man, and found himself so moved that he was speechless. As he regained his composure, someone in the audience stood up and quoted solemnly: "Stand still and see the salvation of God." Immediately, "a wave of emotion swept over the congregation like an electric shock." The awaited revival had begun. Physical manifestations and speaking in tongues made it "like the day of Pentecost and none was careless or indifferent."[106]

Local revivals continued sporadically throughout the early nineteenth century. Methodist circuit riders like Peter Cartwright kept the revival fires burning in the West. During the 1820's and 1830's Charles Grandison Finney brought revivalism to the cities of the East, and "new measures" were devised to help ensure the frequency of spiritual renewals.

Meanwhile, continental Europe also experienced "seasons of refreshing." In 1817, Gustav von Below, a Pomeranian army officer, experienced a profound and life-directing conversion as a result of independent Bible study. Shortly thereafter, his two brothers had similar experiences, and the three young Lutheran aristocrats opened their estates to any who wished to join them in informal study and worship. The rationalism which pervaded much of the contemporary state church in Prussia and elsewhere in the Germanies had made such gatherings unusual and aroused opposition. Worshippers took increasing part in the services and patterned their practices after those of the early Christians. Soon the gifts of the Holy Spirit, including tongues, appeared. Among these people, tongues were sung rather than spoken: people sang "spiritual songs" (Eph. 5:19) in languages unknown ("fremden Sprachen") to the singers and unrecognized by the hearers. An ecclesiastical commission sent to investigate the strange phenomenon declared it to be of God. After a period of extra-ecclesiastical existence, Gustav von Below and his followers returned to active involvement in a newly awakened state church. [107]

During the 1820's, revival came to Buch bei Schaffhausen, and David Spleiss saw remarkable transformations in his Swiss congregation. Children as well as adults were "seized by conviction" and cried out for mercy until they received a personal certainty of forgiveness. The revival continued for several months, until it had penetrated nearly every home in the vicinity. [108]

The *Erweckungsbewegung* (revival) penetrated French-speaking Lausanne as the *Réveil*, with Prof. Alexandre Vinet (d. 1847) its chief spokesman. While Vinet was much interested in spiritual manifestations, on which he wrote in 1831 and 1842, and in Jansenism, which movement did include the gift of tongues, there is no evidence that Eglise Libre du pays Vaud experienced glossolalia (despite the proximity and memory of the Camisards), but otherwise the movement shared fully in the universal revival.

In the next decade, a "tongues movement" captured the attention of Great Britain. What the fervent acclaimed as the "latter rain" (Joel 2:23) had begun to fall. Edward Irving (1792-1834), lifelong friend of Thomas Carlyle and popular Scottish Presbyterian minister to a fashionable London congregation, became the man around whom the new tongues movement centered. His initial involvement was at least partially the result of his interest in prophecy and millenarianism. His premillennialism brought him into contact with the growing number whose convictions were moving in that direction and led him to accept the invitation of Henry Drummond (d. 1860) [109] to a conference at Albury Park south of London in 1826. Through his participation in that and later Albury conferences, Irving was stimulated to seek for and expect a restoration of spiritual gifts to the church. [110] He made this a matter of diligent personal and congregational concern. A popular—though lengthy—speaker, Irving meanwhile extended his influence and saw his Regent's Square church experience significant growth. Early in 1830, reports of the appearance of the gifts of tongues and healing near Glasgow reached London; Irving investigated and was intrigued by what he discovered.

Among those who had been yearning for the restoration of the gifts was the Campbell family of Fermicarry in the vicinity of Glasgow in western Scotland. One Sunday the family gathered for prayer in the room of the invalid daughter, Mary. During their devotions, "the Holy Ghost came with mighty power upon the sick woman as she lay in her weakness, and constrained her to speak at great length and with superhuman strength in an unknown tongue, to the astonishment of all who heard, and to her own great edification and enjoyment in God. . . ."[111]

Irving, in London, immediately began special prayer meetings with the sole object of receiving the gifts, especially the gift of tongues. The magnitude of the yearning was attested by the crowds in attendance at the 6:30 a.m. services. By July, 1831, tongues and interpretations had begun to occur. At first, Irving restrained them, but the illogical position of admitting that they were utterances inspired by the Holy Spirit and yet trying to restrain them became increasingly untenable. His decision to permit tongues in any service isolated his more sedate parishioners, who objected to the frequent disruptions during the Sunday morning sermon. "All a tumult yonder, oh me!" observed Carlyle, who also admitted: "Sorrow and disgust were naturally my own feeling: 'How are the mighty fallen'; my once high Irving come to this, by paltry popularities, and Cockney admirations, puddling such a head!"[112]

The situation for Irving did, indeed, quickly assume tragic dimensions. He himself never spoke in tongues; but his inability to lead those who did cost him significant support and evoked the ridicule of the fashionable classes who had once thronged to hear him and the alienation of those whom at a spiritual distance he actually trusted. Expelled by his Scottish presbytery (Annan) on issues of both Christology and tongues, Irving became a victim of his own spiritual and innovative comprehensiveness. Those who possessed the "gifts" claimed the spiritual authority to reorganize themselves as the Church of the Spirit, separate from the Regent's Park parish. All the more grievous to him, they claimed the authority to direct all aspects of church life and they silenced their leader in the name of the Holy Spirit. He died in 1834, a still young, much worn, and lonely proclaimer of the place of tongues in the context of a premillennial eschatology. His work continued, without due recognition, in the hands of "prophets" and "apostles" under the banner of a sacramental Catholic Apostolic Church, which was Catholic in its use of incense, vestments, and creeds based on Roman Catholic, Orthodox, and Anglican rites, and Apostolic in its endorsement of tongues and in the active roles assigned to deacons, elders, prophets, and apostles in its ministries and polity.[113]

The notoriety which inevitably accompanied the rapid transformation and relocation of a fashionable London congregation as a "fanatical" sect did not prevent the extension of Irving's influence beyond the confines of Great Britain. In the United States and continental Europe, convinced Irvingites made contacts with small but interested Christian groups of various affiliations.

In southern Germany, a Roman Catholic priest named Johann Lutz had begun to sense a spiritual need among his parishioners in Karlshuld. He consequently preached with exceptional fervor on New Year's Eve, 1827. A few hours later he was awakened by a crowd of penitents desiring to confess, and a revival had begun. For many weeks prayer meetings were held almost continuously until on Ash Wednesday, in an all-night prayer vigil, people suddenly began to speak under inspiration. "Der Herr wird seinen Geist wieder ausgiessen wie im Anfang" (the Lord will again pour out his spirit as in the beginning") became their confident message. The revival lasted several years and was accompanied by operations of the gifts of the Holy Spirit. In 1831 Catholic authorities decided to silence Lutz, but after a brief and disappointing experiment with Protestantism (in which he was repelled by the rampant rationalism) Lutz returned to Catholic obedience. While a priest at Oberroth, he made the acquaintance of the Irvingite, W. R. Caird. Formally excommunicated by his Catholic bishop in 1856 because of his involvement with the Irvingites, Lutz permanently transferred his allegiance to the Catholic Apostolic Church.[114]

While London watched the Irvingite spectacle, a new American sect was emerging. The Church of Jesus Christ of the Latter Day Saints (Mormons) consisted of the growing number of those who gave credence to the revelations claimed by Joseph Smith (1805-44). Although the Mormons may be classified as post-Christian (because of their acceptance of the Book of Mormon as a revelation supplementary to the Bible), their reading of Scripture made them advocates of the place of the apostolic gifts in their church. "We believe," Smith wrote, "in the gift of tongues, prophecy, revelation, visions, healing, interpretation of tongues, etc."[115]

The gift of tongues first appeared among Mormons in Pennsylvania and became widespread among them during their stay in Kirkland, Ohio, where they built their first temple. There Brigham Young received the gift several weeks after his baptism while praying with some friends: "The Spirit came on me, and I spoke in tongues, and we thought only of the day of Pentecost." The Saints anxiously awaited the arrival and the verdict of their Prophet, Joseph Smith. When he came, he informed Young that his gift of tongues was "the pure Adamic language."[116] Shortly thereafter, Smith himself received the gift.[117]

Early Mormons considered the hands the "natural channel through which those who are filled with the Holy Ghost . . . can communicate it to others" and practiced the laying on of hands for the Holy Ghost mentioned in Acts 8 and 19.[118]   They also laid hands on the sick for healing.[119]

A man who lived among the Mormons as an elder for eight years published an account of his "adventure." Included in it were some critical comments about the Mormon experience of glossolalia. He accused some of the speakers in tongues with stopping at a "gin shop" on their way to meeting and arriving "beastly drunk with whisky." As a typical example of the use of the gift in a service, he recalled that one would jump up, "put forth his arm, stretch out his neck, shut his eyes, and at the top of his voice" begin a series of disjointed utterances. When he had finished, he collapsed, and, at his last "fiz," another arose to interpret. Some who doubted were not content merely to mock, however. One day a skeptic arrived and delivered a memorized Latin "message in tongues" which a fervent Mormon promptly—and wrongly—interpreted.[120]

Reports of speaking in tongues naturally resulted in some attempts at objective discussion of the gift among those who had no firsthand knowledge of it in main-line Protestantism. The widely different conclusions that were reached can be demonstrated by considering what two mid-nineteenth-century Congregationalists argued. Horace Bushnell's *Nature and the Supernatural* included a defense of the credibility of Edward Irving's experiences. Against those who charged that the reported spiritual gifts were "mere hallucinations," he contended that the Scotch families involved were of "unimpeachable character" and that Irving himself was "a man of great calmness" and "well poised in the balance of his understanding." There was nothing in the gift of tongues "that could any how become a temptation to the enthusiast or the pretender." That this gift and that of interpretation should function cooperatively was entirely reasonable:

> The gift of tongues seems, at first view, to be an exercise so wide of intelligence, as to create no impression of respect. And for just that reason it has the stronger evidence when it occurs; for, notwithstanding all that is said by the commentators about tongues imparted for the preaching of the gospel, I have found no one of all the reported cases of tongues, in which the tongue was intelligible, either to the speaker or the hearers, except as it was made so by a supernatural interpretation—which accords exactly, also with what is said of tongues in the New Testament. And yet, on second thought, they have all the greater dignity and propriety, for just the reason that they require another gift to make them intelligible. . . . For so it is with all revelations of the Spirit, they are not only uttered or penned by inspiration, but they want a light of the Spirit in the receiver, to really apprehend their power.[121]

Bushnell recognized, of course, that religious "delusion" existed, but he steadily refused to dismiss the gift of tongues as mere enthusiasm. It meant little to him that educated men argued against the authenticity of such gifts. Their negative approaches signified only "that the human mind, as educated mind, is just now at the point of religious apogee; where it is occupied, or preoccupied by nature, and can not think it rational to suppose that God does any thing longer, which exceeds the causalities of nature." Bushnell probed beyond the superficial in an effort to link speaking in tongues with his theory of language. The gift, he suggested, possibly pointed to the fact that all languages are from "the Eternal Word, in souls; there being, in his intelligent nature as Word, millions doubtless of possible tongues, that are as real to him as the spoken tongues of the world."[122]

Of his New England contemporaries Bushnell remarked: "Nothing is farther off from the Christian expectation of our New England communities, than the gift of tongues." He reported, however, that that gift and the gift of interpretation had appeared at a gathering of New England Christians concerned with their need of sanctification. He also recounted several recent healings in the vicinity. Bushnell remarked that the answers to specific prayers to which Pietists had testified had often been deemed too strange for serious consideration. He knew personally of so many direct and remarkable answers to prayer, however, that he ventured to suggest that they were "even common" among certain classes:

> In that humbler stratum of life, where the conventionalities and carnal judgements of the world have less power, there are characters blooming in the holiest type of Christian love and beauty, who talk, and pray, and, as they think, operate apostolically, as if God were all to them that he ever was to the church, in the days of her primitive grace.[123]

In contrast to Bushnell, David Green, Secretary of the American Board of Commissioners for Foreign Missions, took a much less positive attitude toward the renewed interest in tongues. Green first of all took issue with the teaching that a gift of tongues would enable the recipient to preach in foreign vernaculars. Tongues had not been a permanent endowment of the church, but rather a supernatural sign of confirmation of the "divine authority of Christianity," and attempts to preserve or resuscitate this gift had inevitably led to confusion such as that in the church at Corinth.[124]

At mid-century the waning of the revival moods in the "Atlantic community" was suddenly quickened beyond expectations by a new series of spiritual awakenings, this time first in Cornwall, England (1851), then spreading through the United States, then to Wales, Ireland, and other parts of England beyond Cornwall. Glossolalia was not reported in this renewal, but fervent prayer, spontaneous shouts of praise, exuberant singing, and joyful testimonies were evidences of transforming spiritual experiences. The Holy Spirit came "with wondrous power," one observer of the Irish awakening reported. Cases of prostrations were common, and some of the physical manifestations were "very violent." Healings often accompanied experiences of salvation.[125]

In the United States, this pre-Civil War revival was largely a lay movement. During the first half of the century, the phenomenal spread of Methodism had introduced into American revivalism a strong emphasis on an experience of sanctification. Wesley's teaching on the availability of a "second" definite work of grace (see I Thess. 5:5-23; Heb. 3:19; 4:1) was modified and popularized through the itinerant ministry and the publications of Walter and Phoebe Palmer.

The quest for holiness was not confined to Arminian Methodist ranks. From his position at Oberlin College, Charles Grandison Finney (1792-1875), Presbyterian-turned-Congregationalist, with his colleague Asa Mahan, expounded a related version of perfectionist doctrine.[126] William Edwin Boardman, a Presbyterian, published *The Higher Christian Life* in 1859. This quickly became a classic expression of the teachings of many who aspired to an experiential understanding of the Wesleyan dictum: "Go on unto perfection."

During the second half of the nineteenth century, this pre-Civil War interest in a religious-crisis experience subsequent to conversion was channeled into a structured Holiness movement. Originating at Vineland, New Jersey, in 1867, the National Camp Meeting Association for the Promotion of Holiness was initially a Methodist organization. The association attracted some of that denomination's most illustrious leaders and soon expanded its activities beyond the confines of camp meetings. Local Holiness revivals and special publications devoted to holiness teaching drew the attention of non-Methodists and gave the movement a broad evangelical base. The Holiness revival renewed emphasis on a normative Christian experience, variously termed entire sanctification, second blessing, perfection, perfect love and baptism with the Holy Spirit, and it popularized the terminology which was subsequently adopted by organized Pentecostalism.[127]

Considerable concern with a "deeper," "higher," or "happy" Christian life was also demonstrated outside of the auspices of the Holiness associations. Albert Benjamin Simpson, Presbyterian founder of the Christian and Missionary Alliance, preached a fourfold Gospel of Christ the Saviour, Healer, Sanctifier, and Coming King.[128] His premillennial and divine healing emphases formed an accepted part of the common holiness message of "Jesus Christ the same, yesterday, and today, and forever" (Heb. 13:8). Simpson was among the most creative of Holiness contributors to the Pentecostal movement in process of separate denominational organization. (The presbyterian polity of Simpson's Christian and Missionary Alliance has been adopted by the largest Pentecostal body, the Assemblies of God.)

The vocabulary of the Holiness movement pervaded much of American Evangelicalism in the last three decades of the century. The revivalist Dwight L. Moody (d. 1899) had a remarkable Spirit baptism and often urged upon participants in his Northfield Conferences their need for a similar outpouring.[129] He frequently requested his associate and successor, Reuben A. Torrey, to preach his sermon on the baptism with the Holy Ghost which claimed that spiritual baptism resulted in power for service.[130] Torrey was a prominent participant in the annual British Keswick Conventions in the Lake District, which had resulted primarily from the efforts of the American Quaker couple R. Pearsall and Hannah Whitall Smith. Leading Keswick speakers like the Dutch-Reformed South African, Andrew Murray,[131] and the German-born British Baptist, Frederick Brotherton Meyer, frequently visited Northfield and contributed an international perspective to American Evangelical holiness teaching.

The dramatic inroads of holiness doctrines and the concomitant revival spirit, alas, fostered division as well as cohesion. In the South, a black preacher of holiness, Charles Price Jones, was not only locked out of his church—an attempt was made on his life.[132] In Tennessee the struggling group which later emerged as the influential Church of God (Cleveland) found their church building demolished one Sunday morning. Their homes were frequently stoned, and they were harassed.[133]

By 1894, the Methodist Episcopal Church (South) had second thoughts and issued a statement deploring the independent nature and activities of the Holiness Associations. The opposition of the last decade of the century proved decisive: a number of groups emerged as independent Holiness denominations.

THE HOLINESS MOVEMENT AND THE DIFFERENTIATION OF PENTECOSTALISM INTO MAJOR DENOMINATIONAL FAMILIES ON A GLOBAL SCALE

The Holiness movement endured disparagement, persecution, and divisions. Yet, serious indeed were the questions raised from within and the confusion that the ambiguities in the holiness teaching fostered.

At this point we must become clear about the problem of the *ordo salutis* (the order of salvation), of which baptism with the Holy Spirit signified by tongues is a phase or a theologically, scripturally, and experientially discreet moment, because that order would inevitably differ from the start as between those who had had a pedobaptist background and those who presupposed, in any case, believers' baptism, usually by immersion. For some Pentecostals of a pedobaptist background, there would naturally be a predisposition to repudiate the water baptism of one's infancy.[134] Thus we must be prepared to find in the Pentecostal movement in modern times some difference in usage between those groups in which experiential conversion was followed by immersion as a requisite (hence anabaptism) and those groups in which the new life would be signalized and understood by some other action or theological formulation. Pentecostal groups, whether pedobaptist or believers' baptist in background, differ as to whether there are two or three discreet moments. Approximately half of all American Pentecostals today hold to the bipartite view: experiential conversion (followed by immersion) and baptism with the Holy Spirit, of which tongues is the initial evidence. The other half hold to the tripartite: experiential conversion, entire sanctification or the second blessing, and the baptism with the Holy Spirit, of which baptism the speaking in tongues is the initial manifestation to be followed by other fruits of the Spirit.[135]

Moreover, even within these two basically different orders of successive moments in the career of salvation, there have been lesser distinctions that have often aroused acrimonious debate, leading sometimes to schism. In general, however, in the believers' baptist line, water baptism would be regularly interposed as the outward sign of conversion while very frequently immersion (i.e., anabaptism) would also be expected, even of those in the pedobaptist tradition.

During the last few years of the nineteenth century, a number of prominent Evangelicals, none of whom was associated with the Methodist wing of the Holiness revival, published books dealing with the baptism with the Holy Spirit. R. A. Torrey, Adoniram Judson Gordon (pastor of Boston's Clarendon Street [Baptist] Church and founder of Gordon College), and Cyrus Scofield were all associated with D. L. Moody's Northfield Conferences. A. B. Simpson expressed similar views independently.

Gordon's *The Ministry of the Spirit* was the first of the four to appear. The Holy Spirit had come to abide in the church at Pentecost, he claimed, but every believer nonetheless needed a definite experience of infilling of the Spirit. "We conceive that the great end for which the enduement of the Spirit is bestowed is our qualification for the highest and most effective service in the church of Christ."[136]

Torrey's *The Baptism with the Holy Spirit* was published the next year (1895). He contended that such a baptism was always connected with testimony and service, and he took issue with the holiness teaching that it involved the eradication of sinful nature: "The Baptism with the Holy Spirit is not for the purpose of cleansing from sin, but for the purpose of empowering for service."[137]

Simpson's *The Holy Spirit, or Power from on High* appeared at almost the same time. In it he gave expression to ideas which were influential in the subsequent formulations of Pentecostal doctrine. The baptism with the Holy Spirit was not an influence, notion, feeling, or power, but a union of the individual with "the living personality of the Spirit." Its functions were diverse: penetrating, purifying, consuming, refining, quickening, energizing, protecting. While Spirit baptism undoubtedly resulted in "power for service," it was not primarily that: "It is power to receive the life of Christ; power to be, rather than to say and to do. Our service and testimony will be the outcome of our life and experience." Simpson's premillennialism made him expect increasing prominence of the gifts of the Spirit in these "last days before the coming of the Lord Jesus Christ." His own activities included an extensive healing ministry. These gifts bestowed by the Holy Spirit would, however, remain secondary if kept in the proper perspective. The true object of Spirit baptism was "to bring Jesus upon the canvas, and make him real to us, while the blessed Actor is, in a measure, out of sight," for "the Holy Ghost never comes to us apart from Jesus."[138]

Cyrus Ingerson Scofield was pastor of the Moody Church in Northfield, Massachusetts, when he published his *Plain Papers on the Doctrine of the Holy Spirit* in 1899. He developed a view which significantly converged with and diverged from those of Gordon, Torrey, and Simpson. Spirit baptism was not to be sought as a discrete experience, for it was the "present possession" of all the regenerate. On the other hand, subsequent fillings resulted in "special enduement for distinctive service."[139]

Since interest in the baptism with the Holy Spirit focused on the day of Pentecost, it proved impossible to ignore the significance of glossolalia. Torrey puzzled over the place of speaking in tongues in Spirit baptism until he decided, on the basis of I Corinthians 12:30 ("Do all speak with tongues?"), that it was not necessarily a normative part of the experience, and he established other criteria to ascertain the reality of Spirit baptism.[140]

For many Holiness people the Briton, William Arthur, of the Wesleyan Church, provided in his *Tongue of Fire* (1856) an explanation of Spirit baptism in its relation to the gift of tongues. Arthur dealt with the place of tongues in the experience of spiritual baptism in some detail. The gift, he claimed, was a lower gift than that of prophecy. Both had been given in New Testament times to serve as miraculous evidence that the Gospel message was indeed of supernatural power. The gift of tongues was not, however, a "permanent privilege" of the church:

Not adapted to edify the Church, or to bring ignorant unbelievers to repentance, and fitted only to be a sign under exceptionable circumstances, this gift does not seem clearly designed to be either universal or perpetual. We are not called upon to say that it will never be restored to the Church; for that is never said in the word of God; nor should we ridicule or talk disrespectfully of the faith of any Christian who devoutly expects its restoration. All we say is that we have not scriptural ground to claim it as one of the permanent gifts of the Spirit; and we may add that, if it ever return to the Church, it will be, not a mystification, but a miracle; a real speaking with "other tongues," not a speaking in some unheard-of, unknown tongue.[141]

The idea that the gift of tongues had not been a permanent endowment found support and able expression in another small nineteenth-century group which was destined to exert an influence on Evangelical Protestantism out of all proportion to its numerical strength. The Plymouth Brethren were followers of John Nelson Darby (d. 1882), an Irish Anglican priest who left the church to lead a restorationist, anti-institutional movement. In the United States he found few who were willing to endorse the "come-outism" he advocated, but many sympathized with his dispensationalism and premillennialism. The most enduring and effective contribution of his sympathizers to the American religious scene was the C. I. Scofield Reference Bible, which was prepared under the direction of such prominent Fundamentalist Evangelicals as James M. Gray and Arthur T. Pierson and appeared in New York in 1909. In the notes of the Scofield Bible was developed what has remained the restrained teaching of Fundamentalism on tongues.[142]

The baptism with the Holy Spirit as given at Pentecost was not intended, according to Scofield, as an enduring part of normal Christian experience. Indeed, Spirit baptism was not even subsequent to conversion, but occurred as part of conversion (experiential regeneration, as distinguished from regeneration during water baptism). The permanent legacy of Pentecost to this "Church Age" was simple: "Every believer is born of the Spirit; indwelt by the Spirit, whose presence makes the believer's body a temple; and baptized with the Spirit, thus sealing him for God."[143]   The Holy Spirit became one's portion at conversion, and subsequent experiences of infilling were not to be "confused" with baptism. Despite Scofield's reserve concerning glossolalia, his dispensationalism was appropriated by Pentecostal organizations like the Assemblies of God, and the Scofield Bible is widely used by Pentecostals.

Meanwhile, as Darbyites formulated their dispensational teachings, confusion abounded in certain segments of the Holiness movement. The problem was clearly discerned and ably expressed by the committed but eminently sensible Hannah Whitall Smith (d. 1913). Mrs. Smith deplored emotional excesses of any sort and was deeply disturbed by those who followed irrational leadings under the guise of obedience to the Holy Spirit. In her capacity as an exponent of Keswickian holiness doctrine, she was thoroughly familiar with the various modes in which it was expressed. She had observed how the quest for certainty had too often resulted in the elevation of particular manifestations over concern for authentic experience. Some claimed that a certain dance or laugh was sure evidence of Spirit baptism; others found that undue emphasis on the "holy kiss" led to unfortunate consequences.[144]

There are many accounts of sporadic outbreaks of tongues in the period between 1865 and 1906, and not all were confined in Evangelical contexts. William James reported his unsuccessful attempt in the 1870's to convince a young woman who claimed she was speaking in tongues that her "nonsense-syllables" (which were "a very curious thing to hear") were mere "psychic automatism." He also presented his readers with an account of a man whose incomprehensible utterances he attributed to the same source. But the man remained convinced of the authenticity of the languages he spoke and kept records of the messages and interpretations, cherishing a vain hope of discovering his "tongue." An old Catholic man in Boston was also reported to have spoken in old Latin under inspiration.[145]

In 1886, in the mountain region where Tennessee, North Carolina, and Georgia converge, a small group withdrew from a local Baptist church and organized a Holiness group known as the Christian Union. Several small churches were eventually associated with this Union, but for about ten years their prayer for renewal seemed unanswered. In 1896, however, revival came, and with it came a strange and awesome phenomenon—that of tongues. Here the languages spoken were not understood, but the manifestation continued. All who had ecstatic experiences in that revival—regardless of where or when they occurred—"spoke in tongues, or languages, unknown to those who listened in wonder and hope." Out of this Christian Union has grown the large and influential Church of God (Cleveland), the oldest Pentecostal Church.[146]

In other parts of the world, similar phenomena occurred. Shortly after 1880 reports of glossolalia came from a Moravian mission outpost. In the course of a revival in which many were shaken and compelled to cry out for mercy, such gifts of the Holy Spirit as prophecy and tongues, together with visions and dreams, began to appear among the awakened. One missionary reported that he heard a man speaking in an unknown tongue while engaged in his daily tasks. During the services some were observed moving their lips as if speaking unusually fast but emitting no audible sounds.[147]

In Sweden in 1902 Lewi Pethrus, a young Baptist minister, had limited contact with the Salvation Army and Methodism, which left him aware of his need for a fuller religious experience. However, his Baptist mentors explained to him the errors of holiness teachings and made him wary of both groups. After meetings in Lillesand, Pethrus was invited to spend the hours before his departure for Oslo with a group of friends whose experience included contact with the healing ministry of John Alexander Dowie (d. 1907), founder of Zion City in Illinois (1900)[148] and with the Norwegian Holiness movement. After a night spent together in prayer, these friends accompanied Pethrus to the pier and saw him embark on the 4 a.m. boat. As he stood on the deck alone, praying, and watched the sun rising over the ocean, Pethrus was overwhelmed: "Tears streamed down my cheeks while I was overflowing with joy.. A current of power and sweetness went through my entire being, and I spoke strange words which surprised me a great deal."[149]

In 1904 a revival broke out again in Wales which surpassed expectations and brought many to observe who departed to proclaim. Throughout that little country, thousands were added to the "churches, chapels and mission-rooms."[150] Remarkable demonstrations attended the ministry of Evan Roberts, the itinerant youth whose piercing words brought conviction wherever he went. His meetings were marked by outbursts of song, spontaneous praise, fervent prayer, and enthusiastic testimony. Curiously, many who were ordinarily unable to converse in the Welsh tongue had experiences during which they prayed, testified, or sang at length in fluent Welsh.

It was during the Welsh Revival that William F. P. Burton first heard glossolalia. Burton later became a pioneer of Pentecostalism in England and a co-founder of the Congo [Zaire] Evangelistic Mission. When he first heard tongues in 1906, he was not greatly impressed, nor did he understand their significance.[151]

In both Wales and the Highlands, where the population was almost wholly bilingual by the end of the nineteenth century, there was a preaching phenomenon closely related to the gift of tongues. In the Highlands and Isles it was called the Highland wail, and in Wales, *hwyl*. In Scotland, where communion was held four times a year as in Calvin's Geneva, with one additional service just before New Year's, the preparation for the event was so intensive, involving repentance and thanksgiving, that the two weeks preceding the actual solemnity were called "communion season"; and during this period the Highland preachers in high, intensive singsong Gaelic induced a special spirit of repentance and solemn joy that approached ecstasy. *Hwyl* was similarly used, in circumstances less closely connected to communion, to describe the afflatus (divine gust or mighty wind) which seems to have inspired Welsh preachers and descended upon their congregations with compelling urgency and chapel-filling power.[152] The Welsh revival provided a powerful stimulus to a growing desire for authentic renewal. The prayer groups which began as a result provided the setting for the Pentecostal awakening which soon arrived.

Meanwhile, at the turn of the century, a small, isolated group of American Christians embarked on the same project which had led R.A. Torrey to deemphasize tongues while continuing to preach a baptism with the Holy Spirit. They began to search for a biblical doctrine of evidence. Their conclusions were radically different, however. From Topeka, Kansas, emanated the teaching which was to become a basic Pentecostal distinctive: glossolalia was the initial evidence of Spirit baptism, the third in a series of spiritual marks, the first mark being conversion, usually signalized by believers' water baptism, the second being sanctification as a "second blessing" in the tradition of John Wesley.

Charles F. Parham had brought his holiness message to many midwestern rural areas as a Methodist revivalist and later as an independent preacher of healing and sanctification before he opened his "faith" Bible School in Topeka in October, 1900. One objective of those whom he gathered there was literal obedience to all the commands of Christ. By December, consensus had been reached on such subjects as repentance, conversion, healing, and the Second Coming, but the question of evidence for Spirit baptism proved more difficult. Parham recognized a need for agreement, instructed his students to search the Bible for an irrefutable doctrine, and left them at the task while he conducted meetings in Kansas City. He returned on 31 December 1900 and convened the students to discuss their conclusions. The forty students unanimously affirmed that in the Bible tongues were the "indisputable proof" of spiritual baptism.

That night about 135 people gathered for the New Year's Eve service. One of the students requested that others lay hands on her so that she might be filled with the Holy Spirit. Parham's initial reluctance gave way to the insistence of his students; and Agnes Ozman began to speak in tongues. Parham declared that "a glory fell upon her, a halo seemed to surround her head and face, and she began speaking in the Chinese language, and was unable to speak English for three days." Miss Ozman's experience served as a powerful incentive, and soon Topeka newsboys shouted in the streets: "Pentecost, Pentecost, Pentecost, read all about the Pentecost." One after another spoke in tongues. Parham recalled one meeting at which twelve ministers, representing several denominations, sang Charles Wesley's "Jesus Lover of my Soul" simultaneously in six different languages. According to his testimony, all who received the baptism in the Spirit spoke known languages, many of which were understood by observers. There was no "chatting, blabbering, or stuttering."[153]

Parham and his willing students closed their Bible School to become itinerant exponents of the full salvation. They were primarily evangelists, but the Gospel they proclaimed commenced rather than culminated at conversion. He whose death had purchased salvation was also an omnipresent, omnipotent healer. And, best of all, one's yearnings for a deeper experience need no longer promote the frustration which had so often accompanied ambiguity. One could know when he had received the baptism with the Holy Spirit, for he would speak in tongues!

Parham's initial activities were concentrated in the southern Middle West. It was in Houston, Texas (where he had moved his headquarters in 1905), that he met the black Baptist holiness preacher through whose ministry his teaching would command widespread attention. As much as Southern racial mores would then permit, William Seymour sat under Parham's teaching. Seymour learned from Parham that the baptism with the Holy Spirit (which is evidenced by tongues) *was not to be equated* with sanctification or the second blessing but was rather the third in a series of three discrete experiences, leading to "service." Seymour carried this complex psychological-religious doctrine with him to Los Angeles in 1906.

Called to a small black Holiness mission, Seymour preached his first sermon on Acts 2:4, although he had not himself yet spoken in tongues. Expelled from the black Holiness mission because of his identification of tongues with the baptism with the Spirit (which was offensive to the Holiness people, who had identified this spiritual baptism with sanctification), Seymour and his sympathizers moved their services to a private home. Speaking in tongues continued unabated in the resultant new black mission after April 9, when Seymour and others received their spiritual baptisms, and the crowds attracted by the unusual phenomenon soon became interracial. Meetings were moved to an abandoned Methodist church building, and the fame of the Azusa Street revival was quickly "spread abroad." Azusa Street in Los Angeles became the temporary center from which the doctrine of tongues as initial evidence of the final phase of the whole *ordo salutis* went forth in both its stabilizing and its divisive aspects.

As a stabilizing influence, the concept of tongues as initial evidence of the completion of the *ordo salutis* ended an ambiguity inherent in holiness teaching and provided an organizing principle for the emerging independent Holiness groups and separate denominations. On the other hand, this concept split Holiness ranks and alienated some who had contributed most creatively to the preparation for a Pentecostal revival by developing its vocabulary, theology, hymnody, and international missionary expansion.

Fundamentalist Evangelicals like Torrey, whose teachings and meetings had helped to quicken the spiritual longings which had given birth to the revival, could not accept the doctrine of tongues as "initial evidence" and became increasingly opposed to the emerging Pentecostal groups based on this principle. Arthur T. Pierson also cautioned Evangelicals against ready acceptance of the teaching.[154]

All American Holiness groups were forced to take a position on tongues. Some leaders, like Alma White of the Pillar of Fire Church, went so far as to associate tongues with demon possession. Of William Seymour, who had visited her Denver headquarters en route to Los Angeles in 1906, she declared: "I had met all kinds of religious fakirs and tramps, but I felt he excelled them all."

G. B. Cashwell had a different reaction. A member of the Pentecostal Holiness Church, a Southern holiness denomination, he went to Los Angeles to investigate the new teaching which distinguished sanctification from the gift of tongues. While there, he spoke in tongues, and on his return many caught the intense fervor and sense of expectancy that motivated him. The "tongues movement" quickly took hold in the area. From Dunn, N.C., Cashwell toured the South.

By early 1907 the General Overseer of the Fire-Baptized Holiness Church, J. H. King, had spoken in tongues; but A. B. Crumpler, leader of the Pentecostal Holiness Church, refused to be convinced of Cashwell's credentials. When Crumpler realized that the plenary Pentecostal view had been adopted by a majority in his denomination, he withdrew.

In 1911 the Fire-Baptized Holiness and Pentecostal Holiness Churches merged to form the Pentecostal Holiness Church.[155] Ambrose Jessup Tomlinson, father of Milton and Homer (both destined to be major Pentecostal leaders) and head of the growing Church of God (Cleveland), spoke in tongues under Cashwell's ministry and brought that group into the Pentecostal movement.[156]

Under the leadership of Charles Price Jones and C. H. Mason, the Holiness revival flourished among blacks in Alabama, Mississippi, and Tennessee. This group, as others, was divided by the tongues question. Mason's journey to Los Angeles convinced him of the validity of the Pentecostal distinctive, but Jones was unwilling to endorse tongues. In 1907, Jones' group withdrew the right hand of fellowship from Mason and all who agreed with his views. Mason left Jones' Assembly in Jackson, Mississippi, and convened another in Memphis, where it was decided to retain the name "Church of God in Christ" and to add a paragraph endorsing tongues to the original articles of faith. Mason's black group has exerted significant influence on the whole Pentecostal Movement in the United States and has grown into the second largest Pentecostal denomination. Jones changed the name of his body to the "Church of Christ (Holiness) U.S.A." It continues to function, with headquarters in Jackson, Mississippi.[157]

In the Christian and Missionary Alliance, it became clear that the position of the founder, A. B. Simpson, on tongues would be crucial.[158]   As news of the Los Angeles revival had spread, a number of Christian and Missionary Alliance churches accepted tongues. By May, 1907, the Pentecostal revival reached the Missionary Training Institute (Nyack College) at Nyack, New York. David McDowell, a student of Simpson, was sufficiently impressed by what he saw there to seek "the blessing" for himself. He received it at a camp meeting where he prayed with his arms raised for over an hour. When he lowered his arms, his hands fell on the heads of two women, who, in turn, immediately began to speak with tongues. This was the beginning of a long and fruitful ministry for McDowell. By August, when he told an audience of nearly a thousand at Nyack that this was "the Latter Rain for which we have been praying for years," almost everyone rose to pray for a personal Pentecost.[159]

A. B. Simpson did not, during the initial period of association with the movement, question the validity of speaking in tongues. Indeed, he acknowledged that what was recorded in Acts 2 had not necessarily been limited to Apostolic times: "[T]here appears to be no reason why this gift should not appear at any time in the history of the Church. It was not always employed in the Apostolic Church as the vehicle of preaching to people of other languages, but rather as a channel of direct worship and adoration."

But what came to trouble him about the phenomenon and associated doctrine was not that tongues were associated with the baptism with the Holy Spirit, but rather the dogmatic insistence of those who carried the Azusa Street message that tongues were the initial evidence of Spirit baptism in the tripartite *ordo salutis. An* evidence they might well be, but tongues as *the* evidence was, in his mind, unscriptural. Simpson reflected sadly on the error of the disposition "to make special manifestations [tongues and other charismatic phenomena] evidence of the baptism of the Holy Ghost, giving to them the name of Pentecost, as though none had received the Spirit of Pentecost but those who had the power to speak in tongues. . . ." Reluctantly but resolutely, Simpson announced his opposition to the teaching which found expression in organized Pentecostalism and stated his policy as "seek not, forbid not."[160]   As a result, whole churches and an impressive list of young and able ministers severed their connections with Simpson's Christian and Missionary Alliance in order to join the growing Pentecostal ranks. Many of them eventually joined the Assemblies of God when these organized as a distinct denomination in 1914, and provided judicious leadership during the stormy, decisive period of modern Pentecostalist development.

Bramwell Booth, who succeeded his father, William, as General of the Salvation Army, sadly but not necessarily accurately observed that tongues had tended to deflect from the "interest of Salvationists in evangelism":

> We have to be suspicious of any voices or gifts which make men indisposed to bear the Cross or to seek the Salvation of others, and although some of our own people have received what is spoken of as a gift of tongues, we have almost invariably found that one of the consequences has been a disposition to withdraw from hard work for the blessing of others and from fearless testimony to the Saviour. I recognize the dangers which attend the whole subject, and while I believe that these things, as I have witnessed them, are Divine in their origin, I do not forget that in some instances they may have been mixed with what is the very reverse.[161]

The Church of the Nazarene was created in 1908 by the merger of several quite small Holiness groups. It was originally known as the Pentecostal Church of the Nazarene, but the implications of the word *Pentecostal* became increasingly offensive to those who rejected the notion of glossolalia as initial evidence of Spirit baptism, although in some Nazarene assemblies, members spoke in tongues. Meanwhile, as organized Pentecostalism expanded, Nazarene opposition to glossolalia began to harden. This disposition culminated in 1919 with the deletion of *Pentecostal* from the official name of the church.[162]

Elsewhere, the doctrine of tongues as the final phase of the *ordo salutis* gave direction to revival but also fostered controversy and schism. A Methodist minister in Oslo, Norway, B. T. Barratt, an Englishman by birth, while in the United States on a fund-raising mission heard of the revival in Los Angeles; and on 15 November 1906 he spoke in tongues at a Pentecostal meeting in New York City. "I was filled with light and such power," he recalled,

> that I began to shout as loud as I could in a foreign language. I must have spoken seven or eight languages, to judge from the various sounds and forms of speech used. . . . The most wonderful moment was when I burst into a beautiful baritone solo, using one of the most pure and delightful languages I have ever heard.[163]

Barratt returned immediately to Europe, full of the exuberance of his new experience and soon had crowds attending his meetings. News of the revival in Oslo attracted Lewi Pethrus, who returned to Sweden more fully committed to the movement.[164] By 1916, Barratt had the largest dissenter congregation in Norway and Pethrus had been called to Stockholm's Filadelfia Church, which under his ministry became one of the largest Pentecostal assemblies in the world.

Barratt was invited to England by Alexander Boddy, the vicar of All Saints' Church, Sunderland, near Newcastle. Boddy had already observed Barratt's ministry in Norway: "I stood with Evan Roberts in Tonypandy [Wales]," he recalled, "but have never witnessed such scenes as those in Norway." Under Barratt's ministry, the Los Angeles revival extended to England. Handley G. Moule, Bishop of Durham, Boddy's superior and leader in the Keswick Movement, offered no remonstrance, and the revival flourished.[165]

News of events in Norway drew the Lutheran pastor Jonathan Paul, leader of the German Holiness Association, the Gnadauer Verband, to Oslo. Paul came as a curious observer and returned to declare: "I found there a revival which prompted a yearning for a deeper cleansing through the blood of Jesus and a fuller experience of the baptism and gifts of the Holy Spirit."[166]   The visit of two Pentecostalist representatives from Oslo to Germany reinforced Pastor Paul's observations and stimulated interest in speaking in tongues.

As the movement gained increasing support, however, opposition appeared. By 1908, under Paul's leadership, the pages of the new *Pfingstgrüsse* attempted to defend the German modification of the Azusa Street teaching and win the support of Holiness leaders. Speaking in tongues, Paul admitted, was in itself not an evidence of Spirit baptism. The *fruits* of the Spirit were rather the real tests of experience: "We do not want to consider tongues more significant than does the Bible." Despite this remarkably moderate gesture to his skeptical colleagues, Pastor Paul and those who preached and practiced the speaking in tongues were read out of the Gnadauer Verband and forced to unite independently in the Mühlheimer Gemeinschaft organized in 1909.

These early Pentecostal leaders never encouraged anyone to pray for the experience of speaking in tongues. Seekers were consistently directed to desire a fuller revelation of Christ within, and tongues were considered a sign that he had moved into one's life and assumed complete control. The baptism with the Holy Spirit (evidenced by glossolalia) was not the apex of spiritual experience, but rather marked the commencement of an ever deepening relationship with the indwelling Christ and the conferral of power "for life and for service" upon the committed disciple.

By virtue of their acceptance of the doctrine of tongues as initial evidence of Spirit baptism, congregations in the United States and Europe became distinctly Pentecostal.[167]   From its inception, the revival included a strong missionary impulse. Missionaries on furlough who attended the Azusa Street meetings in Los Angeles brought its message back to their fields. Reports of spiritual renewals at home stimulated desires for revival abroad, and the newly awakened soon swelled missionary ranks. Early Pentecostal expansion was frequently without organization or pledged support. Following spiritual leadings and equipped, as the apostles had been, by their "personal Pentecosts," missionaries went into all the world. As the

American and European movements coalesced into denominational organizations, newly created mission boards increased the efficiency with which Pentecostals responded to the Great Commission (Matt. 28:19, 20).

The Pentecostal movement has grown remarkably in South America. The revival come to Valparaiso in 1908-1910 through Methodism, and today Chilean Pentecostalism embraces at least 14 percent of the total population. In Brazil the Assembleias de Deus, founded by the two Swedish-American missionaries Gunnar Vingren and Daniel Berg, has experienced growth "unparalleled in recent church history."[168] With at least 70 percent of Brazilian Protestants as members, the several Pentecostal bodies represented there constitute the largest single evangelical group in that country. Pentecostals have also established schools and strong indigenous churches in other parts of Latin America and in Asian and African nations.[169]

By 1916, Pentecostalism had assumed a relatively stable character. In the United States, several independent bodies had emerged. The Pentecostal Holiness Church (Franklin Springs, Georgia), the Church of God (Cleveland, Tennessee), and the Church of God in Christ (Memphis, Tennessee) had their origins in the Holiness revival of the late nineteenth century. The Assemblies of God was created by the merger of several independent associations at Hot Springs, Arkansas, in 1914. Since 1916, when the Assemblies of God clearly defined its stand on several controversial issues, the several American-based international Pentecostal denominations have adhered to their traditional standards.[170]

From the beginning, these groups were divided into two factions, nearly equal in size, over the question of sanctification. The Assemblies of God (and later Aimee Semple McPherson's Four Square Church)[171] accepted what was known as the "finished work" theory of the atonement, which regarded sanctification as "positional and instantaneous" and "practical and progressive." In this view, salvation included a fundamental transformation of human nature.[172] Those Pentecostals with roots in the holiness tradition, on the other hand, agreed with non-Pentecostal holiness bodies like the Church of the Nazarene that sanctification was a distinct experience, a "second blessing."

For several years a growing group within Pentecostalism had begun to insist on rebaptism in water "in the name of Jesus" (Acts 2:39). In the Assemblies of God, the "Jesus Only" teaching, with its unitarian implications, gained a significant foothold. The Assemblies of God, though numerically weakened by the withdrawal of a sizable "Oneness" faction, emerged from its decisive 1916 General Council in St. Louis strengthened by a new unity and stability in its ranks. Organized independently, the "Oneness" Pentecostals have experienced significant growth while continuing to evoke the criticism of other Pentecostal bodies.[173]

After a difficult period of persecution and stabilization, Pentecostals assumed a prominent place in American Evangelicalism in the formation of the National Association of Evangelicals in 1942. During the past fifteen years, Pentecostal phenomena have emerged in such Christian communions as the Protestant Episcopal Church and American Catholicism.[174] Pentecostal denominations provide structure and stability for a movement that is particularly prone to enthusiasm and fanaticism, and distinctive theological tenets give denominational Pentecostalism continued reason for separate existence.

Together with independent, indigenous groups, European and third-world counterparts of the major American Pentecostal families constitute the international Pentecostal community. Triennial World Pentecostal Conferences (first convened at Zürich in 1947) provide a meeting place at which the common heritage of these many Pentecostal organizations is recognized.

CONCLUSION

We can summarize our two-millennial survey of reports on glossolalia and related gifts of the Spirit by asserting that, in addition to groanings and ejaculations in ecstasy and the invocation of a few sacred names or terms of a half-remembered language, there have also been instances of speaking in living or dead or subliminal languages and of understanding such evangelical proclamations. The collective phenomenon of glossolalia in the three above senses is not wholly unrelated to rhythmic oracles and prophecies. In any case the affected person participates in some kind of communal-spiritual way in a corporate consciousness, presumably among Christians, under the power of the Holy Spirit. We have concluded furthermore that this Spirit, taking possession of the will and of the heart—but specifically, above all, of the mind—moves the tongue of the glossolalic to give voice to the deepest level of human experience. Thus, whatever light psychology, group psychology, and parapsychology can help throw on the strange phenomenon, these three forms of glossolalia do testify to an individual-transcending Power at work in a faithful, though often unsophisticated, community.

In Acts 2, Luke beheld in the seeming miracle of diverse languages being mutually understood in the upper room under the impact of the Spirit of Christ the first signs of the healing of the division caused by man's presumption in erecting into heaven, as it were, the Tower of Babel. Mutual semantic understanding was the onset of the new unity in the Second Adam. It is therefore regrettable that in the course of Christian history the great scene constructed by Luke has repeatedly led to divisiveness and factionalism among Christians. Paul himself had listed glossolalia and its interpretation as only two of many gifts of the Spirit, and he did not even place them high on his list.

Nevertheless, glossolalia in its fullest range and depth surely has been no more divisive in Christian history than other doctrines such as predestination or other practices such as baptism and the eucharist, and it should not therefore be singled out for special opprobrium. Rather, *in* this phenomenon and *behind* it and *beyond* it we may now and in the future seek to ascertain what the Spirit is groaning for within and through some of us—to heed whatever voice may be in the process of emerging among us in the charismatic movement that may prove to be the healing word for our time.

Glossolalia may be a kind of rhythmic syllabic ejaculation unrelated to any ordinary language, or it may be the gift of swiftly communicating in a hitherto unknown language through the missionary or evangelical urge to communicate the Gospel (more a matter of genius perhaps, and swift linguistic acuity), or perhaps it is a parapsychologically-explicable but still authentically Spiritual communication in which a dedicated charismatic in a Spiritually-created community, sharing the mind of Christ (I Cor. 2:16), communicates love, healing, and power. In any event, it is evident even from our brief survey that we have been in touch with something mysteriously operating through the sensitization of that most marvelously complicated form of matter, the human brain, and its principal means of communication, the tongue. The whole of creation has been groaning and sighing in travail until now (Rom. 8:22f.), waiting for divine adoption amid the alienations of the world.

Notes

The three standard histories of the Holy Spirit in Christianity deal scarcely at all with the experiential Spirit of glossolalia or the manifestations of the Spirit outside main-line ecclesiastical development: H.B. Swete, *The Holy Spirit in the New Testament* (London, 1909), *The Holy Spirit in the Ancient Church* (London, 1912), and H. Watkins-Jones, *The Holy Spirit in the Medieval Church* (London, 1922).

1. "And they were all filled with the Holy Ghost, and began to speak with other tongues, as the Spirit gave them utterance." (All biblical citations are from the King James version.) The historian must reckon here with the probability that Luke was fully conscious, as he recounted the Pentecostal event, of the confusion of tongues at the tower of Babel (Gen. 11:9). While the author of Chapter 6, John Kildahl, is skeptical about the authenticity of the language spoken in ecstatic speech, the authors of this chapter trace what they regard as lingual ecstasy, ranging from inarticulate utterances to true languages, either actively communicated or receptively understood.
2. "And God hath set some in the church, first apostles, secondarily prophets, thirdly teachers, after that miracles, then gifts of healings, helps, govern-

ments, diversities of tongues. Are all apostles? are all prophets? are all teachers? are all workers of miracles? have all the gifts of healing? do all speak with tongues? do all interpret? But covet earnestly the best gifts" (1 Cor. 12:28-31). "For he that speaketh in an unknown tongue speaketh not unto men, but unto God: for no man understandeth him; howbeit in the spirit he speaketh mysteries. He that speaketh in an unknown tongue edifieth himself; but he that prophesieth edifieth the church. I would that ye all spake with tongues, but rather that ye prophesied; for greater is he that prophesieth than he that speaketh with tongues, except he interpret, that the church may receive edifying" (1 Cor. 14:2, 4, 5).

3. Cf. John Kildahl, *The Psychology of Speaking in Tongues* (New York, 1972).

4. The translation "unknown tongue" is a peculiarity of the King James version, used only in 1 Corinthians 14:2.

5. Carl-Martin Edsman, *Le Baptême du feu*, Acta Seminarii Neotestamentici Upsaliensis IX (Leipzig, 1940); Per Lundberg, *La Typologie baptismale dans l'ancienne Eglise* (Leipzig, 1942).

6. "For we know that the whole creation groaneth and travaileth in pain together until now" (Rom. 8:22). "Likewise the Spirit also helpeth our infirmities: for we know not what we should pray for as we ought: but the Spirit itself maketh intercession for us with groanings which cannot be uttered" (Rom. 8:26).

7. It is true that the ability to speak in tongues has not necessarily always been accompanied by a new intensity of spiritual experience or been evidenced by the fruits of the Spirit (Gal. 5:22, 23). Donald Gee, *All With One Accord* (Springfield, Mo., 1961) discusses this in the context of Pentecostal theology and negates the claim that Spirit baptism necessarily signifies spiritual maturity.

8. For a typical Pentecostal exposition of this distinction, see Carl Brumback, *"What Meaneth This?" A Pentecostal Answer to a Pentecostal Question* (Springfield, Mo., 1947).

9. "And it shall come to pass afterward, that I will pour out my spirit upon all flesh; and your sons and your daughters shall prophesy, your old men shall dream dreams, your young men shall see visions: and also upon the servants and upon the handmaids in those days will I pour out my spirit" (Joel 2:28, 29).

10. In an address entitled "Lesser Known Sources in the Roman Catholic Tradition of Charismatic Piety," delivered at the annual meeting of the Society for Pentecostal Studies in Oklahoma City in November, 1972, Stanley M. Burgess of Evangel College (Springfield, Mo.) discussed three different historical phenomena which can be classified as speaking in tongues: (1) glossolalia, or speech in an unknown tongue; (2) xenolalia, or speech in a foreign language; (3) heteroglossolalia, or the miraculous understanding of a foreign tongue.

11. Ignatius, writing to the Philadelphians: "For if some wished to deceive me after the flesh, yet the Spirit is not deceived, being from God. . . . I cried out while I was with you [in Philadelphia, not far from Phrygia, the province of Montanus], I spoke with a great voice, the voice of God." This is a prophecy rather than glossolalia, but a closely related phenomenon vividly attested to in a personal letter.

12. Stuart D. Currie, "Speaking in Tongues," *Interpreter*, XIX (1965), 288. Currie notes that the earlier apologist, Justin Martyr (d. 165 A.D.), in his *Dialogue with Trypho* (39.2), when he mentions the gifts of the Spirit, expressly omits tongues (p. 281).

13. For the Gnostic references, see Irenaeus, *Against Heresies*, I, xxi, ed. W.W. Harvey (Cambridge, 1857), I, 183ff., where an effort is made to reconstruct the original Semitic formulas surviving in Greek and Latin transliteration. See further *The Books of Jeu*, eds. Carl Schmidt and Walter Till, *Koptisch-gnostische Schriften* (Berlin, 1954), I, 308 *et passim;* J. Doresse, "Le Livre Sacré du grand Esprit Invisible," *Journal Asiatique*, CCLIV (1966), 317-

435, esp. pp. 344f. and 416-21 where single Greek vowels and consonants repeated many times, along with some fabricated Greek phrases, are set forth in Greek characters in the Coptic text as expressive of "the ineffable" and "a secret mystery inexpressible," proceeding, presumably, from the depths of the Great Invisible Spirit through which the higher powers, including the Ultimate Silence, bring benediction to the devotees. We are indebted to Professor George MacRae, S.J., for some of these references.

14. On the early history, up to the papal monopolization of the Corinthian test, see Albert M. Koeniger, "Prima sedes a nemine judicatur," *Festgabe A. Ehrhard* (Bonn, 1922).

15. Eusebius, *Ecclesiastical History*, V, xvi, 7, *Nicene and Post-Nicene Fathers* (Grand Rapids, 1971), 1st series, I, 231 (henceforth *NPF*). Though Eusebius dates the movement from 177 A.D., Epiphanius gives 157; and the latest study, based on startlingly new archaeological finds in Turkey, favors the earlier date of origin. See Elsa Gibson, "Montanism and its Monuments," doctoral thesis, Harvard University, 1974. See further Pierre de Labriolle, *La Crise montanists* (Paris, 1913) and *Les Sources de l'histoire du montanisme* (Fribourg, 1913); cf. Hans von Campenhausen, *Kirchliches Amt und geistliche Vollmacht* (Tübingen, 1953). In *The Riddle of the Didache* (1938), F.E. Vokes conjectures that the *Didache* may be an archaizing Montanist effort to repristinate earlier usage.

16. Eusebius, V, xvi, 8, *NPF*, loc. cit.

17. Tertullian, *A Treatise on the Soul*, ix, *Ante-Nicene Fathers* (Grand Rapids, 1973), III, 188 (henceforth *ANF*).

18. Tertullian, *Against Marcion*, V, viii, *ANF*, III, 447.

19. *Ibid.* In his *Treatise on the Soul*, Tertullian reports how, through the ecstasy in the Spirit, a sister was moved during divine service to share revelations; and in *Veiling of Virgins* he further reports special revelations and presumably glossolalia inspired by the Spirit, in appealing to the promise of the Paraclete as vicar of Christ, who said in John 14:26 and John 16:12f. that he would send "supervening things." Currie (op. cit.) quotes the same text in the Harvey edition as III, ix, 6.

20. Irenaeus, *Against Heresies*, III, xii, 1, *ANF*, I, 430.

21. *Against Heresies*, V, vi, 1, *ANF*, I, 531.

22. Origen, *Against Celsus*, VII, ix, *ANF*, IV, 614.

23. Origen, *De Principiis*, II, vii, 2, *ANF*, IV, 285.

24. Novatian, *Treatise Concerning the Trinity*, xxix, *ANF*, V, 641.

25. Hilary of Poitiers, *On the Trinity*, II, xxxiv, *NPF*, 2nd series, IX, 61.

26. *On the Trinity*, VIII, xxxiii, *NPF*, 2nd s., IX, 147.

27. Ambrose, *Of the Holy Spirit*, II, xiii, *NPF*, 2nd s., X, 134.

28. Chrysostom, *Homilies on First Corinthians*, XXIX, *NPF*, 1st s., XII, 168.

29. Augustine, *Homilies on the First Epistle of John*, VI, x, *NPF*, 1st s., VII, 497-98. See also Basil the Great, *On the Holy Spirit*, *NPF*, 2nd s., VIII, 1-50; Gregory Nazianzen, *On Pentecost*, xv, *NPF*, 2nd s., VII, 384; Jerome, *Letters*, XLI, *NPF*, 2nd s., VI, 55-56, and *Against the Pelagians*, I, xvi, *NPF*, 2nd s., VI, 457. These may all be cited as accepting only the literal sense of Acts 2:4. Jerome suggested that specific experiences like those at Pentecost should not be expected to recur. John Chrysostom, while also accepting the literal sense of Acts 2, simply stated that he had no personal knowledge of the gift of tongues.

30. Leo the Great, *Sermons*, LXXV, ii, *NPF*, 2nd s., XII, 190.

31. *Acta Sanctorum quotquot toto orbe coluntur, vel a catholicis scriptoribus . . . nostra illustravit Joannes Bollandus* (Antwerp, 1643-1931), May III, 319, 342.

32. John Meyendorff, *A Study of Gregory Palamas* (London, 1964). Much later, something akin to tongues in the sense of unintelligible but seemingly oracular ejaculations appeared among the heretical Khiltzy.

33. The Venerable Bede, *In Acta Apostolorum Expositio*, *Works*, ed. J.A. Gile (London, 1844), XII, 15-16.

34. Bede, *A History of the English Church and People*, trans. Leo Sherley-Price

(London, 1968), pp. 250-53. Others who sang under inspiration include Hildegard von Bingen and Ranters and Quakers; see notes 36 and 64 below.

35. Strong inspiration from Joachim continued well into the sixteenth century, appearing in the Radical Reformation, and traces thereof continue in recognizable form even in modern times. See Marjorie Reeves, *The Figure of Joachim of Fiore* (Oxford, 1972); Ernst Benz, *Ecclesia Spiritualis* (Stuttgart, 1934).

36. Hildegard von Bingen, *Wisse die Wege: Scivias* (Salzburg, 1954), pp. 169ff.; Johannes May, *Die heilige Hildegard von Bingen* (Munich, 1929), pp. 129ff. Much later, Jacob Boehme (d. 1624), although he did not speak in tongues, likewise claimed for his esoteric language divine illumination. See Ernst Benz, "Zur metaphysischen Begründung der Sprache bei Jakob Böhme," *Dichtung und Volkstum, neve Folge des Euphorion,* XXXVII (1936), 340-57.

37. *St. Dominic: Biographical Documents,* ed. Francis C. Lehner (Washington, D.C., 1964), pp. 52-53; *Acta Sanctorum,* June 11, 1094; *Acta Sanctorum,* August II, 687.

38. From the *Legenda Prima,* quoted by Raphael Huber, *St. Anthony of Padua* (Milwaukee, 1948), p. 54.

39. *Annales Minorum seu trium ordinum a S. Francisco institutorum* (Florence, 1931), II, 191.

40. Stanley Burgess made similar observations in his address noted above.

41. Aquinas, *Summa Theologica* (New York, 1947), a.7, I, 225; a.4, I, 1138; a.1, II, 1919; a.2-14, II, 1920; a.1, II, 1929.

42. Luther, *Lectures on Isaiah,* eds. Helmut Lehmann and Jaroslav Pelikan, *Works* (joint American edition), XVI, 302 (all future references to Luther's *Works* are to the American edition).

43. Luther, *Selected Psalms,* ed. Jaroslav Pelikan, *Works,* XII, 294.

44. *Selected Psalms,* p. 295.

45. Luther, *Against the Heavenly Prophets,* ed. Conrad Bergendorff, *Works,* XL, 142.

46. *Ibid.*

47. Luther, *Table Talk,* ed. Helmut T. Lehmann, *Works,* LIV, 53-54.

48. This form of the verb is well established in Pentecostal hymnody and homily.

49. Luther, *Sermons on the Gospel of St. John,* ed. Jaroslav Pelikan, *Works,* XXIV, 405.

50. Luther, *Lectures on the Minor Prophets,* ed. Hilton C. Oswald, *Works,* XX, 182.

51. Luther, *Lectures on Genesis,* ed. Jaroslav Pelikan, *Works,* VI, 330. See also *Predigt am Pfingstmontag,* Weimer Edition, XXXIV:1 (1908), 476-86.

52. John Calvin, *Commentaries: The Gospel According to St. John* (Grand Rapids, 1959), I, 34.

53. Calvin, *Commentaries: The Acts of the Apostles* (Grand Rapids, 1965), I, 51.

54. Genesis 11:7.

55. Calvin, *Acts,* I, 51.

56. E.g., Cornelius in Acts 10.

57. Calvin, *Acts,* I, 318.

58. George H. Williams, *The Radical Reformation* (Philadelphia, 1962), p. 133.

59. Peter Kawerau, *Melchior Hoffman* (Haarlem, 1954).

60. Koeniger, *op. cit.,* where it is suggested that the council was made up of bishops from all tongues, while they most commonly spoke in the single language of the Greek or (later) the Latin oikoumenē, were inspired by the Holy Spirit as at Pentecost and at the first Council in Jerusalem (Acts 15).

61. Menno Simons, *Treatise on Christian Baptism, Collected Works,* trans. and ed. Leonard Verduin (Scottdale, Pa., 1956), pp. 276f.

62. Williams, *The Radical Reformation,* pp. 698ff.; Stanislaw Cynarski, *Raków Ognisko Arianizmu* (Cracow, 1968), pp. 51-80.

63. *Acta Sanctorum,* October V, 322-23, 382, 481, 483; *Monumenta Xaveri-*

ana et autographis vel ex antiquioribus exemplis collecta (Madrid, 1912), II, 224, 546-47, 555, 689, 694, 698; Benedictus XIV, *Opera omnia in corpus collecta et nunc primum in quindecim tomos distributa* (Venice, 1787), III, 250.

64. For the visions and inspired utterances of a sixteenth-century Familist see Tobias, *Mirabilia opera Dei* (London, 1575). Geoffrey F. Nuttall comments on Quaker and Ranter experiences in *Studies in Christian Enthusiasm, Illustrated from Early Quakerism* (Wallingford, Pa., 1948).

65. George Fox, *Journal, passim;* Hannah Whitall Smith, *The Early Friends* (Philadelphia, n.d.).

66. André Ducassé, *La Guerre des camisards* (Paris, 1946).

67. John Lacy, *A Cry from the Desert* (London, 1708), pp. v-vi. This includes reminiscences of Camisard refugees in England.

68. *Ibid.*, p. vi.

69. De Brueys, *Histoire du fanatisme de notre temps* (Paris, 1692), p. 137.

70. *Ibid.*, p. 89.

71. Lacy, p. 14.

72. *Ibid.*, p. 15.

73. *Ibid.*, p. 32.

74. P.F. Mathieu, *Histoire des miraculés et des convulsionnaires de Saint-Médard* (Paris, 1864).

75. John Greenfield, *When the Spirit Came* (Minneapolis, 1967).

76. John Roche, *The Moravian Heresy* (Dublin, 1751), p. 44.

77. Vinson Synan, *The Holiness Pentecostal Movement* (Grand Rapids, 1971), p. 13.

78. Conyers Middleton, *A Free Inquiry* (London, 1749), p. xxi.

79. *Ibid.*, p. xxii.

80. *Ibid.*, p. xliii.

81. *Ibid.*, p. 120.

82. John Wesley to Conyers Middleton, 4 January 1749, *The Letters of John Wesley*, ed. John Telford (London, 1931), II, 365.

83. John Wesley, *Journal*, ed. Nehemiah Curnock (London, 1938), II, 180.

84. *Ibid.*, pp. 184-85.

85. *Ibid.*, p. 216; see Gerald Cragg, *The Works of John Wesley* (Oxford, 1974), V. When Wesley returned to the London area, he reported that "convulsions" were frequent in the society meetings there.

86. N. Spinckes, *The Pretenders to Prophecy Re-examined* (London, 1710), pp. 41-50.

87. *Ibid.*, p. 17.

88. Robert Southey, *The Life of John Wesley* (New York, 1847), I, 240.

89. Wesley, *Journal*, III, 496; Wesley, *Works*, ed. John Emory (New York, 1856), VI, 556. Wesley frequently extolled the early Christians and urged others to follow their example. George Whitefield, too, as he journeyed to the American colonies in 1739, wrote to the societies in England and Wales: "Take then, my Brethren, the Primitive Christians for your Ensamples; and while you endeavor in all Things to follow them as they did Christ, no Power upon Earth can lawfully forbid or hinder you." Quoted from Whitefield, *A Letter to the Religious Societies, lately set on Foot in several Parts of England and Wales* (London, 1740), p. 5.

90. Wesley, *Letters*, IV, 379-80.

91. Wesley, *An Account of Mrs. Elizabeth Johnson* (Bristol, 1799), pp. 48, 69.

92. *The Manners of the Antient Christians*, trans. John Wesley (Bristol, 1771), p. 48.

93. John Fletcher, *Works*.

94. Henry Moore, ed., *The Life of Mary Fletcher* (New York, 1840), pp. 270-324.

95. Wesley, *Journal*, II, 220. Wesley heard the prophecies of a French prophetess. She spoke, he recalled, "all as in the person of God, and mostly in Scripture words of the fulfilling of the prophecies, the coming of Christ now at hand, and the spreading of the gospel over all the earth." Although

some of his companions were "much affected," "it was in no wise clear" to Wesley himself that she spoke by divine inspiration. Wesley, *Journal*, II, 137.

96. Nathan Tiffany, "Testimony of Nathan Tiffany," and Benjamin Whitcher, "Testimony of Benjamin Whitcher," *Testimonies Concerning the Character and Ministry of Mother Ann Lee*, ed. S. Y. Wells (Albany, N.Y., 1827), pp. 153, 169.
97. Abijah Worster, "Testimony of Abijah Worster," *ibid.*, p. 138.
98. Jethro Turner, "Testimony of Jethro Turner," *ibid.*, p. 80.
99. Samuel Johnson, "Testimony of Samuel Johnson," *ibid.*, p. 113.
100. Haskett, *Shakerism Unmasked* (Pittsfield, Mass., 1828), p. 189.
101. *Ibid.*, pp. 190-91.
102. *Ibid.*, p. 194.
103. Richard M'Nemar, *The Kentucky Revival* (Cincinnati, 1808), p. 32.
104. *Ibid.*
105. *Ibid.*, p. 68.
106. Quoted in Guion G. Johnson, "Revival Movements in Ante-Bellum North Carolina," *North Carolina Historical Review*, X (January, 1933), 30.
107. Karl Ecke, *Durchbruch des Urchristentums* (Nürnberg, n.d.), pp. 13ff.
108. *Ibid.*, pp. 9-12.
109. Drummond later became an Irvingite leader. He should not be confused with Henry Drummond (d. 1897), associate of D.L. Moody and author of *Ascent of Man* (1894).
110. For a summary of the significance of the Albury conferences in the context of premillennial thought, see Ernest R. Sandeen, *The Roots of Fundamentalism* (Chicago, 1970).
111. Edward Irving, quoted in Jean C. Root, *Edward Irving* (Boston, 1912), p. 71.
112. Thomas Carlyle, *Reminiscences* (London, 1932), p. 298. Irving published his explanation of the charismatic phenomenon in a series of articles in *Frasers Magazine* in 1832.
113. See Andrew L. Drummond, *Edward Irving and His Circle* (London, 1937).
114. *Ibid.*, pp. 233-34, 286ff.; Ecke, *op. cit.*, pp. 28-33.
115. "The Wentworth Letter," March, 1842, reprinted in William Mulder and A. Russell Mortensen, *Among the Mormons: Historic Accounts by Contemporary Observers* (Lincoln, Neb., 1973), p. 16. See also Moroni, Chapter 10, *The Book of Mormon*.
116. Brigham Young, "The History of Brigham Young," *The Latter-Day Saints Millennial Star*, XXV (11 July 1863), 439.
117. Joseph Smith, *History of Joseph Smith, the Prophet* (Salt Lake City, 1902), I, 296.
118. *Millennial Star*, XVII (28 July 1855), 483-84.
119. James Talmage, *A Study of the Articles of Faith* (Salt Lake City, 1949), p. 225. The *Millennial Star* contains many testimonies of healing, e.g., XVIII (27 September 1856).
120. S. Hawthornthwaite, *Mr. Hawthornwaite's Adventure Among the Mormons* (London, 1857), pp. 86-93; William Kirby, *Mormonism Exposed and Refuted* (Nashville, 1893), pp. 91-92.
121. Bushnell, *Nature and the Supernatural* (New York, 1859), pp. 46-67.
122. Cf. the observation at note 36.
123. Bushnell, pp. 478ff.
124. David Green, "The Gift of Tongues," *Bibliotheca Sacra*, XXII (January, 1865), 99-126.
125. William Gibson, *The Year of Grace* (Boston, 1860), pp. 203-04.
126. See the forthcoming doctoral thesis, "The Public Life of Finney," by Garth Roselle, University of Minnesota.
127. In an unpublished paper, "From 'Christian Perfection' to the 'Baptism of the Holy Ghost'," Donald Dayton (graduate student at the University of Chicago Divinity School) has noted the shift of terminology among advocates of Christian perfection which helped introduce the vocabulary of later Pentecostalism.

128. See A.E. Thompson, *A.B. Simpson* (New York, 1920), for a brief historical account.
129. Torrey, *Why God Used D.L. Moody* (New York, 1923).
130. Torrey's views were most fully expressed in his book, *The Baptism with the Holy Spirit* (Chicago, 1895).
131. Andrew Murray, *The Full Blessing of Pentecost* (London, 1908).
132. Charles Price Jones, "Autobiographical Sketch," *History of Church of Christ (Holiness) U.S.A.*, ed. Otho B. Cobbins (New York, 1966), pp. 27-30, 410-11.
133. The early struggles of the Church of God are ably recounted in Charles Conn, *Like a Mighty Army* (Cleveland, Tenn., 1955). The *Diary* of A.J. Tomlinson, edited by Homer A. Tomlinson, contains personal reminiscences.
134. E.g., Pastor Paul in Germany, or the Pentecostal Holiness Church, Franklin Springs, Georgia.
135. Cf. diagram in Walter J. Hollenweger, *The Pentecostals* (London, 1972), p. 25.
136. Gordon, *The Ministry of the Spirit* (New York, 1894). The original edition contains an introduction by the Keswick and Northfield Conventions speaker, F.B. Meyer.
137. Torrey, *Baptism*, p. 14. Torrey's teaching was similar to that of the British Keswick Movement at the time.
138. Albert B. Simpson, *The Holy Spirit, or Power from on High* (New York, 1895), I, 31-37; II, 107-27.
139. Scofield, *Plain Papers on the Doctrine of the Holy Spirit* (Grand Rapids, 1966), pp. 40-53.
140. Torrey, *Baptism*. See forthcoming dissertation by Edith L. Waldvogel, Ph.D. candidate in church history, Harvard University.
141. William Arthur, *The Tongue of Fire* (New York, 1856), p. 108. In the last line, Arthur refers to the fact already noted that the Greek text of Acts 2 indeed refers to "other" tongues.
142. Scofield was instrumental in the founding of Dallas Theological Seminary, a bastion of classical Fundamentalism and a theological center of opposition to the distinctive tenets of organized Pentecostalism.
143. Scofield, notes to Acts 2, p. 1163 of Reference Bible.
144. Hannah Whitall Smith, *Religious Fanaticism*, ed. R. Strachey (London, 1928).
145. A number of instances of glossolalia in Evangelical Protestantism have been collected by Stanley Frodsham, *With Signs Following* (Springfield, Mo., 1941). See also Albert LeBaron, "A Case of Psychic Automatism, Including 'Speaking with Tongues'," communicated by William James, *Proceedings of the Society for Psychical Research*, XII (December, 1896), 277ff. James did not deal with glossolalia in his classic *Varieties of Religious Experience*.
146. Conn, *Like a Mighty Army*, p. 13.
147. Leonard Steiner, *Mit folgenden Zeichen* (Basel, 1954), p. 156.
148. Dowie had in mind a congeries of theocratic communities. When utopian Zion City collapsed in 1906, many devotees joined the Pentecostal movement, bringing with them their traditional emphasis on healing as well as their scriptural literalism.
149. Lewi Pethrus, *A Spiritual Memoir* (Plainfield, N.J., 1973), p. 22. Pethrus is one of the few living participants in the emergence of European Pentecostalism; he has exerted vast influence on its development.
150. Awstin, *et al.*, *The Religious Revival in Wales, 1904* (Cardiff, Wales, 1905), p. 25.
151. Burton, "My Personal Pentecost," *World Pentecost*, I (1973), 19; Ramon Hunston, "The Welsh Revival 1904-05," *ibid.*, pp. 10-11; Eifion Evans, *The Welsh Revival of 1904* (London, 1969).
152. We appreciate the help of Professor Gerald Cragg and Jean Rittmueller in tracking down these references. It should be noted that the Highland wail is not the same as keening (*caoine*): that was a form of lamentation confined to women at the time of death and burial. The wail was, in contrast, related

to the Welsh *hwyl,* which etymologically implies frenzy. See H.I. Bell, *Development of Welsh Poetry* (Oxford, 1936).

153. Sarah Parham, *Charles F. Parham* (Joplin, Mo., 1930), pp. 51-55.

154. Arthur T. Pierson, "Speaking with Tongues," *Missionary Review of the World,* XV (July, 1907), 487-92. The global tour of Torrey and Charles Alexander, 1904-05, has been credited by their contemporaries as having exerted significant influence on the increasing revival spirit. The tour itself was the result of a revival spirit in Torrey's Moody Church, Chicago. See George T.B. Davis, *Torrey and Alexander, The Story of a World-Wide Revival* (New York, 1905).

155. Cashwell's influence is discussed by Synan, *The Holiness Pentecostal Movement,* pp. 126ff.

156. Ambrose Jessup Tomlinson, *Answering the Call of God* (Cleveland, Tenn., n.d.).

157. Cobbins, *History of Church of Christ (Holiness) U.S.A.,* pp. 431-33.

158. Mrs. Simpson is reported to have strongly opposed speaking in tongues. In his study of the Welshman Howel Harris, Geoffrey Nuttall suggests that the reason for the absence of tongues in Harris' experience may well have been his marriage to Anne Williams instead of to a Mrs. Griffith. Carlyle's wife (who was once courted by Irving) reportedly said that, had Irving married her, there would have been no tongues. Nuttall, *Howel Harris* (Cardiff, Wales, 1965).

159. Carl Brumback, *Suddenly From Heaven* (Springfield, Mo., 1961), pp. 89-91.

160. See Christian and Missionary Alliance Pamphlet entitled "The Gift of Tongues: seek not, forbid not" (n.d.).

161. Booth, *Echoes and Memories* (New York, 1925), pp. 57-58. Bramwell Booth's nephew, William Booth-Clibborn, was the first of his family to receive the baptism with the Holy Spirit. He eventually became a leader in certain segments of American Pentecostalism. See William Booth-Clibborn, *The Baptism in the Holy Spirit, a Personal Testimony* (Portland, Ore., 1936).

162. Timothy L. Smith, *Called Unto Holiness* (Kansas City, 1962).

163. Quoted in John Nichol, *Pentecostalism* (New York, 1966). Reprinted as *The Pentecostals* (Plainfield, N.J., 1971).

164. Pethrus, *A Spiritual Memoir,* pp. 24-34.

165. Quoted in Nichol, *Pentecostalism,* p. 62.

166. Steiner, *Mit folgenden Zeichen,* p. 55. See also Jonathan Paul, *Ein volles Pfingsten* (Basel, n.d.). Paul regarded the Pentecostal movement as an actualization of the Evangelical heritage; it gave experiential meaning to old doctrines:

> Ja, stimmet an die alten Lieder,
> Legt auch Gebet und Herz hinein
> Und lasst das euer Flehen sein:
> Heilger Geist, kehr bei uns ein. (p. 159)

167. In *All With One Accord* (Springfield, Mo., 1961), the late British Pentecostal leader, Donald Gee, comments that before the Los Angeles revival, well over a thousand had spoken with tongues in the years just prior to 1906. Isolated instances of glossolalia, however, had not been significant in launching the far-reaching revival that was the result of the association of tongues and Spirit baptism.

168. Hollenweger, *The Pentecostals,* p. 79.

169. See Henry Pitney van Dusen, "The Third Force," *Life,* XLIV (June 9, 1958), 122-24. The author later put this experience in an historical and new theological setting in *Spirit, Son and Father.*

170. Although some Holiness and Pentecostal congregations have felt that snake-handling was a sign (Mark 16:17, 18; Acts 28:3-6), the larger Pentecostal organizations have taken a stand against testing the power of God (Matt. 4:7).

171. Mrs. McPherson was a member of the Assemblies of God from 1919 until 1922.
172. For a detailed discussion, see Myer Pearlman, *Knowing the Doctrines of the Bible* (Springfield, Mo., 1937), pp. 249-67.
173. David Reed is currently working at Boston University on a Ph.D. dissertation which deals with the origins of the "Oneness" Pentecostal groups.
174. See Kevin and Dorothy Ranaghan, *Catholic Pentecostals* (New York, 1969); Dennis J. Bennett, *Nine O'Clock in the Morning* (Plainfield, N.J., 1970). Apart from the general religious stirrings in the United States that would account for this outbreak of tongues, one might adduce the fact that the translation of the Latin mass into the vernacular left Catholics without the linguistic sense of mystery that Latin had provided (the consequence of the Second Vatican Council, 1962-1965).

5 THE CHARISMATIC GIFTS IN WORSHIP

JOSEPHINE MASSYNGBERDE FORD

The Pentecostal[1] phenomenon is a prayer movement which from time to time throughout history has swept through the Christian church to rekindle devotion and has borne as its characteristic features the more dramatic gifts of the Spirit. These are the utterance of wisdom and knowledge, faith healing, miracles, prophecy, discernment of spirits, various kinds of tongues and interpretation of tongues (1 Cor. 12:8-11);[2] the "fivefold" ministry, as it is frequently called in nonconformist tradition, namely apostleship, prophecy, evangelizing, working as pastor, teaching (Eph. 4:11); prophecy according to our faith, service *(diakonia)*, teaching, exhorting, helping, performing acts of mercy (Rom. 12:6-8; 1 Peter 4:10-11).[3] All these can be present in the church (and here I speak of all denominations) as and when God pleases.[4]

I will be giving special attention to glossolalia, the gift of speaking an unknown language under the influence of the Holy Spirit. At the beginning of this essay I wish to stress that this does not mean that I believe either that it is an essential gift or the most important charismatic gift. On the other hand there is little evidence to say that it is the least gift.[5]

TONGUES

Genuine speaking in tongues is a prayer gift which comes without human intervention. Suddenly the recipient finds that he or she can speak, and very often sing, in a language which has not been learned through any human art. The words flow easily and the speaker can

Dr. Josephine Massyngberde Ford was born in England, received her early education in convent schools there, and received her Ph.D. from the University of Nottingham. She is a specialist in Rabbinics and New Testament studies and has taught at the University of Durham, England, and at Makere University College, Uganda. She came to join the Department of Theology at Notre Dame in 1965 as one of the first two women faculty members.

Dr. Ford is active in the charismatic movement and is a frequent contributor to scholarly journals. She has published a number of books, including *A Trilogy on Wisdom and Celibacy* (1967); *The Spirit and the Human Person* (1969); *The Pentecostal Experience* (1970); and *The Ministries and Fruits of the Spirit* (1973).

begin and cease at will. This gift is called glossolalia and is to be distinguished from the "strange sounds" called *xenophoneō* which occurred in the early church within a group of schismatic Christians called the Montanists.[6] When the Montanists spoke strange sounds they did so in para-ecstasy, that is, they were not in control of themselves but were seized by a power beyond them. The church examined the Montanist movement for a long time and eventually ruled that it was not orthodox and that the genuine prophet does not speak in para-ecstasy but is in control of himself and knows what is happening. Thus the genuine glossolalist is not in a state of trance.[7]

Perhaps the most important thing about glossolalia is that it is a noncerebral prayer gift. In an excellent paper read at the second meeting of the Society for Pentecostal Studies,[8] Dr. Richard Baer (himself a glossolalist) notes that the current charismatic movement is often seen as a threat to peace in the churches, but argues that the strangeness of glossolalia has tended to make people overlook the "fundamental functional similarity between speaking in tongues and two other widespread and generally accepted religious practices, namely Quaker silent worship and the liturgical worship of Catholic and Episcopal churches."[9] Dr. Baer believes that all these practices free one from intellectual and analytical functions and open one to other parts of the person which can be touched by God. It is not a question of the emotions being concentrated to the exclusion of the mind, for the gift of tongues is not always accompanied by emotion. Indeed, when the novelty of tongues diminishes so does the emotional side, and Dr. Baer reports that "at times the glossolalic feels a singular *lack* of emotion while speaking in tongues" (his italics).

Dr. Baer gives four reasons for using this gift: for praising God; as an expression in deep sorrow; for intercession; and for petition. He also mentions the use of tongues for the "healing of the memories," that is, healing trauma—probably childhood trauma—of which one is not wholly conscious. Dr. Baer then proceeds to compare glossolalia with Quaker silent worship. Here the worshippers follow the leading of the Spirit and the individual may speak or not at will, just as in tongues there is no "Spirit-possession" in the sense of trance or para-ecstasy. Dr. Baer rightly claims that in Quaker worship there is "a resting of the analytical mind," a refusal to let deliberate, objective thinking dominate the meeting for worship. Rather, one tries to "center down" and become open to the inner light within himself, to "that of God in every man," to the "leading of the Spirit."[10] At a Quaker meeting a person may add a comment to that which is spoken by another, and Dr. Baer finds this analogous to the interpretation of a tongue spoken at a public meeting. The utterances at a Quaker meeting speak to the depth of one's being rather than attempting to change one's ideas or appeal to emotions, logic, or eloquence. Again there is a similarity with glossolalia.

Dr. Baer then turns to liturgical worship. He himself is accustomed to the Episcopal liturgical worship. He concedes that the ritualistic repetition of the same prayers and movements week after week may appear annoying, but he compares it to one's learning to dance. At first it is more graceful to walk. When the technique is learned, however, a certain "wisdom of the body" takes over and one follows the beat of the music and rhythm of the dance. So it is with the liturgy. In the liturgy the analytical mind is permitted to rest and the accustomed prayers reach to the depth of one's being. Also, there is no conscious effort to manipulate the emotions in the liturgy.[11] Dr. Baer quotes Romano Guardini:

> The liturgy has perfected a masterly instrument which has made it possible for us to express our inner life in all its fulness and depth without divulging our secrets. . . . We can pour out our hearts and still feel that nothing has been dragged to light that should remain "hidden."[12]

Dr. Baer contends that there is a playfulness and reverent laughter in glossolalia which frees one from undue solemnity and pomposity. There is also a certain playfulness—perhaps we should say a dramatic-artistic quality—about the liturgy. It is performed for itself, not as a means to an end—he quotes Guardini again concerning the necessity of learning "to waste time for God"[13] (an exquisite phrase).

I have cited at length from Dr. Baer's paper because it is perhaps the most sensitive essay I have read on the question of glossolalia. In my own work[14] I have pointed out that the gift of tongues may be one of the spiritual "senses"[15] which has been revived, the genuine gift of tongues being a sign of the "restoration of the organ which is necessary for giving vocal praise to God and communicating Divine Inspiration to others." I have also noted that together with the gift of tongues the recipient often develops poetical, musical, or other artistic qualities which he or she did not possess before. For example, the present writer can sing in tune in tongues but is not able to do so in an ordinary way. She also knows a religious sister who receives songs in the Spirit, commits them to writing and notation, and then uses them at prayer gatherings. Of course, this may be the origin of many of the hymns or litanies which we use in our own services or liturgies. The Jews regarded the Holy Spirit as the inspirer of all the arts. Thus the genuine gift of tongues appears to be one which is noteworthy in private devotion and in prayer meetings. But how can it be incorporated into the liturgy, especially the eucharistic liturgy and vespers?

First of all, it seems necessary to distinguish three types of tongues. First, there is the genuine gift of tongues which is received without human intervention. Classical works on spirituality refer to this phenomenon as occurring quite spontaneously and usually to those who have been long in the service of the Lord. Nowadays, God appears to be giving this gift more freely—or perhaps it is being recognized more frequently—in order to help those who are weak in faith. However, great attention should be paid to Dr. Kildahl's thesis as found in the present collection of essays. Although I do not believe that Dr. Kildahl has recognized fully that there is a genuine gift from God which does not bring about undesirable results, yet his hypothesis that the conditions for receiving induced glossolalia and those for hypnosis are similar must not be overlooked. In my own opinion, charisms such as tongues, healing, miracle-working, and prophecy cannot be transmitted in the same way as the charisms or spiritual fruits for offices within the church, such as bishops, priests, deacons, and deaconesses, which are in apostolic succession. One transmits such fruits as wisdom, understanding, counsel, might, knowledge, and fear of the Lord (Isa. 11:2-5) for the upbuilding of the church to those who are called to permanent ministry. These qualities must always be in the church, for they are essential. But praeternatural[16] gifts are given only when God sees a special need; they are *extra-ordinary*, not ordinary and normative. It is wisest, therefore, to refrain from techniques which have as their goal making people yield to tongues, for it is when this is done that divisiveness, dependence on authority figures, retrogression of the ego, histrionic display, group camaraderie, etc. occur. All these are a sign that the "tongues" possessed by these individuals are not a genuine spiritual gift, but are "induced tongues" which are an imitation of the genuine gift. However, this is *not* to say that either those who induced the tongues or those who allowed themselves to be induced are sinful.[17] They usually act out of the highest motives and out of ignorance of the psychological forces at play. Tongues may be found in diabolical obsession[18] or possession, but this does not happen to Christians who do not invite diabolical intervention. It would seem to occur when people have been dabbling with the occult.[19] If someone converts from such dealings, the pastor might do well to caution against the use of tongues.

In summary, I should say that those who have received tongues as a genuine gift, without self-inducement or intervention from others, should feel free to use this gift (at the discretion of the pastor) at the liturgy and the paraliturgy. For example, tongues are used at Pentecostal Catholic eucharists during the synaxis or preparatory section of the mass and after the reception of Holy Communion. Also choral singing in tongues at these points can be deeply moving. All sing together in different tongues and different tunes, but *mirabile dictu* all seems to harmonize.[20] This also can happen at weddings and baptisms.

Other gifts may also be used in the liturgy, again subject to the pastor's discernment. I emphasize this discernment because the institutional side of the church is as necessary to the Body of Christ as a skeleton to a physical body. For it is not sufficient to permit only the Pentecostals to decide who should be their leader, it is the whole church who should do this. When the bishops formally ordain the ministers, they become facilitators of all the charisms within that part of Christ's body which is under their care. This is not to say that no one else may express an opinion. But it is the pastor who ultimately decides when and where tongues may be used in the liturgy. He also decides how much silence should be employed. St. Paul's instructions about tongues-speakers and prophets should be followed; there should be no more than two or three and each should speak in turn (1 Cor. 14:26-33). St. Paul's most exhaustive treatment of the Pentecostal gifts lies close to his teaching about baptism (1 Cor. 10:1-5) and the eucharist (1 Cor. 10:14-22 and 11:17-34); this should be a guide to us that such gifts have a place in liturgical worship.

PROPHECY AND THE UTTERANCE OF
WISDOM AND KNOWLEDGE

The other gifts of the Spirit may be even more precious than tongues. These are prophecy (which St. Paul counts as greater than tongues),[21] the utterance of wisdom and knowledge, healing, miracle-working, evangelization, and teaching. My attendance at Pentecostal prayer meetings has led me to think that probably there is more utterance of wisdom and knowledge than prophecy. That which is labelled as "prophecy" is often an utterance of wisdom very much akin to either the sayings in the biblical book of Proverbs or other wisdom literature,[22] and it should be accepted as such. The utterance of wisdom does not bring with it the atmosphere of mystery and grandeur that the word prophecy tends to arouse. One leading psychologist from California has expressed much greater reservation about prophecy than about tongues. She maintains that people look up to and reverence the prophet and are apt to interpret his or her words and put them into action. This is especially so when the words are expressed in an authoritative tone by one of the leaders. But prophecies should not be interpreted. Like Mary we should ponder them in our minds and then allow God to bring about an event which will cast light upon the prophecy. The two examples which I usually cite are those of Isaiah and St. Francis of Assisi. Isaiah probably did not realize that he was speaking about a virginal conception in Isaiah 7:14; but when the event occurred, St. Matthew and others were able to recognize the deeper meaning of the prophecy. Similarly, St. Francis was told by God to restore the church, and he began to repair a ruined building until he discovered that God

meant him to renew the church spiritually not materially. I can say
that this has happened several times in my own life. In prayer a
thought has come which I did not understand. Months or perhaps
years later an event has proved that those words were from God.
Again the pastor is the one who should guide the recipients of
prophecy and guide the community.[23]

The utterances of wisdom and knowledge, like interpreted glossolalia, speak to our inmost beings and kindle our hearts with love for
God. It is to be hoped that they will produce in us the desire to live a
more loving life, loving to God and to our neighbor, but they are not
calculated to lead us to specific acts. If we feel this is so, we must
resort not only to more prayer (and some think fasting) but also to
counsel from someone trained in this field. So the synaxis of the
eucharist, especially after the reading of the Scripture, and the post-
communion, can be special times to hear the utterance of wisdom
and knowledge, prophecy and interpretation of tongues. The practice
of the dialogue homily, namely, the pastor delivering the main
address and then members of the congregation adding their remarks,
gives ample scope for the Pentecostal gifts. However, this is easier in
a small congregation and it needs a very skilled facilitator. One word
of warning. The Pentecostal element in the worship should not
protract the service so long that the synaxis is completely out of
proportion to the eucharistic prayer or to the Scripture readings. The
canon (anaphora) which includes the words of institution "this is
my body and this is my blood" is charism in the deepest sense of the
word, performing the miracle of the transforming of bread and wine
into the very Presence of the Risen Lord.

EVANGELIZATION AND TEACHING

"Evangelization" is all too often associated with emotional revivalist
meetings and sometimes deemed beneath the dignity of the historical
churches. However, in this time of the Jesus Movement, of rather
dramatic conversions to Christ and the necessity to open the church
to the needs of the newly converted, we must leave room for
evangelization. The evangelist, in contrast to the teacher, is not
necessarily trained in his or her work but is called merely to witness
to the facts of his own or other people's relationship to the Lord
Jesus. The historical churches have had almost no opening for this in
their traditional services. But nowadays, it seems to me, such witnesses, or testimonies, as they are often called, might well occasionally take the place of the homily, with a word or two of introduction
by the pastor. Again these testimonies need to be carefully selected
and the person witnessing asked to be succinct—for a rare gift for the
Spirit to bestow on Pentecostals is the gift of brevity! The witness

might be about conversion, about physical or psychological healing; or it might provide a new insight into Scripture or a new idea for social action.[24]

Teaching also is a gift which may be used in the same position in the eucharistic liturgy or morning or evening prayer. Where a parish has specialists in various fields, a homily from one of these laymen or laywomen (especially women, who have little chance to minister actively in the historical churches) about such current issues as the pro-life movement, the peace issue, and death and dying would give the church the circumstances to use all the charisms of the laity. The reason it is so important that these talks be given at the service rather than at special parish functions is that many people attend church only for Saturday or Sunday Mass and it is perhaps they who need to receive information about these topics. Naturally, too, the prayer atmosphere opens the mind and heart to these teachings.[25]

It is also of great importance not to forget those confined to their homes because of illness or disability. With modern media it should be possible for even a quadraplegic to be carried to church and witness to the people how a relationship to Christ helps one to bear the cross. Neither must one omit braille-reading Christians, who should frequently be invited to read the lessons and perhaps to expound upon them from the inner light which they seem to receive when their physical sight fails. The text of Scripture can either be typed out in braille for them or they can bring their own books to church. Often these Christians have good reading voices and the psychological effect of asking them to participate is very great—both for the congregation and the lector.

HEALING

Faith-healing is another subject from which the historical churches have often shrunk, through fear of excesses or because this phenomenon belongs to the Catholic veneration of Mary (especially at Lourdes) or to the invocation of the saints or to tent revivalist meetings. Certainly there is danger in the faith-healer who exerts magnetic power over his or her audience. Simony, making godliness the source of gain, is not always avoided. The movie Marjoe exhibits the temptations attached to such ministries. But misuse does not mean that we cannot use a ministry. It would seem that Kathryn Kuhlman, who conducts healing services on television, has approached this gift in the right way. She does not impose hands upon any patient and openly avows that she has never cured anyone: It is only the Holy Spirit who cures, and those who feel a cure should come up to the altar or stage to give thanks not to Miss Kuhlman, but to God. Healing services such as these might be excellent once or twice a year and might also attract the sick and disabled to church. If hands are imposed it would seem to be a safeguard to let a number of people take part in this action so that the gift of healing is not attached to one person but is seen as the Spirit working through the community.

However, perhaps more important is the modern approach to the sacrament of anointing. Nowadays this is not seen as a preparation for death, but as a sacrament which may indeed bring healing to the body and also strength to the soul. It might be good to allow anyone who wished to impose hands on patients at a public Unction service after the priest has anointed the person. The new Roman Catholic rite of anointing has very meaningful Scripture readings and prayers. It should also be mentioned that family and parochial participation in the Unction service, if the patient is able to come to church, gives great support not only to the sufferer but to relatives or friends. Should healings occur, either from a healing service or from the Unction service, then the patient should be examined occasionally for the next few months or years until it is finally established that the cure was supernatural. The doctor's presence at the service might also be sought. It is very important not to overstress faith-healing or to suggest that a patient is not improving because he has too little faith. Paul left Trophimus sick, our Lord did not cure everyone, and the false hope of a cure may actually impede the necessary growth of faith and courage which are essential, especially for a long disease.

These, then, are some of the ways the Pentecostal gifts can be fitted in to the life, liturgy, and paraliturgy of the historical churches. Why has the Pentecostal movement arisen in the twentieth century? Pentecostals aver that they find a certain dryness or even necrosis in the traditional churches and that their experience of the Spirit brings them, sometimes for the first time, into a personal relationship to God. Certainly, one can admit that in the Roman Catholic communion the removal of the Latin mass and the substitution of the more "cerebral" liturgies with too little silence and too much creative novelty in them have catered too much to the mind rather than the heart. Traditional devotions, especially with regard to the communion of the saints, have largely disappeared and left a communal void. So the Pentecostal movement supplies the "heart prayer" and the prayer supplementary to the formal liturgy which was formerly catered to by rosary and benediction, the Way of the Cross, and novenas.[26] But Pentecostalism does not only answer a spiritual need, it also speaks clearly to a psychological and social void, and it is culturally conditioned. The change in family life, the lack of counselling within the church, and the depersonalization of society through technology all contribute to this void. All this draws people into communes, whether these be religious or not, and into

Pentecostalism. This is not the first time that such a phenomenon has occurred in the church. Ever and anon God brings about these movements of the Spirit.[27] And always in the wake of these, some groups eventually break from the church.[28] Our task today is to foster unity and use all our knowledge, especially in theology, psychology, and sociology, to prevent such schisms.

Notes

1. I use *Pentecostal* because I believe that all those who have a personal relationship to Jesus are *charismatic*, making this term broader than *Pentecostal*.
2. All biblical references are to the Revised Standard version.
3. For a simple discussion of all these ministries, see the author's *Ministries and Fruits of the Spirit* (Notre Dame, Ind., 1973).
4. Some of the charismatic elements, such as tongues, prophecy, and healing, do not appear to be permanent manifestations of the Spirit in the church; but certainly they are not confined to the early church.
5. It is not listed last in I Corinthians 12:27-31.
6. Eusebius, *Ecclesiastical History*, V, xvi, 7, *Nicene and Post-Nicene Fathers* (Grand Rapids, 1971), 1st s., I, 231.
7. Trance, however, need not be viewed as something which is wrong in itself. Many of the saints underwent trances, e.g., Dr. Catherine of Siena when she dictated her *Dialogue*. A feature of genuine trance, however, is that the recipient responds to a request or command from a superior and comes out of the trance at the bidding of the superior.
8. Richard A. Baer, Jr., "Quaker Silent Worship, Glossolalia and Liturgy; Some Functional Similarities" (unpublished essay). The author kindly gave me a typescript, and the citations will be given according to that pagination. The whole will be published with the *Proceedings of the Pneuma Conference of the Society for Pentecostal Studies*, 1973, Logos Press.
9. *Ibid.*, p. 2.
10. *Ibid.*, p. 6.
11. I would say, however, that some "guitar Masses" may influence one in this way.
12. Baer, p. 11, quoting from Romano Guardini, *The Spirit of the Liturgy* (1935).
13. Baer, p. 14.
14. See *Baptism of the Spirit*, Claretian Fathers (Illinois, 1972), pp. 79-133. This paper also appeared in *Theological Studies*, XXXII, 1 (1971), 3-29. It is a review of the biblical interpretations of the passages concerning tongues and a reflection on the contribution which tongues make (a) to the life of the individual, and (b) to the life of the community.
15. The spiritual senses are sight, hearing, touch, taste and smell. See A. Poulain, *The Grace of Interior Prayer*, trans. Leonora L. Yorke (London, 1957), pp. 88-113. For a similar thought in Judaism, see J. Abelson, *The Immanence of God in Rabbinical Literature* (London, 1912), pp. 82-115, 212-223.
16. Praeternatural gifts are those which are directly supernatural and cannot be learned or received through human means.
17. The Roman Catholic neo-Pentecostals have a series of seminars designed to facilitate the reception of the "baptism of the Spirit." These are printed in the *Team Manual for The Life of the Spirit Seminars* by Stephen Clark, obtainable from Box 12, Notre Dame, Indiana, 46556. In the first edition of *The Team Manual* there were over thirty references to tongues in 101 pages. In the second edition there is even more emphasis. One may make four comments: (1) The manual appears to equate baptism with the Spirit and tongues in several places, or at least thinks of them together (pp. 6-8, 20,

27). (2) The manual rules that a team member should have yielded to tongues himself: "It is very difficult for someone who has not yielded to the gift of tongues to help someone else to do so" (pp. 26, 116, 145). The team leader teaches the people to sing in tongues, they do so in a chorus together, and he exhorts them to pray in tongues every day. (It is interesting that tongues are advocated for daily use but that the eucharist is not.) If someone has not prayed in tongues, the team leader coaxes him to do so (p. 153); those who are making babbling sounds are encouraged to go on, so that this may turn into tongues (pp. 148-49). (3) Tongues are seen as a very important gift—almost, I should say, as essential (pp. 151, 157). (4) The commitment prayer which the recipients are encouraged to say includes a direct prayer to God for the gift of tongues (pp. 147, 150-157, 171). It would seem that tongues are of very special importance to those who prepared this manual and that their stress on this gift, together with various techniques which they employ to induce tongues, and the importance of the authority figure (p. 152), presents an enormous risk of hypnosis followed by regression of the ego and personality transference. My own advice would be to abstain from this emphasis, these techniques, and from praying over people for tongues, and to leave the gift entirely to the Holy Spirit. I believe that there is a genuine gift of tongues bestowed by God without human intervention.

18. "Obsession" means that a person is attacked by the devil; "possession" means that his personality is actually taken over by the devil.

19. See Poulain, pp. 428-443.

20. St. Paul's discussion of glossolalia in the context of the eucharist and baptism (I Cor. 11-14) would seem to suggest that there is scriptural authority for tongues at the liturgy.

21. I Cor. 14:5: "Now I want you all to speak in tongues, but even more to prophesy. He who prophesies is greater than he who speaks in tongues, unless someone interprets, so that the church may be edified." However, Pentecostals often quote only the first part of the verse: "Now I want you all to speak in tongues." This alters the entire meaning of St. Paul's statement.

22. E.g., Job, Canticle of Canticles, Wisdom of Solomon, Sirach, and some of the Psalms. Isaiah 40-55 might also be the utterances of wisdom and knowledge expressed by the Jews exiled in Babylon and then collected under the name of the prophet Isaiah.

23. For further views on prophecy, see Ministries and Fruits of the Spirit.

24. Perhaps even non-Christians might be invited to speak, for we can learn from everyone.

25. In the Roman Catholic Church there has arisen the practice of the prayers of the faithful, or intercessory prayers, offered after the homily. These are akin to the ancient bidding prayers. In large congregations these are recited by the pastor or lector: in small, groups, especially where people are invited to leave their pews and stand round the altar, the congregation offers individual prayers especially associated with the Scripture readings which have been proclaimed and also with any social activity which is being implemented by members of the local church. This has tended to foster a great spirit of community.

26. Certain prayers or services repeated for nine days.

27. E.g., the Franciscan movement.

28. E.g., the Jansenists.

6 *PSYCHOLOGICAL OBSERVATIONS*

JOHN P. KILDAHL

In the past twelve years, hundreds of letters have been sent to me by persons who speak in tongues. I have been helped enormously in my research into glossolalia by these letters, and am grateful for the persons who have shared their experiences with me. For this chapter, I have collated the common denominators of these letters into one composite letter which will form the introduction to this chapter. The chapter will consist of nine psychological observations about speaking in tongues. Each of those observations is illustrated in the following letter.

Dear Sir:

"It was with a great deal of interest that I read the findings of your research on glossolalia.[1]

"It is of particular interest to me since I received the baptism of (by, in, or with) the Holy Spirit when I was eighteen years old (I am now twenty-eight) after fasting and praying during my school lunch period for about ten days. Those ten days had been a time of serious struggle for me, both spiritually and in every other way. I had been seeking for answers to the great turmoil and uncertainty in my life. I was having trouble sleeping, studying, getting along with people, and even eating. I was a religious person, thoroughly grounded in Scripture, and had been seeking guidance and answers in my struggle. During the preceding ten days I had gone to prayer meetings at one

Professor and Director of Programs in Pastoral Psychology at New York Theological Seminary, Dr. John P. Kildahl also conducts a private practice in psychoanalysis and psychotherapy. Dr. Kildahl received his B.A. from St. Olaf College and his B.D. from Luther Theological Seminary in 1953. He then entered New York University and in 1957 received his Ph.D. in Clinical Psychology. He continued postdoctoral studies in that field, and he now serves as a consultant and lecturer in a number of medical and mental health institutions. He is presently organizing a Center for Personal Growth in New York and is also developing educational programs to provide new combinations of classroom learning and psychotherapy.

Professor Kildahl is the author of numerous articles and reports in psychological journals, and he has conducted a ten-year research project on tongue-speaking, financed by the National Institute of Mental Health and the American Lutheran Church. In 1972 he published a book based on these findings, entitled *The Psychology of Speaking in Tongues*.

of the local churches in which speaking in tongues and the gifts of the Spirit were much in evidence. I was greatly taken by the warmth and Christian spirit of the group, particularly by the minister, who seemed to be positively Christ-like. Finally I received the baptism, during my lunch period when I was sitting alone in an empty classroom. I had been prayed for fervently the night before, with the laying on of hands, and had felt strange urgings inside me, but it was not until the next day that I received the baptism. The evidence to me of his incoming was speaking in tongues. This gift of tongues I have continued to use through the years, primarily in private prayers and praise, particularly praise.

"I had earlier accepted Christ as my personal Savior but I had not had the baptism of the Holy Spirit. This came only through travail and prayer and worship, and finally when the Holy Spirit entered in for the first time, it was an experience of burning all through me. I felt chills and great beads of perspiration. And yet for me, it was a very quiet experience. But a change had taken place all through me and I became the temple of God's Spirit, which was evidenced by the speaking of an unknown tongue. There was no need for me to know what I was saying—the Spirit knew what I was in need of and he gave me utterance when I was thanking and worshiping the Lord. I felt that I could take all the joy, love, thrills, and lusts of the flesh that the world could offer and roll it up and it couldn't compare to the joy, the thrill, the peace, and the excitement of that experience.

"You have mentioned in your writing the importance of the leader, but I say to you the only leader was Christ and the Holy Spirit. The group of Christians in that church where I found the baptism were only weak instruments of the Holy Spirit. I could recognize that they were crude channels of the Holy Spirit but all glory belongs to Christ himself. I came to love and trust them, not for what they were as individuals, but because I knew the Lord spoke through them.

"This gift was tremendously helpful to my spiritual life, since the physical evidence of God's presence this way made a serious lack of faith in him impossible. I had that which, to me, was irrefutable evidence of God's power and concern for me, and I felt that his wishes influenced my actions in the many times I asked him to guide me.

"I left home after graduating from high school and was in the service. Later, my work called for me to travel a great deal. I moved about a lot, and during months and sometimes years of carelessness, I would not pray, so naturally I did not pray in tongues. I suppose that I could have prayed in tongues if I had wanted to, but the thought never occurred to me. But in times of need I would come back to the Lord, and when I moved close enough to God to speak to him, I again started praying in tongues. I might add that praying, or, as was the general rule, praising, in tongues was practically always accompanied by a definite lifting of my spirit and a deep feeling of thankfulness for his care for me and for his goodness to me.

"During the time when I strayed from the Lord, I was almost continuously among strangers for months at a time. From time to time during those years I would find myself troubled in spirit and would make my way to a church where I could find Bible-believing Christians. I might add that I had had a solid foundation in the Bible in my youth and knew from that what God expected of me. I only accepted as God's revelations to me what was consistent with conservative Bible doctrine. I felt most at home in those churches where the pastor preached the Bible and believed in the baptism of the Spirit.

"Believe me, doctor, while I know nothing of the depth and strength of your own faith in a personal God or your consciousness of the indwelling Holy Spirit I can testify to you that knowing that his Spirit lives in you, and orders, with love, your comings and goings, is not to be described—it can only be experienced. Let me point out as strongly as I am able that speaking in tongues to me, and to most others so gifted, is merely an outward evidence of something infinitely greater within.

"Other outward evidences of what is within me are expressed in the movements of my hands when I pray. Sometimes I touch my forehead with my fingertips, and at other times the palms of my hands turn upward and my arms spread. Also, sometimes I raise my face, and other times I lower it. All these movements, and others, as with the words I speak in tongues, are instinctive, though I am as conscious of what I am doing as if it were a formal liturgical action. At those moments, I know that God is directing my whole being, not just my tongue.

"Since I use my gift of tongues primarily in private, I do not have much experience with the interpretation of tongues, and I myself do not have that gift. I feel that a tongue is the language of God and not for man. It is the Spirit of God speaking to God directly through me. There is no need for me to know what is said. I am, of course, curious about exactly what it is that is being spoken and how it happens. I have wondered about the possibility of not merely recording the messages on a tape-recorder, but of measuring the source of the message, just as radio and TV waves can be identified. However, this may not be permitted because 'His ways are past finding out,' and this might not be of faith. I can add that a number of interpretations that I have heard in the past ten years have concerned warnings and rebukes to God's people as well as instruction and comfort. In all cases, the genuine message was appropriate to the immediate need or situation. I also think that you can't take a supernatural blessing bestowed from God and bring it down to a common denominator or natural level. The Gospel of John says 'The wind bloweth where it listeth, and thou hearest the sound thereof but canst not tell whence it cometh and whither it goeth: so is everyone that is born of the Spirit.'

"As I said, I do not know what my own tongue means, and I do not know if it is a language spoken anywhere in the world. Maybe I would have found out more if I had used my gift more publicly. But here is an example of the language I most often speak:

> Un te a tiki, un se;
> un se, un se;
> te a tiki un se.

I pronounce the *t* with my tongue pressed hard against the roof of the mouth just behind the teeth, similar to the sounding of *th*, except the tongue is forced forward while the breath is expelled with enough force that it makes a slight sound. I hope you will find this example of my own speech useful in your work. If you do have any information about whether this is a true language, please let me know.

"I think you may also be interested in knowing that having the baptism of the Holy Spirit and the gift of tongues has never made me successful in business, but it has cast out fear of people and has made me a strong leader and salesman—a person who loves God and tries seriously to put him first and tell others about his wonderful Son, Jesus Christ. For me, the indwelling of the Holy Spirit can be considered *bona fide* only if the person shows a deep love for Christ in that which he promotes. By the same token a person who doesn't show a profound love for Christ very possibly does not have the Holy Spirit in him.

"As a psychologist, it should be easy for you to see that a person who has experienced, or regularly experiences (as in the matter of speaking in tongues), a miracle within himself should be more convinced and convincing than one who has not had any such experience with God.

"My own experience of the baptism has tended to make me a poor follower, since I generally feel that I know what God wants and expects of me; and I trust my judgment more than that of many who would presume to tell me what I should do. When I am subject to authority it is generally with well-defined reservations—usually expressed, so there is no misunderstanding. In order that you may better understand my attitude toward my pastor and other church leaders, I might say that I think of myself as an apostle, subject first to God, and to people only when there is no conflict of interest. Normally, there isn't. Nevertheless, this attitude has caused me to change churches a number of times. But while I had never entertained the thought of being an Episcopalian[2] before last year, I find that I have had more freedom and opportunity to work in my Episcopalian church than I have had for over twenty years. My present project, which I undertook with the church's blessing, is to try to activate inactive members. I find that my hours of visiting, writing, and phoning are paying off and that I am more effective than someone who does not have the Holy Spirit in him, even though that person may be a true Christian. The chances are that evangelism for that person is work, rather than a source of deep satisfaction.

"As an example of how strongly I feel about my opinions, I have always felt that it was God's will that I marry my Presbyterian wife. Furthermore, I feel that it was his will that I take my two children out of the Presbyterian church and prevent them from getting enmeshed in it at all. As a matter of fact I am quite sure that my Presbyterian wife will soon learn to depend on Christ instead of the Presbyterian church, if she doesn't already.

"In closing, may I caution you to be at least neutral in this investigation, since it is easy for a person to feel that 'if he doesn't have it, it can't be important'; or worse, take a pharisaical attitude toward it, assuming that if it isn't approved 'by the Board of Trustees' it can't be of God.

"The fact remains, whatever conclusions you come up with, that through the centuries God has blessed people—sometimes few and sometimes, as now, many—with this gift of tongues, and he will continue to do so.

"I hope you will excuse the length of this letter, but I recognize that you are in a position to do a great deal of harm, especially since reason is much more popular than faith—although it alone has little value before God. Many people continue to go to hell, we can be sure, because faith isn't recognized by the common senses, so these people will have none of it. Let me urge you to remember that you will stand before God much longer than you will stand before men. So please be careful.

Truly yours,
John Doe

"P.S. Doctor, this letter is an example of my doing what I felt God would have me do. The results or your attitude toward it are no concern of mine. I feel I have contributed my bit under his direction, and that is all I am expected to do. I am merely a small cog in an intricate machine, a cog which doesn't even know what product is being produced, except that it is something for the glory of God. Truly, JD.
P.P.S. I hope this has helped you. I am enclosing a card of our church, where I guarantee you will witness the manifestations of the Spirit. Truly JD."

This composite letter, then, reflects the common features in the autobiographical statements of tongue-speakers. I would like now to develop nine observations from the letter.

Observation one: There are five steps in the process of one's coming to speak in tongues. Each of these five steps may be seen in the testimony of John Doe. First, the person who is about to speak in tongues has a great sense of personal distress, often called an existential crisis. In his distress, he is openly seeking and is open for someone who will tell him what to do and provide relief from his suffering. Second, he is generally drawn to a person who is a leader whom he trusts or eventually comes to trust. In his sense of weakness and dependency, he looks for a person with certainty, for someone who has a sense of definiteness and strength. Third, the charismatic leader is surrounded by a supporting group of fellow believers. The credibility of the leader is enhanced by the presence of this group of followers, who are almost equally firm in their convictions that a solution and an end to suffering lies in following their own path. Fourth, a comprehensive rationale is offered to the initiate to explain what tongue-speaking is, and how it may be understood. Fifth, there is an intense emotional atmosphere at some point in what I have come to call the induction process.

Let us now explore each of these five steps. Again, it is well to remember that the danger of oversimplification is great, and that there surely must be some exceptions to every rule.

Persons who begin to speak in tongues have suffered before they began to speak with the strange sounds that appear to be a language. This suffering and distress is usually intense, with feelings of confusion or estrangement or isolation. The distress may be environmental, physical, or emotional in origin. Or more likely, it is caused by a combination of circumstances. Marital difficulties, financial concern, ill health, feelings of depression are common. At times the crisis is ethical or religious in nature and involves concerns about spiritual values, a sense of guilt, or questions about the ultimate meaning and purpose of life. Preoccupation with one's internal psychology seems to create the atmosphere in which a person is open to finding answers for one's problems. Persons who are generally anxiety free or who are not feeling any particular distress are less likely to seek answers to existential questions, and are therefore less susceptible to the induction of a glossolalia experience. Note that John Doe turned to speaking in tongues during his travels whenever he fell into periods of profound emotional distress.

One of the common features of a person in distress is that he has a powerful sense of dependency. When a swimmer tires, he looks about for someone to lean on or to clutch for safety. A dependent and distressed person can be likened to a tired swimmer. He wants to find someone or something who can do for him what he feels he cannot do for himself. What he generally looks for at those moments is a perfect parent. While John Doe says that his only leader was the Holy Spirit, it is possible to see that he had a great admiration for the leader of his group who served as the channel for the Holy Spirit. He came to trust this leader, which is the second precondition for beginning to speak in tongues.

Doe also presents an interesting variant on the usual pattern, inasmuch as he reports that he very rarely took advice from other persons who offered it. He reports that he trusted his own thinking more than that of others. This is a case that might be described psychologically as counterdependence. Mr. Doe appears to be a man who is quite fearful of being dependent upon others, and bends over backward not to be influenced by others. And yet, under situations of extreme distress he did return to a church fellowship where he found support. Some people who are independent seem to go 180 degrees in the opposite direction intermittently, and become what appears to be the opposite of independent. One example of this behavior is the case of a minister who was actually in the middle of preaching a sermon against tongue-speaking when he suddenly broke out into speaking in tongues himself. A belligerent skeptic may in fact be quite susceptible to the experience—which is an example of the psychological mechanism called reaction formation. In Shakespeare's words, "Me thinks he protesteth too much" may well indicate an underlying desire to conform.

The comradeship of the group is the third factor in the induction process. The warmth of the group provides acceptance. Enthusiastic members of the group promise relief from turmoil. It appears to me that once having begun to speak in tongues, relatively few persons continue it with any degree of importance unless they keep in touch with an ongoing group of fellow believers. This is a consistent finding with other groups, including members of Alcoholics Anonymous, who derive great support from their fellow members. Without follow-up group support, it seems that many psychological changes will dissipate.

The fourth feature in the induction process is providing a rationale so that making these strange sounds appears to be part of some comprehensible plan. Perhaps no one would make the strange sounds of tongue-speaking without having a rationale to explain that these sounds are indeed a special gift and not just nonsensical babble. I do not know of any persons who have begun to speak in tongues without knowing that there was such a thing described in religious literature. It appears that no one begins speaking in tongues until he or she has some grasp of the New Testament explanation of what it is.

A heightened emotional atmosphere is the fifth element in the induction process. Some leaders are more effective than others at preparing the emotional atmosphere which is optimally effective in inducing the experience. A skilled leader may have a number of effective rituals which he feels are beneficial for the initiate. This systematic activity may generate a great deal of emotional feeling, sometimes even to the point of fatigue or exhaustion. In these instances the advent of tongue-speaking is all the more euphoric or dramatic. One noted tongue-speaker now reports that he is able to preach a sermon during which he never mentions the gifts of the

Spirit, or even the Holy Spirit, and nonetheless at the end of his sermon, or even during it, initiates begin to speak in tongues for the first time. This leader's reputation is so great that persons come to his meeting already aware that indeed they may be seized with the impulse to speak in tongues. His reputation has preceded him, so that he needs to make very little conscious effort to induce people to speak in tongues. Nonetheless, the overall rule holds true, that a heightened emotional atmosphere is what has brought the onset of glossolalia.

I am therefore advancing the hypothesis that glossolalia is a learned experience, and that these five factors constitute the steps in the learning process. These five steps closely parallel the essential steps for religious healing to take place.[3] James Hanson agrees that speaking in tongues rarely develops spontaneously without some kind of coaching. He himself reports that he would not have received this gift if someone had not coached him.[4]

It is not my purpose in this chapter to make a value judgment on the induction process or on the hypothesis that glossolalia is a learned experience. Rather, my purpose here is simply to observe that the evidence is strong that one may learn to speak in tongues under certain prescribed conditions.

Observation two: The capability of being hypnotized and the capability of speaking in tongues are closely related.

Tongue-speakers begin to speak in tongues through the help and direction of a leader who actively initiates the neophyte into the experience. It appears essential that the initiate develop a deeply trusting and even submissive relationship to the person who is his or her mentor. If the initiate holds back, if he is only partly involved in the experience or has strong reservations about the credibility of the leader, then he or she will not begin to speak in tongues. If, for example, a group of twenty persons are exposed to a charismatic leader, those persons in the group who trust the leader the most have the best chance of becoming glossolalists. In subordinating one's own ego to that of the authority figure, the initiate is able to regress psychologically to a level of childlike openness, dependency, and suggestibility.

The ability to submit oneself to a mentor appears to be a precondition for speaking in tongues. This capacity to regress exhibits the same general traits as the trait of hypnotizability. Hypnotizability requires that one be trusting enough to turn himself rather fully over to someone else and to place one's momentary destiny in the hands of the other person. Some persons tend to hang on to their own psychological controls and do not develop the trusting relationship which is the precondition for hypnosis. However, many persons who at first cannot give themselves up will gradually come to trust the mentor and in time will allow themselves to regress enough to be hypnotized.

Hypnotizability constitutes the *sine qua non* of a glossolalia experience. If one can be hypnotized, then one is able under proper conditions to learn to speak in tongues. While people who speak in tongues are not hypnotized, the induction of glossolalia is very similar to the induction into hypnosis. There is a further connection. After a person has been hypnotized for the first time, it becomes increasingly easy for him to be hypnotized on repeated occasions. This holds true also for the tongue-speaker. Once he has begun to speak in tongues under the conditions of a trusting dependence and regression in the face of the mentor, then the tongue-speaker himself is able to repeat the tongue-speech without repeated induction efforts by the mentor. Once the tongue-speaker has been able to regress and let go of the conscious controls so that glossolalia is produced, then it is easy for him to repeat the same or similar sounds under a wide variety of conditions, whether kneeling in the quiet of a church or driving along the freeway.

Observation three: The feelings of well-being experienced by the new tongue-speaker are caused by his or her feeling of acceptance by the leader and the group of fellow tongue-speakers. The feeling of euphoria is not caused by the actual making of the sounds of glossolalia itself.

The feelings of well-being are caused by the belief, as reinforced by the group, that this is an act of God's intervention in one's speech. The actual verbalizing is a neutral experience. It is one's belief that this is a gift of God which brings an experience of euphoria.

The new tongue-speaker has been told for days or weeks or months or years that once he begins to speak in tongues there will be a variety of benefits. It is a sign of God's approval, physical evidence that the speaker has been singled out for a special blessing. Many new tongue-speakers have been striving with a great deal of energy, curiosity, and perseverance to experience this phenomenon. When one has striven diligently to reach a goal, and that goal is seen as one which will produce tremendous benefits in one's life, then a feeling of relief and elation will occur when one reaches the goal.

It is known that when a person has been hypnotized and been given post-hypnotic suggestions that he will feel more relaxed or more confident, these benefits will actually occur, at least for a time. The hypnotized person begins to experience the mood which has been suggested to him. This is precisely what happens with the new tongue-speaker. He exhibits those results in his life which he has been led to expect.

Whether or not these suggested benefits will persist appears to depend upon whether or not the experience is reinforced by one's fellow practitioners, and whether or not these persons continue their support and encouragement. Psychologically, there is a common experience of feeling let down after a major experience in one's life. We are familiar, for example, with post-graduation letdown. This may also happen with tongue-speakers who are not surrounded by a group of fellow believers who buoy each other up. If they continue to feel that they are a company of special people, the subjective feelings of euphoria seem to continue. But the new tongue-speaker who is soon cut off from a supportive group or who has conflicts with his group so that he comes to put less stock in their comradeship seems to derive relatively less psychological benefits from the experience. He may have felt special at the moment, but he needs continuing reinforcement from his fellow believers if he is to continue to feel that he is one of a select fellowship. Otherwise glossolalia becomes relatively less meaningful for him.

The actual making of the sounds is not what makes a person feel good. It is rather the belief that God Almighty is moving his tongue. It is a physical experience, but it is confirmed by one's intellectual understanding that it is a gift of the Spirit, and is combined with emotional support from one's fellow believers. When all these factors are present, it is understandable that tongue-speakers are less depressed as they continue to believe in the special gift of God that is given to them.

Four examples will illustrate my point here. While being interviewed on a television program, I was surprised to hear the master of ceremonies begin to speak in tongues. He did so to give the television audience an example of what glossolalia sounded like. He explained that he had not made those sounds for twenty years. As an adolescent he had belonged to a religious fellowship in which he spoke in tongues, but had discarded the practice as he moved away from home and left the fellowship of his church. Twenty years later he could still demonstrate the ability to make the sounds, but they had no emotional or spiritual impact for him. Twenty years previously, he had felt a warm, inner glow when he made those sounds, believing that this was God speaking through him.

Speaking in tongues is practiced in non-Christian religions, particularly among the Hindus in India.[5] The physical manifestations appear to be analogous to what happens in a Christian context, though the belief system connected with the experience is quite different. Similarly, the subjective experience is correlated with what each religious group teaches will be the results of what happens subjectively when one speaks in tongues.

A linguist has reported that he has been able to teach members of his linguistics class how to speak in tongues.[6] This experience was developed outside any religious beliefs about the practice. And as would be expected, no particular feelings of euphoria developed as a result of the linguistics class members learning to speak in tongues.

Acting classes encourage students to develop a type of glossolalia called "turkey talk" as part of training in acting. Class members are encouraged to use verbal expression without using a known language. Actors and actresses under these conditions are able to speak a "language" which sounds like glossolalia, but is simply an exercise in the free flow of emotion and verbal expression without intellectual content. Actors and actresses will speak somewhat different "languages" when they are asked to talk a language that conveys joy, warmth, sadness, etc.

In summary, it is not the speech itself, but rather the belief about what the speech is, that makes glossolalists feel good.

Observation four: Subjective experience alone cannot determine the value of an experience. Tongue-speakers, especially beginning tongue-speakers, report very positive subjective feelings. However, positive subjective feelings can be produced in a wide variety of ways. And the subjective feelings can be equally euphoric, even when produced by very different kinds of stimuli.

LSD users, for example, have said that nothing can compare with the heights of ecstasy which they feel when they are on a good trip. They often say that if one hasn't tried it, one should not knock the experience. Nothing can compare with the unfathomable beauty of a leaf rustling in the wind when on an LSD trip, someone has said. And the true inner nature of a Beethoven symphony can best be grasped when using LSD, someone else has said.

An Oxford University professor of English literature once told the story of having been hypnotized by Adolf Hitler during a mass meeting in Nazi Germany during the 1930s. This professor was a British citizen on a visit to Berlin, when he decided to observe at first hand a Nazi rally. Before the meeting was over he found himself standing on his seat (along with thousands of others), cheering wildly for Hitler, waving his arms, stamping his feet and shouting Nazi slogans.

Hours later in his hotel room he wondered what had possessed him to act in a way so totally out of character. He thought not only that he was an undemonstrative man temperamentally, but that he had also been and continued to be opposed to the Hitler movement. In fact, a year later he was no longer allowed to enter Germany because of his opposition to Nazism. But that night, he said, during Hitler's speech he had felt a wonderful kind of wholeness and enthusiasm. He later said that he felt completely convinced about the rightness of what he was doing, and would have sworn that he was fully in possession of all his faculties, and was psychologically "together." He said later that during the Nazi rally perhaps nothing could have convinced him that he was not doing the right thing. For the moment, he became convinced intellectually, he was emotionally supported by thousands of others at the rally, and he was caught up in the subjective sense of euphoria.

LSD users and those hypnotized at Hitler rallies illustrate that different kinds of experience can produce the same euphoria. The spiritual validity of glossolalia, therefore, cannot be proved by how good it makes one feel subjectively. Tongue-speakers often report how marvelous they have felt since they began speaking in tongues. Someone else could report the same feelings after having successfully dieted and lost sixty pounds. Therefore, it is wise to discount the glowing accounts of subjective feelings as determinative of the spiritual value of glossolalia.

Glossolalists will occasionally say that if one has not experienced the phenomenon, one is not in a position to evaluate it. It may be said with equal validity that the person who has experienced the phenomenon may tend to place undue significance on the feelings of well-being that accompany speaking in tongues. To repeat, subjective experience cannot alone determine the value of any phenomenon.

Observation five: The interpretation of tongues raises many questions.

The interpretation of tongues is numbered among the gifts of the Spirit in 1 Corinthians 12:10. Often when someone speaks in tongues during a religious meeting, someone else gets up to report to the group what he understands the tongue-speaker to be saying. The interpreter has a strong conviction that he knows at least the substance of what is being said by the tongue-speaker.

Fewer people claim the gift of interpreting tongues than there are persons who are able to speak in tongues. Only a few persons report that they have the ability both to speak in tongues and to interpret what one's own tongue-speech means, as well as the meaning of some other person's tongue-speaking.

St. Paul in 1 Corinthians 14:26 advises that there be only two or three persons at a meeting who speak in tongues, and that one person interpret the tongue-speaking. He goes on to say that if no one is there to interpret, then the tongue-speakers should keep silence in the church and speak in tongues only to themselves. This pattern is generally followed in neo-Pentecostal meetings. However, there are occasional mass meetings where dozens or even hundreds of persons may speak in tongues all at the same time, and there is no attempt to make individual interpretations of the individual tongue-speaker's words.

Most persons who interpret glossolalia offer interpretations which are quite general. After a tongue-speaker has spoken for several minutes, a typical interpretation might summarize what the tongue-speaker had said in just a few sentences. Most of the interpretations offer the view that the tongue-speaker has been praising and thanking God. Another general theme is that the tongue-speaker has been asking for help, guidance, and strength.

But sometimes—and it may be about one-third of the time—an interpreter will offer very specific interpretations of what the tongue-speaker has been saying. More rarely, the interpreter will translate phrase by phrase what the tongue-speaker has been saying. My colleagues and I have witnessed occasions when the interpreter interspersed his interpretation as the tongue-speaker paused for a comma or a period. It is a remarkable experience to witness this kind of interpretation, because the interpreter implies that he or she knows exactly what is being said, and does not appear to be confused or uncertain about the meaning of each individual word or phrase. We have witnessed occasions when the interpreter's own emotion appeared to reflect the emotion of the tongue-speaker. When we asked how the interpreter knew exactly what each syllable or word meant, we received only general answers about how the interpreter viewed his ability to interpret as he was doing. He simply had a conviction that such and such a phrase meant a certain thing.

Because of our curiosity about these literal translations of tongue-speaking, we wanted to investigate the accuracy of these interpretations. We therefore played taped examples of tongue-speech privately for several different interpreters of tongues. In no instance was there any similarity in the several interpretations given by the interpreters who claimed to do a literal translation of the tongue-speech. For example, a tape-recorded sample of Mr. Jones' glossolalia was taken to three different persons who claimed the gift of interpretation of tongues. One interpreter was convinced that the tongue-speaker was seeking guidance about a new job offer, and another interpreter reported that the same speech was a prayer of thanksgiving for one's recent return to health after a serious illness.

We explained to the different interpreters that someone else had offered a different interpretation of the same example of glossolalia. Without hesitation or defensiveness, the interpreter said that God gave to one interpreter one interpretation, and gave to another interpreter another interpretation. We then asked the tongue-speaker himself what he felt that he was saying, and as is usually the case the tongue-speaker reported that he himself did not know what he was saying. He was uttering things beyond his own understanding; God was giving him a blessing that was beyond his own intellectual understanding of what was happening.

I have gained the impression that interpreters who translate tongue-speech literally are often poorly integrated psychologically. Their view of their gift of interpretation borders on the grandiose. This impression has not been tested clinically, and I offer it to the reader simply to see whether it coincides with the general impression left by this type of interpretation of tongues.

The following example, which I have reported elsewhere,[7] sheds further light on the nature of the interpretation of tongues. We know a man who was raised in Africa, the son of missionary parents, who decided to test the interpretation of tongues. He attended a tongue-speaking meeting where he was a complete stranger. At the appropriate moment, he rose and spoke the Lord's Prayer in the African dialect he had learned in his youth. When he sat down, an interpreter of tongues offered the meaning of what he had said. The interpreter reported that it was a message about the imminent second coming of Christ.

Observation six: Glossolalic speech is not a natural, human language.

Two important questions may be asked in reference to whether tongue-speaking is an actual human language. First, are there examples of tongue-speech which can be translated by a person who knows the language that the person is speaking? Second, do linguists report that tongue-speech has the qualities of human language?

When a person speaks in tongues, it generally sounds like a foreign language to a person who is not familiar with what is being said. The speaker's fluency gives the impression that he is speaking with certainty and with feeling. The sounds appear to a nonlinguist to have the rhythm and the other qualities of a language. And it does not appear possible for the average person consciously to duplicate the fluency and the structure of tongue-speaking. No two persons sound exactly alike when they speak in tongues. It is as if each person were speaking a different language.

Because it sounds so much like a language, there are many reports that glossolalic speech must indeed be a language spoken, say, in Africa, or in some other remote area of the world. Most people who have contact with glossolalia have heard reports that a tongue-speaker had been speaking in Egyptian, or in some Hindu dialect, etc. The story usually goes something like this: A visitor from abroad dropped in on a religious service where tongue-speaking was in progress, and reported hearing his own language spoken by a person who had spent all his or her life in the United States and had never had any contact with the visitor's native language. The report develops that the tongue-speaker was indeed speaking the visitor's language.

Such stories are numerous. However, to the best of our knowledge, these reports are always third-hand. Someone tells the story about someone else having heard that this was indeed the case. There are no reported instances of a glossolalist speaking a language which was then literally translated by an expert in that language. Of the hundreds of thousands of occasions on which glossolalia has been uttered, there is no tape recording that can be translated from a language spoken somewhere in the world. My point is this: If glossolalic utterances were somehow real languages, it would seem that there would exist somewhere in the world evidence that the speaking in tongues was in fact in such a foreign language.

The second question that concerns us here is whether or not tape-recorded examples of glossolalia resemble a natural language. This is a technical linguistic question and the reader is encouraged to refer to the Nida and Samarin material in the bibliography.

Linguists begin with a definition of a natural human language and then see how tongue-speech does or does not meet the criteria implied in the definition of a natural human language. One of the basic methods for characterizing a language is that of Charles F. Hockett.[8] He has suggested sixteen defining features as the universals of a language. He calls them design features of a language, and reports that these sixteen features exist in every language on which we have reliable information. Without describing here what those features are, we may observe that by these standards tongue-speech is not human language. The absence of many of these sixteen features is sufficient to demonstrate the non-linguisticality of glossolalia. The evidence indicates that tongue-speech is not a language spoken anywhere in the world. Some tongue-speakers have countered that perhaps glossolalia is an example of the speech spoken by the angels. We have no answer for that.

Observation seven: Tongue-speakers reported the following positive results:

One of the positive results reported by tongue-speakers was personal happiness. Almost invariably, they said they were more cheerful, more joyful and more optimistic as a result of speaking in tongues. They were less depressed and less pessimistic and had a pervading sense of God's presence and strength within themselves.

In addition to happiness, most tongue-speakers reported a sense of greater personal power. They were more self-confident in interpersonal relationships. They felt bolder and took more risks, whether in their business dealings, or in their marriage relationships, or in witnessing to their faith. Tongue-speakers reported a sense of purposefulness in their lives which provided a feeling of security about who they were and about what they were doing. Often they expressed a sense that God had touched them significantly and they were therefore sure that they were significant people and were doing significant things in the world.

Religious convictions were held more firmly and played a larger part in their lives. They reported a maturing of their own religious and spiritual insights. This was expressed through an intense desire that their friends and fellow church members pursue the same experience. The presence of God in their lives seemed to be a central reality in their existence. Spiritual factors played a large role in almost every conversation with them. Life was most often viewed in spiritual terms, and the jargon of religion was almost always a part of any conversation, regardless of the subject under discussion.

The personal fellowship among tongue-speakers seemed to be joyful and warm. Their sense of community with each other appeared to be genuine and intense. Persons of different intellectual capacities or socio-economic background seemed to be at home with each other. It appeared that their common overwhelming spiritual experience surmounted other barriers of background or class.

However difficult it may be to survey or measure, it seemed that glossolalists had tremendous love and concern and care for one another. According to their own reports, their ways of dealing with life had indeed changed significantly since their experience with glossolalia. They all seemed to report that being filled with the Spirit had made them better able to cope with frustration, and better able to show greater patience and stability in dealing with others.

Observation eight: The following negative results have often been observed in persons who speak in tongues:

Dependency on the leader who introduced the person to tongue-speaking is a prominent factor. Submission to the leader is a necessary factor in the induction in tongue-speaking, and often that dependency continues. The dependence on the leader is then often extended or transferred to a dependence on a group of fellow tongue-speakers. This dependency produces a provincialism among tongue-speakers which isolates them from influences that might give them a more balanced perspective. Many members of tongue-speaking groups are reluctant to make life decisions without getting the permission of their leader or of fellow members of the group. This dependency may often be a form of immaturity in which one is unable to see oneself as an independent and autonomous person. At times, mutual dependency seems to be a mark of the personal insecurity of tongue-speakers.

A special problem is presented by the fact that most tongue-speakers are initiated to this experience after a severe identity crisis. After a profound crisis in which one has nearly lost his moorings in life, the onset of tongue-speaking often is experienced as the rescue from an abyss. One's whole life may begin to revolve around this experience, often with a militant defensiveness against any self-examination. A few seriously upset persons have sought to keep their personal and professional heads above water by clinging to tongue-speaking. In my opinion, this is the situation among some clergy who have been impervious to the counseling of their fellow clergy. Some clergy seem to prefer masochistically to split congregations and terminate their own pastorates rather than cooperate with the guidance or proposals made by their bishops. Such extreme instances are few, but it should be noted that this may be a sign of emotional instability. It is an evidence of how a religious context can be used in the service of one's neurotic or even psychotic needs.

Some tongue-speakers view the way in which God directs their lives as almost magical. Viewed from the standpoint of science, glossolalists give an "irrational" explanation for what they are doing. That is, the explanation offered is that the Holy Spirit is giving the movement to the tongue and the sounds to the speech. This explanation is unverifiable from a scientific point of view. Because of this private type of explanation, it is often difficult to communicate with tongue-speakers. When they say, for example, that God gave them the message, or God spoke to them through glossolalia and it was interpreted by someone else as meaning that they should follow a certain course of action, this is difficult to discuss. There is an exclusiveness to the glossolalia experience that tends to alienate tongue-speakers from discourse with a wider community.

Tongue-speaking is a divisive influence in many congregations. In fact, one bishop of a main-line Protestant denomination, who has asked to remain anonymous, has said that it is the unanimous view of bishops in his church that tongue-speaking has been a divisive influence in every congregation where it has been introduced. The charismatic movement has not made for easy compromise or impartiality. More often it has polarized congregations. In many congregations, those persons who began to speak in tongues left their congregation and went to another or formed a new congregation. The great visibility of the charismatic movement has caused battle lines to be quickly formed. The tongue-speakers' experiences were so overwhelmingly powerful in most cases that they could not keep the experience to themselves. Causes for the divisiveness are the seemingly irrational nature of the act, and the specialness with which the tongue-speakers regard themselves and their gift.

It is easier to be tolerant of one's neighbor if he exhibits behavior that is commonplace and understandable. Tongue-speech is not commonplace, nor is it readily understandable. This makes for suspicion and distance.

Further, the language of the glossolalist serves to alienate him from others. Phrases such as "I have been filled with the Spirit," "I have a special gift from God," "I have had a new experience with God," imply that the listener perhaps is not filled with the Spirit or has not had an experience with God which is special. However careful tongue-speakers are to watch the way in which they describe themselves and others, they often nonetheless betray a subtle disrespect for non-tongue-speakers and towards those who show no interest in joining their group. Non-glossolalists usually report that they are made to feel somewhat inferior in the presence of a tongue-speaker.

Histrionic display is another negative feature of the glossolalia experience. It is evident in only a minority of the situations in which glossolalia is practiced. When speaking in tongues is followed by interpretation of tongues and then by prophecy, three experiences of a basically irrational nature are following one upon another. One cannot critique the value of the sounds glossolalists make; one cannot criticize the interpreter of tongues; and when someone offers a sentence or a paragraph of prophecy, again the speaker will offer the explanation that this is indeed a gift of the Spirit, and the gift was just given to him to say what he just said.

The critic of the movement may offer the explanation that things are not being done decently and in order, nor do the events seem to be edifying the church as a whole. But the person who feels that he has the gift of the Spirit may be impervious to these critiques.

Observation nine: What are the criteria by which glossolalia should be evaluated? A minor criterion is whether it has an upbuilding and uplifting effect on oneself. The major criterion is whether it edifies the community as a whole.

While the fact that tongue-speakers feel good is important, it must be kept in mind that many experiences in life can make one feel good. A religious experience should measure itself by its fruits, and not simply by how it makes one feel. Because of the subjective nature of glossolalia, it is important that other observers contribute their evaluation of the experience and make an attempt objectively to evaluate both its positive and negative effects.

There is some truth to the claim that no one can truly evaluate an experience which he has not had himself. However, the converse is equally true: the person who has had the experience is often in a poor position to evaluate the very experience which he has had.

It is my personal opinion that the experience of glossolalia has the effect of being a security operation, as understood in the way in which Dr. Harry Stack Sullivan, the psychiatrist, used that term.[9] A security operation is a behavior that enables one to cope with anxiety and thus to feel more secure. Speaking in tongues often works as an effective security operation for people; when they do it, their fears and their feelings of worthlessness diminish and they feel much better.

In my opinion the obsessive use of glossolalia is an evidence of an underlying emotional disequilibrium. Those persons who use their tongue-speaking in a more responsible way are emotionally less needy in the first place. They are less likely to use their tongue-speech in the service of their own emotional problems.

It appears to me that the reason tongue-speakers feel so much better after they begin to do it is precisely that they have been going through a fundamental life-crisis and have found a security operation which makes them feel better by helping them to cope with their inner feelings of desperate loneliness or meaninglessness. If they become very dependent on tongue-speaking and the comradeship of a tongue-speaking community, this may indicate their great need for external sources of support by which they compensate for their own inner weaknesses.

In summary: My glossolalia research has convinced me that it is a learned behavior which can bring a sense of power and well-being. It may also lead to excesses resulting in community disruption. It is the use of glossolalia which determines whether or not it is constructive.

Micah said that true religion was to do justice, love kindness, and to walk humbly with God. If the practice of glossolalia produces these fruits, then it appears to me to be a responsible use of the experience.

Notes

1. The writer of the letter is referring to the final progress report, "Glossolalia and Mental Health," a research project supported by the Behavioral Sciences Branch, National Institute of Mental Health, No. MH-10514-01, principal investigator John P. Kildahl, co-investigator Paul A. Qualben. The results of the five hypotheses investigated in this research are the following: (1) glosso-lalists are more submissive, suggestible, and dependent in the presence of authority figures than non-tongue-speakers; (2) glossolalists initiate their speech in the presence of a benevolent authority figure, either in reality or fantasy; (3) glossolalists are less depressed than non-glossolalists; (4) glosso-lalists continued their sense of well-being following a year's interval as they continued the practice of glossolalia; (5) the spoken utterances of glossolalia do not meet the criteria of what constitutes a human language. These findings are further explained in John P. Kildahl, *The Psychology of Speaking in Tongues* (New York, 1972).
2. The denominations mentioned here are not necessarily the ones mentioned in the letter actually being quoted.
3. The reader will find a number of fascinating parallels between the atmosphere for healing and for glossolalia in the excellent work by Jerome Frank, *Persuasion and Healing* (Baltimore, 1961).
4. *The Holy Spirit in Today's Church*, ed. Erling Jorstad (Nashville, 1973), p. 46. This book contains a number of firsthand accounts of people's reactions—both pro and con—to the charismatic movement.
5. L. Carlyle May, "A Survey of Glossolalia and Related Phenomena in Non-Christian Religions," *American Anthropologist*, LVIII (May, 1956), 75-96.
6. William J. Samarin, "The Linguisticality of Glossolalia," *Hartford Quarterly*, VIII (Summer, 1968), 49-75.
7. *The Psychology of Speaking in Tongues*, p. 63.
8. See Hockett, "The Problem of Universals in Language," *Universals of Language*, ed. J.H. Greenberg (Cambridge, 1963).
9. Sullivan, *The Interpersonal Theory of Psychiatry* (New York, 1953), p. 346.

Two American Expressions

7 THE BLACK PENTECOSTALS

LAWRENCE NEALE JONES

The black communities in the United States have made two important contributions to the universal church; their religious music . . . and the Pentecostal spirituality which, since its beginning in a humble black church in Los Angeles in 1906, has swept across the world in a grandiose revival and numbers today somewhere between 25 and 35 millions.[1]

—Walter J. Hollenweger

THE AZUSA STREET REVIVAL

Professor Walter Hollenweger's assertion that Pentecostalism in its modern formulation had its beginning in a "Black Church in Los Angeles" has been vigorously debated among the historians of the movement.[2] But however that debate is decided, it is at least indisputable that the so-called "Azusa Street Revival" of 1906-08 gave critical impetus to a religious phenomenon that has spread throughout the world. Similarly, it is generally conceded that W. J. Seymour, a Black Holiness preacher, was the initiator and principal leader of that revival in its earliest months. Black Pentecostals trace their lineage directly to Azusa Street. Seymour had been a sometime student in a Houston, Texas, Bible school founded by the Rev. C. F. Parham, whom some identify as the true founder of modern Pentecostalism. Parham, who was originally from Topeka, Kansas, taught that the "baptism of the Spirit" was validated in the gift of speaking

Professor Lawrence Neale Jones was born in West Virginia and received his B.S. in education at West Virginia State College. He received an M.A. from the University of Chicago, a B.D. from Oberlin Graduate School of Theology, and a Ph.D. from Yale University. Dr. Jones is currently Professor of Afro-American Church History and Dean of the Seminary at Union Theological Seminary in New York.

Before his ordination into the ministry of the United Church of Christ in 1956, Professor Jones served in the United States Army, taught school in West Virginia, and ministered to a congregation of the Evangelical and Reformed Church in West Salem, Ohio. From 1961 to 1965 he was Dean of Chapel at Fisk University in Nashville and since 1965 he has been at Union Theological Seminary. Professor Jones has among his publications "Is Anybody Listening to Black America?" an essay in *Love and Power*, C. Eric Lincoln (ed.), and has published articles in many religious journals, including the *United Church Herald* and *Christianity and Crisis*.

in tongues. Seymour was convinced of the truth of the doctrine and stressed it in his preaching and conversation. A visitor to Houston, a Mrs. Terry, was impressed with Seymour's preaching and invited him to Los Angeles to become the associate minister of the Nazarene congregation of which she was a member.

The text of Seymour's first sermon was Acts 2:4, "and they were all filled with the Holy Spirit, and began to speak in other tongues, as the Spirit gave them utterance."[3] Though Seymour had not himself received the gift of the baptism of the Spirit and speaking in tongues, he believed that speaking in tongues was a work of grace beyond the holiness doctrine of sanctification. His first sermon was the last sermon he was to preach to this Nazarene congregation, for most of its members found his doctrinal stance offensive. Subsequently, Seymour was befriended by a Mr. and Mrs. Asbury, who were members of the church, and he began to hold services in their home. On April 9, 1906, "seven seekers were baptized by the Holy Spirit" and began to speak in tongues.[4] So great was the impact of their experience that the meeting continued uninterruptedly for three days. These remarkable phenomena can be seen, in retrospect, as being the initial events in a religious revival which attracted such large crowds that Seymour and his followers were forced to seek larger quarters. They found a suitable auditorium in an abandoned Methodist Church in Azusa Street. The services in Azusa Street were virtually nonstop, often lasting as long as fifteen hours!

The nucleus of those persons who continued to meet in Azusa Street eventually called themselves the Apostolic Faith Gospel Mission and began to publish a modest newspaper called *Apostolic Faith*. For three years the revival at the Mission remained intense, and literally thousands of people from the United States and abroad flooded the services seeking the baptism of the Spirit and hoping to be graced by the gift of speaking in tongues. Many of these men and women became worldwide missionaries of the new doctrine.

FROM INTERRACIAL MOVEMENT TO SEGREGATED INSTITUTIONS

An event of significant proportion for the future of Pentecostalism occurred when Elder C. H. Mason of the Church of God in Christ was, in his words, "led by the Spirit to go to Los Angeles, California, where the great fire of the latter rain of the Holy Ghost had fallen on many. It was in March, 1907, when I received Him, Jesus, my Lord, in the Holy Ghost."[5] Mason had been baptized at an early age in a Missionary Baptist Church in Arkansas and was ordained subsequently as a minister by that denomination. After an abortive three-month stay at Arkansas Baptist College (1893-94), he became a traveling revivalist having been shown by "the Lord . . . that there was no salvation in schools and colleges."[6]

By 1896 Mason had joined forces with Elder C. P. Jones of Jackson, Mississippi, and in the next year they established a holiness congregation in Lexington, Mississippi, which they eventually named The Church of God. Shortly thereafter they added the words "in Christ" to distinguish themselves from the Church of God. The seed of this work was a revival conducted by Jones and Mason in Jackson in 1896 where many persons who received the gift of the Holy Spirit were "converted, sanctified and healed by the power of faith."[7] The holiness doctrine, in its main tenets, holds that the believer is converted or regenerated, receives the gift of the Holy Spirit, and is sanctified, i.e., empowered to live a sinless life. Holiness groups may differ as to whether sanctification is an immediate, complete gift of grace or is a more gradual process of growth. A clue to the posture of this church toward other Christians who were "not of its fold" was its watchword, "no salvation without holiness."

In the earliest phase of the Pentecostal revival one of its distinctive aspects was its interracial character. In marked contrast to mainline Protestantism, the Pentecostals fellowshipped together without respect to race. A. A. Boddy, commenting in 1912 upon this phenomenon, wrote:

> It was something very extraordinary, that white pastors from the South were eagerly prepared to go to Los Angeles to the Negroes, to have fellowship with them and to receive through their prayer and intercessions the blessings of the Spirit. And it is still more wonderful that these white pastors went back to the South and reported to the members of their congregations that they had been together with Negroes, that they had prayed in one spirit and received the same blessings as they.[8]

Elder C. H. Mason was to perform an important service to the movement, for he appears to have been the only early convert who came from a legally incorporated church and who could ordain persons whose status as clergymen was recognized by civil authorities. This official recognition was crucial to clergy who wished to perform marriages and other ministerial functions having legal consequences. There also were certain economic disabilities which accrued to clergy who were not identified with officially recognized church bodies, a typical one of which was the failure to qualify for reduced clergy rates on railroads. As a consequence

> . . . scores of white ministers sought ordination at the hands of Mason. Large numbers of white ministers, therefore, were to obtain ministerial credentials carrying the name of the Church of God in Christ. One group in Alabama and Texas eventually made an agreement with Mason in 1912 to use the name of his church but to issue ministerial credentials signed by their own leaders.[9]

This agreement lasted until 1914, when some of the white clergymen who were principals to it called a convention in Hot Springs, Arkansas, which resulted in the establishment of the Assembly of God. Apparently no Blacks, with the possible exception of G. T. Hayward, attended this organizing convention, though the invitation had been extended to all "Pentecostal Saints and Churches of God in Christ." With the founding of the Assembly of God it became clear that as Pentecostals moved toward institutionalizing the movement they would follow the prevailing cultural practice of segregating the races structurally. Thus, a movement which began in a shared religious experience and which was rooted in a theological consensus succumbed early to the acids of racist thinking. However, it should be pointed out that even today several of the predominantly white Pentecostal bodies have Black members.

The so-called interracial period in Pentecostalism did not come to an abrupt end with the establishment of the Assembly of God. Even within the Assembly, Blacks were members of local congregations. In 1916 a controversy developed in the Assembly of God which culminated in the withdrawal of a group popularly denoted as the "Jesus Name" ministers. These clergy dissented from the strongly worded trinitarian statement which the 1916 General Council of the Assemblies of God had adopted. The dissidents organized themselves into a body which they named The General Assembly of the Apostolic Churches. This group failed in its effort to gain official recognition from the federal government, which meant that its clergymen were vulnerable to the military service and similarly had no credentials permitting them to function as clergy with respect to the armed forces. As a consequence of this disability the General Assembly of the Apostolic Churches merged with a West Coast group which did have official standing with the federal government and became known as the Pentecostal Assemblies of the World, with G. T. Hayward, a Black Indianapolis evangelist, as its secretary.[10] Approximately 50 percent of the officers and members of the Pentecostal Assemblies group were Black. But this honeymoon in race relations did not continue for long. At the general conference of the Pentecostal Assemblies in 1924, the white clergy withdrew and left the organization to Hayward and his colleagues. Subsequently the whites organized The Pentecostal Ministerial Alliance in Jackson, Tennessee, in 1925.

During this period (1908-1924) the numerical strength of Pentecostalism was in the South, and it was perhaps inevitable that the regional racial patterns and prejudices would dictate the division of the churches into segregated structures. It should be remembered, however, that segregated structures have been characteristic of the religious establishment in America since the founding of the nation. One of the earliest organizational strategies employed by predominantly white bodies was to place Blacks into separate congregations or judicatories under the supervision of white leadership. The Church of God employed this strategy in a 1926 action when provision was made for its Negro members to have their own General Assembly with the stipulation that the "General Overseer" must always be white. This arrangement was continued until 1966. Similarly, the interracial Fire-Baptized Holiness Church, which had a sizable Black constituency from its founding in 1898, was split ten years later when the minority congregations voted, in the face of pressure from Southern whites, to form their own organization. In 1926 this Black group adopted its present name, The Fire-Baptized Holiness Church of God of the Americas.[11]

BLACK PENTECOSTALISM:
FAITH AND ORDER, LIFE AND WORK

Most Blacks first encountered Christianity under the aegis of Baptist or Methodist churches and the majority of Black Christians maintain this affiliation. It follows that the early Pentecostal movement, like the earlier Holiness gatherings, consisted of persons who had severed their initial denominational ties. They were, and are, often referred to as "come-outers." Holiness and Pentecostal evangelists and missionaries frequently encountered suspicion and sometimes violent resistance from both the established churches and civil authorities. C. H. Mason, for example, reports that he was shot at, personally assaulted, or hailed before the courts on more than one occasion.[12] Persons who were persuaded by the teaching of Pentecostal preachers usually withdrew from their churches and formed small congregations, meeting in houses or other temporary accommodations. In contrast to the mainline churches, some Holiness bodies became Pentecostal in doctrine through accepting tongue-speaking as a sign of the baptism of the Spirit. This was the case with the Church of God in Christ. Elder C. P. Jones, who was a co-founder with C. H. Mason of the church in 1896, was averse to the new doctrine which Mason brought from Azusa Street, and he and those who shared his convictions withdrew the right hand of fellowship from the members holding Pentecostal convictions.[13] Mason and thirteen clergymen who were persuaded by his teaching met shortly thereafter in what is referred to as the First Assembly of the Church of God in Christ.

During the eleven-year existence of the Jones-Mason body a dozen or so churches had been established in Tennessee, Oklahoma, Arkansas, and Mississippi. Following the Jones-Mason break, lawsuits were instituted to determine whether the earlier Church of God in Christ (Holiness) or its schismatic wing could exercise jurisdiction over congregations and their properties. When the litigation was completed, Mason and his followers were given authority over the churches in Tennessee, but their petitions were denied in Arkansas. By 1910 Mason had consolidated his leadership of the Church of God in Christ (Pentecostal) and Elder C. P. Jones continued his leadership in the Holiness body.[14]

To this point we have focused our attention primarily upon the Church of God in Christ because it was so pivotal in the early days of American Pentecostalism and was the first Black Pentecostal denomination, and because it continues to be the largest among the more than two hundred Pentecostal bodies in the nation. The Church of God in Christ asserts that it has a worldwide constituency estimated to be as large as three million. In 1970 the church claimed a membership of one million in the United States alone.

W. J. Hollenweger, in his useful survey of Black Pentecostal bodies in the United States,[15] divides them into five categories as to doctrine: (1) those teaching the three-crisis experience; (2) those teaching the two-crisis experience; (3) the oneness of "Jesus Only" groups; (4) the "Father Only" organization; and (5) those groups which do not fit neatly into any of the above categories. The largest group by far are those that teach the three-crisis experience—i.e., conversion, or regeneration, or justification; sanctification; baptism of the Spirit with tongue-speaking. The two-crisis experience groups are distinguished from the three-crisis experience churches by their insistence that sanctification is a lifelong process which only begins at conversion. The "Jesus Only" groups find biblical proof for their distinctiveness in the baptismal formula "in the Name of Jesus" and in Jesus' statement, "I and my Father are One." The School of the Prophets, which is the only church body identified by Hollenweger as a "Father Only" organization, baptizes in the "Name of the Father."

Whatever differences in doctrine may distinguish major Black Pentecostal bodies from each other, they have certain characteristics in common. As has been pointed out, Pentecostalism among Blacks was a Southern, rural phenomenon in its early years. This fact is reflected in the decision of the Church of God in Christ to set its annual convocations in the period November 25-December 15 so as to conform to the agricultural calendar when "crops were all harvested and enough finances and other provisions were available which would enable them to attend and support a national meeting."[16] Similarly, their membership, like that of their white counterparts, has usually been drawn from the less privileged socio-economic segment of the population.

The polity of Black Pentecostals is episcopal, although the title denominating the person exercising highest authority may be variously that of bishop, superintendent, apostle, or general overseer. Episcopal jurisdictions may be defined by state lines or may encompass larger or smaller geographical areas. Frequently bishops will exercise jurisdictions in territories that overlap. This latter circumstance is due to the fact that most Pentecostal churches have sprung up at the initiative of individual clergy and episcopal jurisdiction is exercised by the prelate to whom that founding clergyman attaches himself. It is also the case that many Pentecostal churches are "free-standing" and are not affiliated with any larger body—thus they are Pentecostal as to doctrine but congregational as to polity.

The worship in Black Pentecostal churches is not distinctive save with respect to tongue-speaking and an emphasis upon healing. The singing, the praying, the dancing, the instrumental music, including horns and percussion, the testimonies, and the vigorous homiletical style of the preachers are also characteristic of other small churches in urban areas. Indeed, the Black Pentecostals continue a worship tradition that developed, in its main features, in Black congregations as far back as the eighteenth century. It is a fact that as Black Christians in the major Protestant denominations began more and more to conform to the worship style of the established white churches, this historic worship tradition was exiled to the unaffiliated, if not alienated, church groups, many of whom were Pentecostal or Holiness in doctrine. In the rural South, however, the historic worship tradition has tended to persist in all churches. While caveats are being noted, it should be observed that this style of worship is not "peculiarly Black" in any essential sense, since it emerged in the course of the evangelical revivals in the first half of the nineteenth century. One distinguishing aspect of worship in Black churches has to do not so much with the content of worship as with the consciousness of the worshippers. This consciousness is informed by the fact that the worshippers are members of an oppressed minority with all the social, economic, and political encumbrances that inhere in that status. This consciousness informs the way in which the worship is carried out, and the way in which its content is appropriated by the believers.

Pentecostalism has grown among Blacks not because of central direction from a denominational bureaucracy, but because of the zeal and conviction of individual clergymen who have literally built their congregations from nothing save perhaps a few relatives and "folks from down home." Often a church meets in a building which is provided by the pastor and may survive in its initial months and years because of his willingness to sacrifice his own salary in order to have the enterprise succeed. As a consequence, Pentecostal churches tend to be dominated by their clergy, who after all have the largest investment of time and funds in their corporate life. The question may be legitimately asked why Pentecostalism has such persuasive appeal—particularly among Blacks, who formerly counted themselves to be Baptists or Methodists. There is, of course, the theological answer: God willed it. But without wishing to limit the freedom of God, one discovers other reasons which may be offered in partial explanation. The movement was born in a time when the civil and social situation of Blacks in America had bottomed out in what Rayford Logan called the "nadir" of the race.[17] Mob violence and lynching were on an upward curve in the South, and Blacks lived on the thin edge of terror. It was also a time of economic dislocation in which survival in the economy of Southern agriculture was very tenuous indeed. The period was marked by a farm-to-city and South-to-North migration which began as a trickle in the 1890's and reached a flood tide during and immediately following World War I. That migration continues, somewhat abated, to the present day. This highly mobile population inundated urban areas of the Northeast, West and Midwest that were totally unprepared to absorb them. These rural Blacks sometimes transferred their church memberships to the established religious bodies in the cities, but many found the churches as little attuned to their needs as were the social, economic, and political sectors of the larger society. Many abandoned the church and were lost, but still others turned to Pentecostalism, which was peculiarly suited to provide a kind of spiritual and religious structure in the midst of a bewildering new environment.

In a religious sense Pentecostalism was an antidote to and a critique of the failure of established church bodies adequately to minister to the personal and religious needs of the new urban dwellers. Though one can point to a number of large Black Pentecostal congregations, they tend to be the exception rather than the rule. The bulk of them have remained comparatively small and have thus retained an intimate character which lends identity, dignity, and a sense of self-affirmation to the "victims" of the impersonal urban culture. Moreover, since most of these congregations have been "preached out," i.e., they were organized and grew under the aegis of their founder-pastor, the personal attention which the members received was reenforcing and provided an institutional benchmark to persons who might not otherwise belong to anything. This ministry to individuals reflects both a pastoral concern on the part of the pastor and a prudential, political stratagem calculated to insure the financial health and stability of the congregation. Of course, this latter observation may be made of non-Pentecostal small churches as well.

Churches are the only institutions in Black communities belonging to and controlled by the people to which access is not proscribed on the basis of social, economic, or political considerations. As such they have always been the primary arena in which leadership, charisma, or other talents, gifts, ambitions, and graces could find expression. Pentecostal churches, like most other Black denominations, have not insisted upon an educated clergy and have rather placed greater emphasis upon doctrinal correctness and a demonstrated capacity for leadership. Familiarity with the Scriptures, firm doctrinal conviction, and experiential testimony are the indispensable credentials for access to clergy leadership in a Pentecostal congregation. These and the conviction that one has received a divine call to preach. It is conventional wisdom that, in addition to its religious function within a given community, the church functions as an important outlet for the various potentials for lay and clerical leadership within the community. This is true in any community, but it is especially crucial in Black communities, where the social fabric affords few other opportunities for service and self-expression.

The steady movement to cities both within and without the South is dramatically illustrated in the fact that whereas in 1900 26.6 percent of Blacks lived in metropolitan areas, by 1970 the percentage had risen to 70 percent. Pentecostalism, like the older Protestant churches among Blacks, has grown mainly in the cities and is not properly classified as a rural church body. I have already referred to social and economic elements in the urban environment which have contributed to the attractive intimacy of the Pentecostal churches. There are religious reasons as well. Pentecostalism as belief, as pietistic life style, and as moral teaching tends to function as a barrier against the erosion of long-held beliefs and also as a protective communal shield against the acids of liberal (rationalistic) or nonspiritual thought.

From the beginning, Pentecostals knew themselves to be under strong discipline insofar as life style was concerned. Pentecostal churches have usually prohibited their members from smoking, drinking, seeking divorce, dancing (outside of the church), and indulging in so-called "worldly pleasures," which may or may not include attending or participating in athletic contests. The degree of strictness with which these demands are enforced varies from group to group, or indeed from congregation to congregation. Some Pentecostal bodies prohibit using cosmetics or wearing such popular dress styles as shorts and mini-skirts. On the other hand, I heard a Pentecostal radio preacher on a New York station encouraging his listeners to attend a fashion show sponsored by his "temple" for the benefit of the building fund. Similarly, it is becoming more and more evident that some more affluent Pentecostal clergy are beginning to outdo their counterparts in some other Black churches with their status-symbol cars, their commodious suburban homes, and the formal "appreciation banquets" they now sponsor. It is this seeming exploitation of the poor as reflected in the dress and life style of the clergy that makes some churches in the Black communities vulnerable to the commonly heard criticism that they are parasitic upon rather than contributing to the upbuilding of the community.

The focus of Pentecostal doctrine and life style is on the assurance of salvation for the individual believer. As a consequence, congregations tend not to be actively involved in the struggle for racial justice. The formal posture of the Church of God in Christ illustrates this point. The preamble to the 1972 version of its Amended Charter, Constitution and By-Laws contains the following statements:

> We believe that Governments are God-Given Institutions for the benefit of mankind. We admonish and exhort our members to honor magistrates and civil authorities and to respect and obey civil laws.
> We declare our loyalty to the President of the United States and to the Constitution of the United States of America. We pledge allegiance and fidelity to the Republic for which it stands
> However, as God-fearing, peace-loving, and law-abiding people, we claim our heritage and natural right to worship God according to the dictates of our own conscience. Therefore, we abhor war, for we believe that the shedding of human blood or the taking of human life is contrary to the teachings of our Lord and Savior Jesus Christ. And as a body of Christian believers, we are adverse to war in all its forms and believe in the peaceful settlement of all international disputes.[18]

This declaration of the church's attitude towards the nation and towards civil authorities was issued at a time when the Black community was becoming increasingly suspicious that the institutions which this preamble affirms were in actual opposition to the best interests of the race. It is also remarkable that this statement duplicates in its essentials similar affirmations made in 1952 without taking cognizance of the momentous changes which took place in the intervening years. One would have supposed that some minimal notice might have been taken of the accelerated quest for social justice even if the liberation rhetoric of the Black nationalists was deemed to be unacceptable. While excessive weight should not be given to the formal principles, their reiteration in 1972 defines the continuing conservative outlook at the highest levels of leadership in the Church. [19] Though we have referred here to the Church of God in Christ, there is no evidence that other Pentecostal denominations have pioneered in these matters either. Nevertheless, numerous instances can be documented in which local churches have engaged in aggressive ministries aimed at improving the quality of life for their members and for the communities in which they are located. I know personally a number of outstanding clergy in the New York metropolitan area who are leading their congregations in community programs including day-care centers, prison ministries, headstart schools, and employment services, and in programs designed to feed the poor, to rehabilitate the drug addict or alcoholic, and to bring the Gospel to everyone. The names of some Pentecostal ministers are notable in the political arena and their support is solicited by candidates for public office. Similarly, some Pentecostal clergy participated conspicuously in the nonviolent movement headed by Martin Luther King, Jr., and are continuing to engage locally in the quest for social and economic justice.[20] One observes also a growing concern for the education of clergy and for the continuing education of clergy and lay persons as well. Bible schools and lay institutes have sprung up throughout the nation sponsored by various Pentecostal groupings.[21] And whatever may be said about the failures of these churches to engage the social, economic, and political inequities in this world with a view towards changing them, their distinctive doctrines are, in the view of their committed adherents, biblically warranted and experientially validated truths of ultimate consequence for one's eternal salvation.

POWER AND POLITICS

The posture of Pentecostal churches towards their Protestant counterparts has traditionally been highly critical and characterized by an arrogance derived from the belief that they, the Pentecostals, have discovered "the truth" and that outside of their circle there is no salvation. This feeling of exclusiveness is still the attitude of some church bodies. Nevertheless, there is evidence that Pentecostal congregations are becoming more ecumenical at the local level. It is not unusual to see denominational officers joining their counterparts in the mainline churches at state or local ecumenical gatherings. There are also signs that "Black consciousness" has had the effect of uniting clergy across denominational lines in causes and projects affecting the community. In this respect it should be noted that despite the nominal power of the bishops in the overall church structure, at the level of the local congregations the pastors and the people are virtually autonomous. Indeed the struggle within some Pentecostal bodies today arises out of the effort of national officials to exert control over property and pulpits which bear the name of the national church. It is the problem of bringing under the hierarchical yoke churches which have been created by the energy and sometimes by the personal funds of individual pastors. The weakness of the episcopacy within some of these groups has also contributed to the excessive proliferation of congregations within given geographical areas. This in turn has had the effect of keeping individual congregations small and impotent. One reason for the limited community impact of these churches is their limited human and fiscal resources. Many pastors work at secular occupations in order to be able to maintain their pulpits. These latter comments would be equally applicable to churches in the Black community where the polity is congregational, as in the case of the Baptist churches, or where the central authority is unable to enforce standards for ordination. There is a sense in which it is valid to observe that the Pentecostal churches mirror the situation of the majority of Black churches in the urban scene. The small size which is conducive to intimacy and in which access to leadership is fairly easy also helps to make them impotent as a social force. The ease with which one can become a leader, fed by the absence of rigorous, enforceable educational prerequisites, means that clergy are generally poorly prepared to cope with the complex problems of urban life. Conversely, it is a tribute to the native ability and charismatic gifts of these men and women that so many do sustain their posts in a highly competitive environment.

The Pentecostal movement has been an arena in which many Black women have been able to rise to positions of congregational leadership. In the more fully organized and centralized church bodies, women tend to fill leadership roles traditionally considered to be "women's work," i.e., as head of women's auxiliaries, as evangelists, and as church "mothers" at both local and national levels. But in many unaffiliated Pentecostal congregations and in some loosely organized national bodies, it is not exceptional to find women clergy as pastors.[22] The best example is in the United Holy Church in America, where women have been ordained and have pastored churches since its organization in 1900.

PROSPECTS: PENTECOSTALISM AND LIBERATION

For all its distinctiveness of doctrine, Black Pentecostalism faces the same future as other Black churches. There are new currents flowing in these communities, and these currents, powered by a renewed ethnic consciousness, are forcing new questions upon Black institutions. In some respects Black churches are just beginning to feel tremors forecasting changes that have reached urgent proportions in white religious bodies. Langdon Gilkey has summarized them very nicely:

> ... The central axis of religion has shifted from matters of ultimate salvation, of judgment and justification before God in eternity, and of heaven and hell, to questions of the meaning, necessity and usefulness of religion for this life—be it self-fulfillment and self-integration, for ethical norms and moral efficacy, for "meaning in life," for self-affirmation, or for what the existentialists call "authentic-existence."[23]

While these religious questions are being asked from within the major white groupings, they are being asked in more strident political terms by persons from outside the Black churches. Moreover, the

Black secular community has developed alternative institutions and ideologies which are self-consciously in competition with the churches. The Black Muslims (Nation of Islam) are an outstanding example of both of these phenomena. The questions that one hears being addressed to the churches time and again are: How can you purge yourself of the religion of your oppressors, which is itself anti-liberation? When will you get on board in the liberation struggle, or does your religion cause you to be satisfied with the status quo? What, concretely, is your institution or your ideology contributing to the struggle? It is no defense to argue that the questions themselves arise out of ignorance of Black religion and its institutions. The mood of the communities is increasingly pragmatic and is notable for its expectation that the end of the world is imminent, brought on not by the activity of God, but through the revolutionary struggle of oppressed people. Neither Pentecostal bodies nor their constituencies have felt the full force of these questions, but in the years ahead such issues will surely be a factor in determining the strength and shape of the churches. It will be no easy task for these churches whose basic posture is individual and eschatological to accommodate a corporate and temporal perspective. The outcome will depend very much upon the ability of the second and third generation of leaders to sustain a creative tension between the emphasis upon a particular religious experience and the demand for the concrete embodiment of faith in actions directed towards the pressing problems of the community.

Notes

1. Hollenweger, "Black Pentecostal Concept: Interpretations and Variations," *Concept*, Special Issue, No. 30 (June, 1970), 9.
2. For a full discussion of this debate, see Leonard Lovett, "Perspective on the Black Origins of the Contemporary Pentecostal Movement," *The Journal of the Interdenominational Theological Center*, I (Fall, 1973), 36-49.
3. All biblical references in this essay are to the King James version.
4. John T. Nichol, *The Pentecostals* (Plainfield, N.J., 1966), pp. 32-33.
5. Joseph Patterson, German R. Ross, and Julia M. Atkins (eds.), *History and Formative Years of the Church of God in Christ with Excerpts from the Life and Works of Its Founder, Bishop C. H. Mason* (Memphis, 1969), p. 17.
6. *Ibid.*, p. 16.
7. *Ibid.*
8. Quoted in Hollenweger, p. 15. Boddy was a long-time leader of British Pentecostalism.
9. Vinson Synan, *The Holiness-Pentecostal Movement in the United States* (Grand Rapids, 1971), p. 169.
10. *Ibid.*, pp. 170-172. Synan provides a quite detailed discussion of this formative period in the Pentecostal movement.
11. Nichol, pp. 104-108. Cf. Synan, pp. 170-173.
12. Patterson, *History*, pp. 23-24.
13. Charles H. Pleas, *Fifty Years of Achievement: Church of God in Christ* (Memphis, 1957), p. 7.
14. *Ibid.*
15. Hollenweger, "Black Pentecostal Concept." See also his larger work, *The Pentecostals* (Minneapolis, 1972).

16. Pleas, p. 19.
17. Rayford W. Logan, *The Betrayal of the Negro: From Rutherford B. Hayes to Woodrow Wilson* (New York, 1965). This book was originally published under the title *The Negro in American Life and Thought: The Nadir, 1877-1901.*
18. "Declaration of Faith and Preamble," *Amendment to the Charter, Constitution, and By-Laws of the Church of God in Christ, Inc.* (unpublished offset copy, Church of God in Christ, 1972). Cf. "The Creed, Discipline, Rules of Order and Doctrine of the Pentecostal Assemblies of the World," quoted in Hollenweger, "Black Pentecostal Concept," p. 63.
19. It is noteworthy that the garbage collectors' strike in Memphis, which Martin Luther King was supporting at the time of his assassination, held its major mass meetings at the Mason Temple, which houses the headquarters of the Church of God in Christ.
20. In the House of the Lord Congregation of the Reverend Herbert D. Daughtry in Brooklyn, New York, there are groups whose purpose it is to participate in marches and demonstrations as a witness of the church and its concern for the world.
21. Pentecostalists have been slow in developing institutions of higher education. The Church of God in Christ supports Saints Junior College in Lexington, Mississippi, a school begun at the instigation of elders in Mississippi in 1917. In addition, the church established the C. H. Mason School of Theology in 1968 as a constituent part of the Interdenominational Theological Center in Atlanta, Georgia.
22. For a statement defining the place of women in the Church of God in Christ, see Bishop O. T. Jones, "Dedicated to the National Women's Convention of the Church of God in Christ," quoted in Pleas, *Fifty Years of Achievement*, pp. 35-37.
23. Langdon Gilkey, "Sources of Protestant Theology in America," *Daedalus*, XCVI (Winter, 1967), 73.

8 THE HOLINESS MOVEMENT IN SOUTHERN APPALACHIA

NATHAN L. GERRARD

The term *Holiness movement* refers generically to dozens of sect-like groups with thousands of churches all over the nation and millions of members who strive to achieve spiritual perfection through strong emotional experience allegedly inspired by the beliefs and practices of primitive Christianity. Speaking in tongues is a frequent part of their religious experience. It has been estimated that there are approximately five million Holiness people in the United States alone.

There is much disagreement as to the most appropriate ways of achieving the state of holiness. The range is from the self-contained piety of the Adventists to the highly visible emotional fury of some "Jesus Only" churches. Although almost all Holiness churches originated as lower-class sects or as sects of newly ascending social classes in evangelical and scriptural opposition to the formalism of the dominant established churches, each social class develops a kind of Holiness church that is congenial to its life style.

Southern Appalachian people, particularly small-town and open-country dwellers, take their religion seriously. A majority of Appalachians still adhere to Protestant fundamentalism; i.e., belief in the literal interpretation of the Scriptures, and Puritan morality, despite the social and economic changes embodying urban values that have taken place in the region during the twentieth century. Fundamentalism is still quite strong in religious groups that at one time evinced sectarian tendencies but are now the dominant churches of the lower and upper middle classes—Baptists, Methodists, and Presbyterians.

Nathan L. Gerrard is Professor and Chairman of the Department of Sociology, Morris Harvey College, Charleston, West Virginia. He received his A.B. and M.A. in urban sociology from the University of Chicago and his Ph.D. at Columbia University, where he specialized in juvenile delinquency. Since coming to West Virginia in 1959, Dr. Gerrard's research interests have included the cultural and social patterns of the "hollows," the communities of the non-farm rural poor in West Virginia. He has maintained continuous and intimate contact with a serpent-handling church for the last ten years. His publications include "The Gang," *British Journal of Criminology* (April, 1964); "The Serpent-Handling Religions of West Virginia," *Trans-action* (May, 1968); and *Churches of the Stationary Poor in Southern Appalachia* (1970), edited by John D. Photiadis and Harry K. Schwarzweller.

The religious heritage of the region, however, is preserved in nearly pristine purity in the churches of the lower classes, particularly in remote valleys or hollows—pronounced "hollers," the communities of the nonfarm rural poor. This heritage is fundamentalistic, sectarian, and experiential. Originating in European religious dissent, it developed against a background of almost two centuries of subsistence agriculture, durable kinship ties, individualism, independence, and egalitarianism. It was shaped in large part and stimulated by the numerous and almost continuous revivals of the nineteenth century, and persisted in almost complete isolation from the urbanization which was going on in most of the rest of American society. The contemporary preservers of this heritage are indeed "Yesterday's People," and to an outsider, their religious beliefs and practices may very well appear strange.

I shall discuss the socioeconomic life style of these "contemporary primitives," the religious beliefs, practices, and structure of their churches, and the social and psychological functions which account for the viability of these churches in the modern United States. I shall call these churches *Holiness churches of the stationary poor.*

A third of the families in Southern Appalachia can be called *poor* according to the standards of an affluent America. But the poor do not constitute a single homogeneous sociological group, and for our purposes we can distinguish two types of poor: the stationary poor and the upwardly mobile poor.

LIFE STYLES—THE UPWARDLY MOBILE POOR

Among the upwardly mobile poor, the heads of the family are regularly employed at tedious and backbreaking jobs as laborers, service workers, and farmers. They themselves have little hope for advancement. They make strenuous efforts, however, to lead respectable lives according to the standards of the middle class of their community. The prospect of welfare assistance is looked upon with repugnance, and they feel humiliated when, because of severe illness or accidents, they are forced to accept aid. The homes in which our upwardly mobile poor live are painted, in good repair, well scrubbed, and tidy. Clothes are clean, although patched, and the family income is carefully budgeted. Children are taught to respect their elders, especially those in authority, such as teachers, and their activities and associates outside the home tend to be supervised. The father, acutely aware that his own upward strivings have been blocked by his meager education, advises the older children to postpone marriage, and encourages them to finish high school. Both mother and father expect their children to enjoy a better life, to have a higher standard of living and a higher social position, than they themselves have, and they raise their children accordingly. Some of the mothers attend PTA meetings, where they observe closely the ways of middle-class mothers.

Parents of the upwardly mobile poor attend church almost as regularly as do the middle classes. The churches they attend are the churches of the lower middle class, the class with which the members of the upwardly mobile poor identify, and to which they aspire. In the rural communities of Southern Appalachia, such churches are likely to be Methodist and Baptist, sometimes Presbyterian. If the need for respectability is accompanied by a nostalgic yearning for the strict fundamentalism and some of the fervor of old-fashioned religion, they may join such evangelical churches as the several Churches of God, the Adventists, Churches of Christ, various Pentecostal churches, the Church of the Nazarene, and the Assemblies of God. Or within the major denominations they may join the Wesleyan Methodist Church, the General Association of Regular Baptists, and the Orthodox Presbyterian churches.

We have called these poor people upwardly mobile because while not many of the parents, particularly those over forty, will manage to move out of the ranks of the poor, their children probably will.

LIFE STYLES—THE STATIONARY POOR

The second group among the poor are those whose children probably will also be poor the rest of their lives. Working adults in these families are mostly unskilled and functionally illiterate. Their jobs tend to be seasonal or cyclical so that there are long periods of unemployment and underemployment. There are periods of hard times, and over the years the family income has to be supplemented by various kinds of welfare payments. Many of these families have been receiving public assistance for two or three generations. It is extremely difficult to save money even for necessities on their low, irregular incomes; getting cash involves a constant struggle. Frequently the family does not know where the next meal is coming from. Food is bought whenever anyone has cash or food stamps. During most of the month, purchases are made only for the day ahead. Members of the stationary poor are sick often and their medical care is poor.

The ceaseless struggle to make ends meet, to take care of the barest necessities, tends to foster a fatalistic outlook on life. This outlook can express itself in two sharply contrasting ways. The first is cynical and pessimistic. The sociologists sometimes call this "anomie." The attitude is: "Nothing good will ever happen to me." It is manifest in squalor, the failure to make the most of the little one has: dirty dishes in the sink; unrepaired, tattered furniture; litter in the rooms and around the unpainted shack; bugs and sometimes rats. It is also manifest in reckless hedonism, the conviction of those leading insecure, unpredictable lives that a pleasure postponed is a pleasure forever lost. A commonly encountered view is: "I'm going to live today. Who cares about tomorrow?" Reckless hedonism results in noisy drinking bouts, illegitimate births, incest, absenteeism or quitting jobs in order to go hunting or fishing, spur-of-the-moment purchases of luxuries when money is needed for necessities, and other kinds of behavior that are incomprehensible from a middle-class point of view.

Among the young adults of the stationary poor, a frequent manifestation of pessimistic fatalism is the attitude that too high a price should not be placed upon human life, not only upon the lives of others but also upon their own. A frequent response to the frictions and frustrations of their impoverished existence is physical violence, usually directed against friends or members of one's family. The bravery of Southern Appalachians in war is well known.

Perhaps the most extreme manifestation of pessimistic fatalism is to be found among the elderly, who have discovered over the years that recklessness inevitably brings painful consequences. They feel that their only alternative is to search for apathy, a state of mind which while devoid of pleasure is also devoid of pain. The quest for apathy is manifest not only in soporific types of alcoholism but also in the very high rates of the type of psychosis loosely called schizophrenia, in which apathy and withdrawal from the external world are central. This apathy is usually accompanied by very low self-esteem. Such persons feel they are so worthless they don't even have a right to complain. The quest for apathy is to be found in its most extreme form in the quest for final oblivion, in suicide. Suicide rates are highest among the stationary poor.

The second way in which the fatalistic outlook can express itself is religious. Religious fatalism is the feeling that one's destiny is in God's hands. Since they conceive of God as loving and forgiving, as well as righteous, many of the religious poor achieve a psychological poise which enables them to carry on despite the trials and tribulations of their position at the bottom of the social and economic pyramids.

In the mine disaster at Hominy Falls, West Virginia, press coverage was extensive. Particular attention was paid to the six men, all but given up for dead, who were trapped in a thirty-six-inch tunnel by rising water. One miner who was rescued after ten days was asked whether he would return to the mines. "I'll have to go over that with God," he said. "Whatever his plans are for me, that's what I'll do." The wife of another rescued man said she never doubted throughout the long wait that her husband would come out alive. "God told me he'd be all right," she said.

Unlike the upwardly mobile poor, the religious stationary poor do not hesitate very long before applying for welfare assistance when they are out of funds and out of work. They take their obligation to keep their families from going hungry more seriously than their worldly pride. I was present at a Holiness meeting when a member of the congregation voiced his opinion that welfare recipients were lazy and worthless. Although not more than one or two members of the congregation actually were receiving welfare, the response evoked was indignant and almost unanimous. The rugged individualist was castigated as unchristian.

As a matter of fact, religious fatalists are much less likely to be on welfare than are the pessimistic fatalists. Sober, scrupulous about money matters, and believing in giving an honest day's work in return for an honest day's pay, they are much less likely to be unemployed. I was informed by the manager of a chain of retail stores that quite a number of his cashiers are petty embezzlers, but that those who belong to Holiness churches are reliable and honest.

Although the women are far from compulsive housekeepers, the homes of the religious fatalists are almost as tidy as those of the upwardly mobile. Children are taught to be courteous and well-mannered. In other respects, the style of life of the religious fatalists of the stationary poor resembles the style of life of the upwardly mobile poor. The central difference is that to the religious fatalists among the stationary poor, success in the pursuit of holiness is much more important than worldly success. Their children are not discouraged from marrying young or from dropping out of school. I know a bright young Holiness man who at the age of twenty-one already has three children. He married at the age of sixteen with the encouragement of his parents because he was marrying a Holiness girl. With an elementary school education and an ever increasing family, he will probably be poor the rest of his life. In the meantime, he and his nineteen-year-old wife attend Holiness church sessions at least three nights a week, taking their children with them, and the general picture is of an affectionate and harmonious family.

THE HOLINESS CHURCHES

The religious stationary poor spend a great deal of time listening to religious radio and television programs sponsored by the established evangelical churches. The elderly, particularly, enjoy the faith-healing of Oral Roberts, and anyone who turns on a radio in Appalachia is aware that there are dozens of radio programs of highly emotional religious content to be heard almost any time of the day.

The religious stationary poor find the rituals of the conventional middle-class churches formalistic and unsatisfying, and they feel ill-at-ease in the presence of the well-dressed and the conventionally polite who go to these churches. They look upon the tight scheduling and the role-stability[1] of the services as both unholy and absurd. They call such churches and their members "stiff-necked."

They do not feel at home even in the established evangelistic churches which allow the members of the congregation some freedom of emotional expression. A member of the stationary poor once attended a Church of God service in his community. While he was listening to the services, he felt he was being moved by the Holy Ghost. He asked the minister for permission to testify. The minister, looking at his wrist watch, told him he could have five minutes, whereupon this member of the stationary poor walked out in indignation, never to return. In telling me the story, he said: "Brother Gerrard, the Holy Ghost does not wear a wrist watch!"

The stationary poor prefer to seek religious fellowship in their own unpainted one-room frame churches, in abandoned school houses, in barns, in crudely constructed tabernacles, in tents, or in each other's homes. There are thousands of such churches in rural Southern Appalachia. They are to be found on secondary and tertiary roads where land values are very low. They are the equivalent of the store-front churches of the city poor. The stranger who passes one of these churches will not recognize it as a church unless he looks closely. Then he might observe a cross on the roof constructed of two-by-fours nailed together, or "Jesus Saves" crudely printed in whitewash on the front or the sides.

Many of these churches do not have names, but are identified by the community in which they are located, such as Camp Creek, Scrabble Creek or Frazier's Bottom. Of those churches which do have names, "Jesus Only" is probably most common. "Church of All Nations" is another frequent name. Or there will be a variety of names preceded by the word "Free."

Even where a church has a name, there frequently is no identifying sign on the building or in the yard. People in the area, when asked, will immediately identify it as "Ed Blankenship's church," or "Brother Homer's church."

These churches are not owned by their congregations but by individuals who built their own churches in order to worship as freely as they pleased. Sometimes the owner dominates the services and lets people in or keeps them out according to personal whim. One very strong personality, the "owner" of his church, changes congregations about every two years. He expels the old congregation and recruits a new one, the converse of middle-class churches in which ministers are sometimes expelled but congregations never. There is much variation, however. Some owners are self-effacing and welcome anyone who comes.

The services and beliefs of these privately owned, unaffiliated mountain churches have been standardized by the almost continuous religious revivals of the nineteenth century, the earliest being the great Kentucky Revival of 1800 to 1803, which spread rapidly to Tennessee and adjacent states.

RELIGIOUS BELIEFS AND PRACTICES IN THE HOLINESS CHURCHES

In general, it can be said that the stationary poor carry individualism in religion to an extreme. Each man is indeed his own Pope. Since they lack the intellectual resources and will for doctrinal elaboration, the main emphasis is on emotional religious experience. Their theology is simple and concrete, and there is great variation in detail from local church to local church—and quite a bit from individual to individual within the same local church. Nevertheless, they all seem to share the belief that their religion represents a return to the purity of the Christians of the first century, and that the larger, more formalized churches are fallen and corrupt.

The theology, or foci of religious belief, of the churches serving the stationary poor can perhaps be best discussed under three headings: fundamentalism, other-worldliness, and perfectionism.

Fundamentalism. In these churches and among a large segment of the Appalachian poor, the Bible is seen as the sole justification of religious practices, with every word divinely inspired and literally true. Knowledge of the Bible is fragmentary, and passages are frequently cited out of context or in garbled form. Often there is no Bible in the church unless a member brings one, but this is not surprising since most members of the congregation, at least among the middle-aged and elderly, are functionally illiterate. Nevertheless, the members enjoy doctrinal disputes, and the older men in particular fancy themselves as biblical authorities. The issues argued, however, seldom involve conflicting interpretations of the same biblical passages, but are more likely to be a confrontation based upon apparently contradictory passages from different parts of the Bible. An outsider may sometimes get the impression that the cited "quotations" have been improvised in the heat of debate—chapter, verse, and all. The arguments in the disputes, like the testimonies and sermons, resemble streams of consciousness rather than logical discourse.

To the religious fatalists among the stationary poor, God is not a metaphysical abstraction but a real person. In fact, they often see him during vivid hallucinations, usually as a smiling, gentle Jesus. One Holiness church member, more literate than most in the congregation, remarked with a smile: "God isn't dead. He wasn't even sick when I talked to him this morning."

These people believe in the reality of the devil, who is hallucinated in various forms: sometimes with stereotyped horns and tail; sometimes as a loathsome insect; and sometimes, perhaps as a result of their economic deprivation, as a well-dressed man with white shirt, tie, and jacket. A Holiness church member once remarked in my presence: "When I think of the devil, I think of Mr. Mullins, the coal company's lawyer."

Other-worldliness. Not able to afford luxuries, the stationary poor often make a virtue out of necessity, and view the pleasures and vanities of the world as incongruent with a way of life guided by the Holy Spirit. Subject to taboo are liquor, movies, athletic events, beauty parlors, jewelry, and makeup. They regard the use of cigarettes and chewing tobacco as "filth of the flesh." Sometimes even coffee and soft drinks are proscribed, but most Holiness people, like other members of the stationary poor, spend a disproportionate share of their income on soft drinks, as much as a dollar a day when they have the cash.

However, despite their strong feelings about the evils of the world, they are completely indifferent to the *social gospel* and take no interest in politics even when temperance is an issue at election time, as it is so often in Appalachia. They believe it is useless to reform the social order, so they concentrate on saving individual souls. Often stigmatized as "ignorant Holy Rollers," they do not participate in the few voluntary associations which exist in mountain communities.

The other-worldliness of these people is also manifest in the fact that many believe in the more or less imminent end of the world by means of a cosmic catastrophe, and what they hear about events in the real world tends to reinforce this belief. They look forward to the second coming of Christ and the establishment of the millennium.

Perfectionism. The stationary poor who are members of Holiness churches believe it is possible to attain in this life, despite man's original sin, a spiritual state of being which is free not only of sinful deeds, but—much more important—of sinful desires. This belief contrasts with the teaching of the Catholic Church, which stresses that a state of holiness can be gradually achieved by a very few through monastic asceticism and meditation, and the teaching of the established evangelical churches, which emphasize that holiness may begin with an experience of emotional regeneration, but that holiness requires a long spiritual growth. However, the stationary poor, it seems, cannot afford to wait. They believe that anyone who believes strongly enough can achieve holiness instantaneously and completely through the direct operation of the Holy Spirit in a violent emotional experience. This is frequently preceded by an emotional upheaval during which the individual, awakened from spiritual indifference, agonizingly repents of his sins.

The experiences of *conversion* and *sanctification* are stimulated and encouraged by such familiar revival techniques as highly emotional sermons and testimonies, repeating and emphasizing the theme of damnation and salvation—especially salvation. Singing by the congregation, with hand-clapping and foot-stomping, is particularly effective. Even the smallest churches have members who play guitars, harmonicas, fiddles, and perhaps even cymbals, tambourines, and accordions. The pronounced beat and rhythm are contagious and create group rapport. The participant tends to lose his self-consciousness and becomes highly suggestible to the central theme of the songs, sermons, and testimonies.

Subjective evidence of *sanctification* is the experience of feeling oneself in direct communion with God, the feeling that one has become a passive instrument of his will, and the attendant feeling of joy and rapture. External evidence is involuntary behavior that cannot be explained except in terms of control by the Holy Spirit: speaking in tongues, shrieking, convulsive dancing, rolling on the floor, jerking, jumping, and even passing into states of unconsciousness. Services in Holiness churches are noisy; the very walls and floors seem to rattle with the activity.

While roles in the church are culturally stereotyped, i.e., dancer, singer, faith-healer, testifier, etc., enactment is almost completely unstructured and spontaneous. Role-playing is very fluid, depending on the individual member's mood at the moment. Members who are passive on one occasion may dominate the meeting on another with their dancing and testifying. This constitutes an important appeal of the church, for if one feels the power of the Holy Spirit, there are almost no structural obstacles to immediate, untrammeled expression. In fact, such obstacles would be considered sacrilegious. This is one important reason why religious sessions are sometimes five or six hours long. No one would consider bringing the meeting to an end until every member who was so disposed had been given the opportunity to express his religious urges fully.

The fact that role-playing is fluid, that no distinction is made between ministry and laity, no record of membership is kept, no dues are collected, and that participants tend to sample other churches in the area indicates a social organization that is almost anarchical. I am not too happy with the terms *sect* or *church* to describe the religious fellowships of the stationary poor. Both terms connote a firmness of structure that does not exist. Perhaps the term *religious band* would be more precise.

The extreme individualism of the participants in the religious bands of the stationary poor frequently leads to religious innovations that most of us would label as queer or immoral or even pathological. The members of one Holiness church in Kanawha County, West Virginia, for example, believe in the immortality not only of the soul but of the body. To them the body is the temple of the soul, and if the soul is pure, the temple will last forever. Members of other Holiness churches refer to this group as the "Neverdies."

Members of another Holiness church in the same county practice a form of polygamy. If a married man talks to a married woman who is not his wife, and both feel the power of the Holy Ghost, they will leave their spouses and start a new "marriage" which they believe has been made in heaven. After the heavenly bliss has worn off, they will return to their spouses, to resume what they call the "marriages made in the world."

SOCIAL AND PSYCHOLOGICAL FUNCTIONS OF HOLINESS GROUPS

Although the evidence is inconclusive and indirect, Holiness churches of the stationary poor appear to be holding their own in rural Southern Appalachia, and are even springing up in Northern cities where there are substantial settlements of rural migrants from the Southern Appalachian region. The precarious nature of physical survival and the loneliness and emotional starvation of social life in the scattered settlements of the frontier explain, in important part, the appeal of revivalism in the past. The problem is to explain the viability of the Holiness churches of the stationary poor in the present, when the level of living has been raised considerably and isolation has been greatly reduced by paved roads, mass communication, consolidated schools, and other innovations embodying urban values.

It would seem that the rural Holiness churches are viable because they serve to alleviate anxieties generated by status deprivation, guilt and illness, and last, but not unimportantly, because they supply recreation in areas of the region where recreational facilities are scarce.

It is not biological deprivation associated with low economic status that bothers the stationary poor so much as status deprivation. Increased contact with urban standards of achievement and success has developed a new awareness of social and cultural advantages they do not possess. Self-esteem based on the egalitarianism of their rural tradition is shaken, and strong feelings of social inadequacy emerge. In the religious fellowship of their church they experience an enhanced sense of personal worth and dignity. They enjoy status security as a member of God's elect.

They have been reared in a guilt culture and thus tend to interpret their present misfortunes and occasional moral lapses as signs of being unworthy of the affection and approval of their primary "we" group. In accordance with their religious beliefs, guilt means "sin," the disapproval of a righteous God, the collective representation of the most important values of their group. The burden of sin is a very heavy one to bear, and unless relieved may lead to mental illness or other aberrations. But in the religious fellowship of the Holiness church they experience conversion and sanctification, they are reconciled with their group—their God—and they gain the psychological poise to carry on in the face of the trials and stresses of their existence at the bottom of the socioeconomic pyramid.

There is a great deal of illness among the poor, and medical facilities are scarce and inaccessible. Especially the older poor suffer from a wide variety of physical ailments. Participation in religious services of the Holiness churches, particularly the faith-healing rituals, enables them to ignore or to minimize their ailments.

Holiness church services are spontaneous, exciting, rhythmical, dramatic, and sometimes even humorous. Unlike many participants in conventional churches, the participants in Holiness churches are seldom bored. The general atmosphere is one of joy and pleasure despite the occasional exhibitions of agony attendant upon the conversion experience and the sober recital of ailments that precede faith-healing rituals. "Jesus is fun" is a cry that is sometimes heard during services, or a preacher might say: "Let's all have a good time in Jesus tonight."

It is well to keep in mind that unlike the pessimistic fatalists the religious fatalists are poor not because they are not thrifty—their religion forbids them to spend money on luxuries; not because they lack responsible work habits—their religion teaches them to be conscientious; not because they lack social skills—their religion teaches them to be loving toward others. They are poor because like the pessimistic fatalists they drop out of school early, work at relatively unskilled jobs, marry young, and have many children. They have many virtues which still have meaning and relevance for social life in the contemporary United States.

THE SNAKE HANDLERS

Perhaps the most numerous of the bizarre churches in Southern Appalachia are the serpent handlers. They are scorned by other Holiness churches as "possessed by the devil" and by the educated as emotionally disturbed. A service in one of these churches is likely to include tongue-speaking, hymn singing, healing prayers, and the other familiar expressions of Holiness worship. But in addition there is a period of ten or fifteen minutes when volunteers from the congregation come forward and pick up snakes as they continue to speak praises of God. The snakes used are rattlesnakes and copperheads. This dangerous ritual adds much to the excitement of the

service, and indeed in the days preceding the occasion it is anticipated with some relish by members of the congregation.

The two or three dozen serpent-handling churches in Southern
Appalachia justify the use of poisonous snakes in their religious
services by quoting Mark 16:15-18:

> ... And these signs shall follow them that believe: In my name shall they cast
> out devils; they shall speak with new tongues; *they shall take up serpents*,
> and if they drink any deadly thing it shall not hurt them; they shall lay hands
> on the sick and they shall recover.

Weston La Barre[2] believes that the founder of Christian serpent-
handling was George Went Hensley, who initiated the ritual in rural
Grasshopper Valley, Tennessee, during the first decade of the twentieth century. Hensley evangelized widely from Tennessee to Florida,
particularly in Kentucky. Serpent-handling became widely diffused
in the South, and in 1945 there occurred the first recorded death
from snakebite suffered in a religious service.

Since then, about twenty-three more deaths have been reported in
the press, taking place in Georgia, Alabama, Tennessee, Kentucky,
and other Southern states. In 1955 Hensley himself, then seventy
years old, died in Florida of snakebite. Five deaths have occurred in
West Virginia since 1961, the most recent in 1974.

Serpent-handling has been outlawed by the state legislatures of
Kentucky, Virginia, and Tennessee, and by municipal ordinance in
North Carolina. Despite the law, however, serpent-handling persists. I
am told that the Harlan, Kentucky, region has more serpent-handling
groups than any other area in the country.

Serpent-handling is still legal in West Virginia. The two centers in
the state are the Scrabble Creek Church of All Nations in Fayette
County, about thirty-seven miles from Charleston, and the Church of
Jesus in Jolo, McDowell County, one of the most depressed sections
of the state. Serpent-handling is also practiced sporadically elsewhere
in the state, usually led by visitors from Scrabble Creek or Jolo.

The Jolo church, located close to the Virginia and Kentucky borders, attracts persons from both sides in addition to West Virginia.
Members of the Scrabble Creek church speak with awe of the Jolo services, where members pick up large handsful of poisonous snakes, fling
them to the ground, pick them up, and thrust them under their skirts or
blouses and dance ecstatically. My wife and I were present at a church
service in Scrabble Creek when visitors from Jolo covered their heads
with clusters of snakes and wore them as crowns.

Serpent-handling was introduced to Scrabble Creek in 1941 by a
coal miner from Harlan, Kentucky. The practice did not take hold in
the area until 1946, when the present leader of the Scrabble Creek
church, then a member of the Church of God, first took up serpents.
The four or five original serpent-handlers in Fayette County met at

one another's homes until given the use of an abandoned one-room schoolhouse in Big Creek. In 1959, when their number swelled several times over, they moved to the larger church in Scrabble Creek, two miles away.

About a dozen members of the church have suffered from snake-bites in the seven years of our study (my wife and I were present on two of these occasions). Although there have been few deaths, each incident has been widely and unfavorably publicized in the area, particularly by members of other Holiness churches who abhor the practice. The serpent-handlers for their part say that the Lord causes a snake to strike in order to refute scoffers' claims that the fangs have been pulled to render the snake harmless. Each recovery from snakebite they see as a miracle wrought by the Lord, and each death a sign that the Lord "really had to show the scoffers how dangerous it is to obey his commandments, and how necessary it is to live with the Lord." Since adherents believe that death brings one to the throne of the Lord, some express an eagerness to die when God decides they are ready. Those who have been bitten seem to receive special deference from members of the church.

The social and psychological functions served by the Scrabble Creek church are probably very much the same as those served by the more conventional churches in the Holiness movement. In addition, the dangerous rituals probably help to validate the members' claims to holiness. The claim that one is a living saint on the same spiritual level as the early Apostles is, after all, extremely pretentious even in a sacred society, and particularly difficult to maintain in a secular society. The fact that one regularly risks his life for his religion is seen as a conclusive test. Serpent-handlers stress over and over: "I'm afraid of snakes like anybody else, but when God anoints me, I handle them with joy." If one is not bitten, or if one is bitten and recovers through prayer, or even if one is bitten and dies—all serve to validate one's claim to holiness.

Our study of the serpent-handlers of Scrabble Creek left us with the definite impression that their worship and fellowship constituted a form of group psychotherapy for individuals who otherwise would be vulnerable to mental and behavioral aberrations because of the deprivations and frustrations associated with conditions of their existence as members of the stationary working class.

Notes

1. By role-stability I am referring to the fact that in conventional churches, the same person delivers the sermon every Sunday, the same person plays the organ, the same people sing in the choir.
2. The following paragraph uses La Barre's account from *They Shall Take Up Serpents: Psychology of the Southern Snake-Handling Cult* (Minneapolis, 1962).

The Impact of Charismatics
on the Local Congregation

9 *A STORY OF INTEGRATION*

RAYMOND W. DAVIS

My first experience with the charismatic movement came at the 1970 General Convention of the Episcopal Church, which met in Houston, Texas. On the first Monday of the convention, I had spent the morning listening to debates in both Houses of the convention. The Episcopal Church was in a state of tension and anxiety and there were dire predictions of schism and division. The atmosphere was gloomy and negative. After leaving the House of Deputies where I had listened to much negative debate, I wandered into the Exhibit Room in the foyer and was drawn almost immediately to a booth where joyful, contemporary music was being played on a recording. I discovered the booth was that of the Church of the Redeemer in Houston, and that the Redeemer was a so-called charismatic church. I knew little about the charismatic movement and what I knew was not generally favorable, but I was impressed with the openness and cordiality of the people at the Redeemer booth. As it was approaching noon, the booth was about to close down because the rector and several laymen who were there said they were going back to the church for a noonday service. I asked if I might go along, and they invited me to accompany them from the convention headquarters to the church. Riding along with the rector and three young laymen, I was impressed by the rector's coolness and sense of quiet calm. I had expected a charismatic to wildly flail his arms in the air! Here was a man who was obviously stable and quiet. On arriving at the church, the parish secretary met the rector in the hall and asked his forgiveness for being angry with him that morning. He met the sexton a few yards further down the hall. The rector and the sexton embraced

---

Rev. Raymond W. Davis was born in Prince William County, Virginia. His theological training was at Philadelphia Divinity School, where he received a Bachelor of Divinity degree. He also studied at St. Augustine's College in England. In 1962 the Philadelphia Divinity School granted him an honorary Doctor of Divinity.

Rev. Davis was ordained into the Episcopal Church in 1943 and has served in the Cathedral of St. Luke in Portland, Maine, at St. Peter's Parish in Morristown, New Jersey, and also as a chaplain in the United States Army. In 1948 he became rector of Truro Episcopal Church, Fairfax, Virginia. Rev. Davis is active in diocesan affairs and is a leader in the charismatic movement.

each other. This was a great revelation to me—that a staff of Christian people could work together in such obvious harmony and Christian love!

The noonday service was a celebration of the Holy Communion, using the new liturgy. The celebrant wore eucharistic vestments. The service was held in the crypt chapel and about forty people were there. As the service proceeded, I was aware of the intense corporateness and the total involvement of everyone present. But two things impressed me even more powerfully: the first was the obvious joy with which everyone present worshiped, and the other was the love which these Christians had for each other. I had never experienced such joy and love in a service before! I remembered that love and joy are the first two "fruits of the Spirit." Obviously, the Holy Spirit was present in a special way in this service, and in this manifestation of love and joy I was experiencing a foretaste of the Kingdom of Heaven.

After the service, a small group of people remained in the chapel to pray for a young Puerto Rican priest to receive the baptism of the Holy Spirit. As the rector laid his hands on the head of this young priest, he started a few syllables in tongues. This was the first time I had heard speaking in tongues, although I was fifty-one years old. It did not frighten me as I had expected it would. It sounded like a few sentences in an Arabic language. It was musical; it was melodic and pleasant to hear.

I returned to the General Convention after the service, and a friend I had met at the convention immediately after my return still remembers the glow of enthusiasm which I brought back with me.

A month later, in November of 1970, the Reverend Derek Prince (a former Anglican layman, now an independent evangelist and teacher) was scheduled to speak for a week at Truro Church. I had invited him for a series of meetings, even though I had never met him, because I was impressed with what I had heard about him and felt that he would have something to contribute to my parish. Derek Prince was a graduate of Eton, and was a student and later a fellow in philosophy in King's College, Cambridge, England, where he was awarded the coveted honor of King's Scholar. During World War II, at a Pentecostal church in Scarborough in the north of England, he was converted from a sterile and routine form of Anglicanism to a living faith in Christ. Since then, he has brought to a ministry of teaching and preaching the clarity of expression and scholarship of his brilliant, academic background, combined with a thorough grasp of the Scriptures and the freedom and power which come from an encounter with the living Christ.

I had not expected that Derek Prince would have anything to say which would apply to me personally, beyond the general helpfulness which might come from listening to some interesting sermons about subjects which might appeal to a number of people. I had not expected that he would influence either me or my people on a deep level. I certainly never intended to enter in the charismatic experience myself, although I had been deeply intrigued by what I had seen in Houston at the Church of the Redeemer.

I had expected that Derek Prince would give his addresses each morning to perhaps twenty-five people who would politely and respectfully pay attention to what he had to say, realizing that his point of view might be somewhat different from their own experience, but being sufficiently open to hear politely what he might say.

On the first morning of the week's mission, when I returned from an appointment in Washington to the service which Dr. Prince was already conducting, I was surprised to find that the parking lot was completely filled and that the chapel where he was speaking was filled to overflowing so that it was necessary for me to sit on the steps leading up to the gallery. On Tuesday, the service had to be transferred from the chapel (which seats 175 people) to the Church (which seats 500 people). As the week proceeded, Dr. Prince challenged me to receive the baptism of the Holy Spirit. I felt that it was not for me, but that I would be polite and willing to discuss it with him. I certainly had no intention of ever speaking in tongues! He set an appointment to talk with me and to pray for me for the baptism in the Holy Spirit on Wednesday. Unexpectedly, he had to cancel this appointment. This gave me a great sigh of relief! We set up another appointment for Thursday, and again this appointment had to be cancelled because of an urgent request for Dr. Prince's ministry from someone else. Again, I breathed a sigh of relief that it would be possible for me to get through the whole week without having this embarrassing confrontation!

On the Friday of the week, another appointment was made for noon just after the conclusion of the 10 o'clock service. Just before I was to meet with Dr. Prince, one of my parishioners—a young woman—went forward to have an interview with him about a personal problem. She knew nothing about the baptism in the Holy Spirit and was not prepared to receive it. Instead of counseling with her at great length, he prayed for her that God's loving, healing power would come to her. She was a young, intelligent, energetic woman who had given a great deal of time to community and political activities. Before my very eyes, I saw a complete transformation take place after a few minutes of prayer! Her face and whole body took on a completely new quality of peace and power after months of strain and anxiety. I respected her sincerity and integrity and knew that this was something that was not false or temporary.

Minutes later, Dr. Prince and his wife and another layman prayed for me in the sacristy and in a few minutes, to my surprise, I spoke in a new language which sounded strangely similar to some of the Eastern Mediterranean languages I have heard. There was no surge of emotion or feeling. It was not a deeply emotional experience for me.

Later that afternoon, I faced a parish crisis and I discovered that I went through it with an unusual degree of calm and tranquility. Within a few days, people began to notice a decided difference in my ministry and conduct of parish affairs.

Two weeks later, after my baptism in the Holy Spirit, I preached at a daughter church, called the Church of the Apostles, which had been formed in 1968 with a nucleus of Truro parishioners. Since they had not been exposed to my ministry for two years, they were in a position to see me more objectively; at once they noted a marked difference—of which I was still unaware.

For twenty-two years, I had been rector of a rapidly growing parish in a community where the population, though transient, was growing rapidly. My parish had grown from slightly over one hundred communicants to something over two thousand. In order to keep pace with growing demands, I had worked hard and had always been under a good bit of strain and tension. Now this tension seemed to be replaced with a new power and confidence. My ministry was characterized by a new note of relaxation and freedom. I had always kept the rubrics and canons of the church faithfully and had been a stickler for a quiet but correct ceremonial; now my ministry was characterized by a new freedom and spontaneity in prayer and worship. After the baptism of the Holy Spirit, I found it easier to relate to people either as individuals or in groups in a more loving, accepting, and helpful manner. Many burdens, which I had carried myself, were now entrusted to the Lord, and I had a sense that I was a channel for God's mighty working rather than the origin and source of his work.

I believe that a decisive act of God occurred on Friday, November 13, 1970, in the sacristy of Truro Church and that the power of God has flowed through me in a new and special way ever since then. I believe the power of God has flowed into the life of Truro Church in a new and special way since that event. In the fall of 1973, one of our senior vestrymen testified to the vestry that, although he was not a member of the charismatic movement, he felt it had brought new life to Truro Church.

In my experience, all sorts of people receive the baptism in the Holy Spirit, just as all sorts of people receive the sacrament of baptism in water. I do not believe there is anything in their personality or style of life which helps or hinders the reception of this gift. I have seen both young and old, conservative and liberal, weak and strong, happy and unhappy people receive the baptism in the Holy

Spirit. Those who have received the baptism in the Holy Spirit at Truro Church have for the most part been strong, effective people in their home life and their work and have enjoyed positions of trust and confidence in the community. A large number are stable, conservative establishment types who could be classified as ordinary Episcopalians and have suddenly found new life and power in their Christian vocation. Nevertheless, looking back after three and a half years in the charismatic movement here at Truro Church, I would say that the Holy Spirit has fallen in a new way on all types and kinds of parishioners. The movement began with some of our strongest parish leaders, but it has spread to the rank and file. I have no way of knowing exactly how many people in my parish have gone through the charismatic experience. I am constantly discovering people who have had this experience for several years who had not previously told me about it, so I would presume that there are many more people who might be called charismatics in the parish than I know. Among those charismatics who are known to me, I would say that a desire for greater meaning in life and a deeper sense of spiritual reality were stronger motivating forces than the desire for renewal after some crisis in life.

After the mission under Dr. Prince in November 1970, we started to celebrate Holy Communion on Sunday evening. Before my baptism in the Holy Spirit I had planned to add an ordinary Sunday evening service to our schedule, but after this event I decided that it should be a freer service with emphasis upon a study of the charismatic gifts. A small handful of people assembled week by week, and within a few months another half-dozen leading members of Truro Church had been baptized in the Holy Spirit.

In February of 1971, the Reverend Graham Pulkingham and Bill Farra came to visit Truro Church from the Church of the Redeemer in Houston for a week's mission. Many members of the parish welcomed their clear emphasis on the parish as the living body of Christ in which the gifts of the Spirit operate in order to carry on Christ's ministry to the world and their emphasis on love as the essential characteristic of this ministering body. Many younger couples in the parish were baptized in the Holy Spirit in the course of that week. The enthusiasm and the love which they demonstrated soon made a positive contribution to the life of the parish. Some parishioners met regularly for fellowship and prayer and formed a firm nucleus of committed Christians who sought to grow in the things of the Spirit. Many of them were people of influence in the community and the church, and the effect of their spiritual renewal was far-reaching in the community.

During the mission under Graham Pulkingham, a large number of the communicants of our daughter church, the Church of the Apostles, also came into the baptism in the Holy Spirit, and since that date the two congregations have shared many services and activities together so that we have become again almost one congregation.

In the spring of 1971 and again in the fall of 1971, we had missions under Derek Prince and a number of charismatic leaders, all of which brought fresh teaching and inspiration.

The Truro Church embraces both those who have gone through the charismatic experience and those who have not had this experience. I minister to all of my people in the same way. I do not distinguish in my mind between those who have the charismatic gifts and those who may not have them. I do not consciously seek to bring those who are not charismatic into the charismatic movement. I am opposed to movements and I am only very reluctantly a part of the charismatic movement. My ways are the ways of the Episcopal Church and I minister to all of my parishioners within the framework of the doctrine, discipline, and worship of the Episcopal Church. I do not want Truro Church to become unusual or peculiar in any way, and I do not want it to be a parish which departs from the traditions of the Episcopal Church. I desire for all my people the fullness of the love and power of God and I realize that for some people this may come through the baptism in the Holy Spirit while for others it may come through the normal sacramental means of grace. I hope and pray that all of the people of Truro Church will become alive unto God in Christ and be filled with the Holy Spirit. I pray that those whose gifts of the Spirit are dormant may have these gifts awakened. Generally, but not always, this awakening comes through a new infilling of the Holy Spirit. I believe that the charismatic renewal as it affects the lives of Christians in all denominations and churches does bring an awakening of dormant gifts of the Spirit, and therefore I am part of that renewal. Yet I believe that the Holy Spirit is creative in many ways, and I do not seek to bring everyone in the parish into a stereotyped experience.

Some people objected strenuously to the charismatic movement and left Truro Church, though it is difficult to determine how many. At almost the same time that the charismatic movement came to Truro Church, a new Episcopal Church was opened a few miles from Truro and a number of people living in the neighborhood of that church transferred to it. Since the departures came at the time of the opening of the new church, it is difficult to say precisely who left because of the new church and who left because of the charismatic movement. Also, at about this time we began to use the new trial liturgies, and since it was reported that we used them more frequently and freely at Truro than in some of our neighboring parishes, it is reasonable to assume that a number of parishioners left because they felt unfamiliar with the new liturgy. I talked with a number of people about their relationship to the parish. In every case, my contacts with them were pleasant and constructive. I would have preferred to have kept all of the people in Truro Church, but I recognize that this was impossible.

A number of those who transferred out in 1971 or '72 have since returned in 1973 and '74. During the time of transition, fifty to a hundred people went to other parishes for a variety of reasons, including the charismatic movement. I had no harsh disagreements with any person. It was simply understood that for the time being those leaving would probably be able to worship better and serve God better in another church. I was impressed with the peaceful, orderly way in which this all took place. I believe it helped enormously that the charismatic renewal was out in the open and that nothing was done secretly. I would counsel any clergyman who enters the charismatic movement to do everything he does openly and with a loving concern for all of his parishioners.

During the three and one-half years that the movement has been a part of Truro Church, no serious difficulties have arisen. The financial support of the parish has steadily increased to a budget of over $200,000. Volunteers are easier to obtain; there is a better spirit of cooperation and a higher degree of order and discipline in the parish. There is far less negativism and criticism, and the worship services have been greatly enriched and renewed.

One of the evidences of the moving of the Spirit in the parish is the desire for Bible reading and prayer. Our parish has a number of neighborhood Bible-study groups, and we hope in the future to have a cell group given to prayer and Bible-study in every neighborhood in the parish. A number of Bible classes meet regularly each week in the parish hall, and the adult education program on Sunday has taken on a new impetus.

The Holy Spirit has raised up a lay ministry at Truro Church which has exceeded my fondest expectation! The mission committee, with the endorsement of the vestry, has initiated a program of *Lay Shepherds*, in which a lay member of the parish, after training and consultation, takes on the responsibility for shepherding a group of twenty families in his neighborhood. Each shepherd is responsible for visiting in the homes of his or her group of twenty families. He is responsible to see that the resources of the Christian community are brought to bear on any person in his charge who is in need or has an emergency. He seeks to develop a Christian community within his neighborhood and in general exercises some of the shepherding responsibilities traditionally assigned to the clergy. The shepherds meet at least monthly for common counsel and training. We now have three full-time clergymen on the staff, but we see our role as persons who are to enable the whole body to release its powers of ministry in healing, teaching, evangelizing, prophesying, shepherding, administering, or other ways. This is being achieved.

Since the charismatic renewal began here at Truro Church in 1970, we have been steadily but quietly trying a series of liturgical experiments, and we have found that the freer liturgies provide greater opportunity to exercise the gifts of the Spirit. The new "third" trial order for the celebration of the eucharist has, with the approval of the bishop, been used almost invariably at the Sunday evening service. It provides a framework for both sacramental worship and the free exercise of the gifts of the Spirit. I have felt that one of my chief vocations is to combine the free charismatic gifts of the Spirit with the sacramental life of the Anglican tradition.

At Truro Church we believe that the established, institutional church needs the gifts and insights of the charismatic movement. Without the full blessing of the Holy Spirit, an institutional church in our day may become dead and formal, with little living faith and little energy for good works. We have also found that the charismatic renewal needs the institutional church. There is a tendency in the charismatic movements outside the institutional church to acquire all sorts of distortions because of extreme individualism. It can lead to distortions of truth and to all the other mistakes and abuses which come when people are not closely bound together in an orderly way of life. The charismatic renewal is probably at its best in the Roman Catholic Church today because it has been purified and made stable by being part of the ordered, corporate life of the church.

I have had no case of discipline or abuse to deal with here at Truro Church. Our charismatic people have been content to stay within the accustomed ways of the Episcopal Church. But in my dealings with charismatics outside of the institutional church I have seen instances of a misplaced emphasis on demonology which would not really come to grips with the full reality of evil, but which would tend to place responsibility for much that was weak in character on demonic forces. I have seen charismatics who were not deeply committed to any church or Christian fellowship but who move from place to place claiming only to have a commitment to the Lord and his guidance. I have known of people whose lives were not lived according to the accepted Christian moral code and who justified this by a claim to direct illumination from the Holy Spirit. Some of the charismatic literature sold in book stores and used by various prayer groups and study groups is merely the old heresy of Gnosticism served in a new form.

However, during the three years I have been in the charismatic renewal, I have seen the movement mature. I believe that this will continue if the movement remains close to the institutional church and profits from the discipline and corporate strength of the historic Christian bodies.

We at Truro Church feel that we have a contribution to make in keeping the charismatic and sacramental together in one household. We see the great church of the future as one which will have the strength of corporate solidarity, in which every member is committed to every other member in love. We see a church which respects the traditions of the past and yet which is ever renewing itself with those fresh gifts of the Spirit which break and purify the molds of the past. We believe that the Holy Spirit is the creator spirit and that within the organized institution of the church he can create new forms of worship, new patterns of ministry, and new ways of living together, and that he is doing this here with us today.

There is no reason in principle why the gifts of tongue-speaking, interpretation of tongues, prophecy, and healing should not be exercised in an orderly way in the ordinary worship of the church and combined with the sacramental and liturgical ministry. At Truro Church these gifts are generally exercised in the course of a Sunday evening service. Eventually, I believe, they may be exercised lovingly and helpfully in the course of our ordinary Sunday worship. However, the important thing about the charismatic renewal is not the exercise of miraculous or spectacular gifts; it is the transformation of character and the building of a Christian life in love and harmony. The true evidence of the power of the Holy Spirit is seen in renewed people, renewed relationships, and renewed churches and institutions. These are more miraculous than any of the more spectacular gifts!

I would counsel any clergyman or member of an institutional church who enters into the charismatic renewal to stay very close to his parish church and not to stray from his denominational background. The organized church certainly needs the fire which comes from the full gifts of the Holy Spirit. On the other hand, any person who is fresh and new in the charismatic renewal also needs the wisdom and corporate strength of the historic church of the ages. To stray from the historic church may lead those who have entered into this new experience into a state of spiritual sterility more frustrating than the deadness of the institutional church. The charismatic movement, too, has its ritual, its dogma, its cultus, and often these are less satisfactory in the long run than those provided by the institutional church.

Above all, it is essential for any person who comes into the charismatic experience to be a part of a loving, Christian community. A person who has been baptized in the Spirit, as the Apostles after Pentecost, needs to be a part of a community which is of one heart and one soul and in which every member is totally committed to the other members, as they all are to the Lord himself. It is only by this commitment to the body of Christ that any Spirit-baptized Christian will find the stability and sustenance he needs. The challenge to the institutional church is to provide such a body into which those who are newly baptized in the Spirit may find a place of acceptance and support for the exercise of their gifts.

10 *A STORY OF DIVISION*

FRANK BENSON

The pastoral nominating committee was a lively mixture of people each very proper looking and as nervous as the prospective pastor. It was the quiet gray-haired lady who dropped the bombshell that caused hasty throat-clearing: "Do you believe in the second baptism?" The fires of Washington, D.C., had raged around this church, but a few months afterwards the primary concern of this committee was not the social upheaval and uncertain temperament of the community but rather the spiritual fires that had scorched some in the congregation and by which several members had been deeply hurt.

When I came to the pulpit it was with the knowledge that there had been a theological disruption the seriousness of which was not easy to gauge. There seemed to be a tendency to eschew mention of it throughout the judiciaries of the denomination. No doubt this was the result of a feeling that a difficult situation had not been well-handled but now, thank goodness, was past. However, the leadership of the congregation had rededicated itself to witness within an indefinitely described parish locality. The community in which the church is set was then rapidly changing in racial content. The full impact of this change took the next three years to manifest itself, during which time the congregation became more black and the community whites became less attached to the church. Now the congregation is about 50 percent black and, nearly six years later, is of diverse theological and practical traditions. The newer members are primarily of Baptist background, though some are from other Protestant or even from Roman Catholic heritages. It should be noted that the neighborhood has not become a ghetto. New white families still move in and associate with this church. The social-racial complexities of the church's situation make an assessment of the

Rev. Frank Benson is pastor of Garden Memorial Presbyterian Church in Washington, D. C. He was born in Scotland and received his M.A. and B.D. degrees at Edinburgh. Rev. Benson attended Union Theological Seminary in New York, where he received an S.T.M. in 1961. Before coming to Garden Memorial Presbyterian Church, he was pastor of Mt. Olivet Community Church in Brooklyn, New York. He has a particular interest in the community outreach of the church's ministry and in pastoral counseling.

theological history of the church a difficult undertaking. One cannot always be certain what motives have prompted what actions. For example, if a white family leaves the fellowship, the reason you find for their action may depend on your color, or on your estimation of their faith, rather than on the actual facts of the matter—which one must assume are hidden in the mysteries of God. During its charismatic period, however, the congregation was, except for two families, all white. Thus we can exclude the racial factor as an element in the developments being treated here.

What I now write is based to a large degree on memories of the members of the congregation who still remain and are willing to discuss the past. Some I have not approached, on the presumption that to do so would hurt them, especially in a situation in which a misunderstanding not only of the charismatic experience but of the basic Gospel message has left them vulnerable. Several excellent sources of information—including my dear gray-haired lady—have moved to warmer climates, and time prevents a detailed correspondence with them. If at times this chapter seems vague, attribute it to the wish of those who are still in the situation not to have old battle wounds reopened. I hope I have not unjustly represented anyone.

How did the normal, though mildly conservative, Garden Memorial Presbyterian Church, a strong church with some community involvement and related to local clergy associations, begin to change direction midway through the pastorate of my predecessor? The change was gradual but progressively hardened. Apparently no one specific event gave birth to this change. No external pressure suddenly assailed the congregation. There is, in the collective memory of the members, no recollection of a sudden revelation of the Spirit; no recounting of a wave of religious zeal from a revival experience.

The events of the late fifties, when the congregation was at its strongest, indicate that the politicians and church people of our generation—as in our Lord's day—do not always read the signs of the times with blessed clarity. Yet the faith and commitment of church people frequently, all things being equal, can enable them to get away with such errors. An extensive building program undertaken in the early sixties provided the church with a beautiful education building and a large mortgage. Only ten years prior to this a new sanctuary had been built on the old location. A mortgage of nearly two hundred thousand dollars was assumed by the congregation. Some would stagger at such a responsibility, but this undertaking was backed by a commitment in faith and a belief in the future growth of the congregation. With a firm conservative and biblical background, the building program went ahead. Within the preaching ministry and through the work of the boards and special committees, a strong emphasis was placed on tithing. A tithe, or 10 percent of one's income, is the Old Testament guideline which we follow today. The congregation responded generously, with the result that all areas of the church's finances were well supported. This included its missionary giving. Those who were not able to give so liberally still gave a proportion of their income.

During the years of construction, when the normal activities associated with an active church were continued, the preaching of the Word and the centrality of the Bible were emphasized—an emphasis which is still maintained. However, a second element appeared wherein the preacher went beyond the conservative philosophy of the congregation. Every word of the Bible was presented as accurate; it was affirmed that there is no error of any description to be found in the Bible. The Bible, our "unique and authoritative witness to Jesus Christ," was reduced to a book of infallible words. This neat little understanding is pregnant with a host of problems, which can cause severe distress. Sunday school pupils, who develop some sophistication, can become adept at finding contradictions in the Bible, real or apparent. The unwary teacher who responds by resorting to his authority is in danger of stifling that young soul's development. He opens himself to the trap of setting himself up as the infallible interpreter of the infallible words. When adults feel they are getting this treatment and develop the impression that if they don't accept what is being preached or taught, then they are not really believers, they go home upset. At a later stage they get angry. Yet it is true to say that some people want their faith given to them so that it will not have to cause them any thought. They are content to eat and forget.

In the beginning stage of the charismatic period, the ruling board, which in a Presbyterian church consists of elected laymen as well as the pastor, began to feel uneasy. Normally, Presbyterian elders talk a great deal to their pastor and usually get their point across. In the course of events a real sharing of ideas develops. But in this case it seemed that communication was now less open and that disagreements were being discouraged. At the same time, activities of the church were being affected. Those which were not expressly biblical were being curtailed. I am referring here to social rather than strictly ecclesiastical activities.

Serving a meal to a church family was accepted as fellowship and thus as a spiritual experience, but serving a meal to a service organization was questioned and ultimately disallowed. This, of course, ignored the element of fellowship which develops among the workers and is of lasting value in their lives. It would appear that, as the new emphasis became more prevalent, the church was becoming less community conscious and less inclined to engage in relationships with social organizations. While a church may be tempted into becoming too commercial, it can also become sanctimonious. In this situation such "gifts" as cooking and serving are suspect while praying and healing are not; but are not the former also gifts of the same Spirit?

I have selected one of several programs which were affected. While this one was actually peripheral to the church program, it illustrates a constricting rather than an expanding approach—an approach which confused people as to the merit of their past labors, which for them had truly been labors of love.

Our Lord healed the sick, as did his disciples. To my knowledge there has not been a time when what we term *faith-healing* has not been practiced. We pray regularly for the healing of our brethren, and fervently for the healing of the nations. When pastors visit the sick in hospitals, in other institutions, and in their homes, that is an integral part of faith-healing. The body and soul and mental-emotional part of man all need healing. Dedicated ministers of the church, in conjunction with other professionals, such as doctors and psychiatrists, spend a considerable part of their time in this ministry. When the pastor at Garden Memorial Church, following either a predetermined timetable or some personal guidance, decided to institute a healing service at an hour apart from the regular worship hour, the officers and congregation received the proposal graciously and participated in the services to a limited degree. The healing service clearly marked a break from the more normal practice of a pastor visiting with and praying for the sick, and an entry into charismatic faith-healing.

Faith-healing is based on three general conditions—first a sincere belief in Christ Jesus, then a confession of sin, and finally a proclamation of forgiveness by the officiating clergyman. The acceptance of that forgiveness by the participants must be sincere. In this new state of grace the participants pray for the healing of one of their members who may or may not be present with them. If the member is present, the laying on of hands and anointing with oil may accompany the healing prayers.

Following this outline, the healing service at Garden Memorial attracted some members of the congregation and increasingly more from outside the church membership. The newer people who associated with the faith-healing group were not really incorporated into the whole, being viewed by the older membership as "different." This factor is usually present in faith-healing situations and played its part in disquieting members at Garden Memorial Church.

When a number of people have gathered expecting to be healed, invariably a number of them will be healed. Of course, some will leave the meeting aware of no change in their condition. Those who are healed praise the Lord and go home rejoicing; those who are not healed patiently persist and begin asking why the healing is denied them. When one member of a family is healed and another is not—and never is—the sick person is left with the impression that he has been denied healing because of his sin or because his faith is weak. That person's estimate of his own worth is greatly reduced. When several others of the congregation who are among his friends also have that impression, the damage to him cannot be measured. Even if that person wishes to claim that the healing service is a fake he is still denied any comfort. People who actually claim to be healed leave no doubt of their conviction. One way or another he must resolve this dilemma.

Faith-healing does not depend solely on the faith of the sick person; in fact the person healed may be a nonbeliever. The faith of the others, those leading and participating in the service, is of prime importance. You may recall the account of Jesus' healing the paralytic who was brought to him. The four friends, despairing of an audience, finally resorted to lowering him through the roof. When the impression of healing as depending on the strength of one's faith or the value of one's Christian commitment developed, it began to set up demarcation lines. Why this impression became prevalent and why its influence was not countered are interesting questions. No understanding of this has been found, and no reason located for its guilt-producing effects. Then, also, there are weak souls who endeavor to show their faith in drastic measures. They may fast inordinately or eschew medical advice. When these endeavors have negative results the effect is not lost on the congregation. Some see this as evidence of error or deception while others become more convinced it betrays a lack of true faith.

It is extremely hard to see a young woman in her early twenties crippled by polio and now confined to a wheel chair who believes that her paralysis continues because she lacks faith. To be convinced that God wills complete health but that lack of faith stands in the way can only result in an intolerable burden of guilt. At the same time, this belief distresses her friends within the congregation, especially when they have been given a similar interpretation. Yet it was her faith in Christ Jesus which sustained her throughout her long hospital stay and daily supported her as she worked to help maintain her household. Confined to a wheelchair, unable to bear children, capable of giving her mother a Christian burial without the false trappings so prevalent in our society, she lives showing her faith, quietly mastering her affliction.

Obviously a flaw in the interpretation of the work and person of the Holy Spirit was being manifested among the members. We recall that the disciples were not always able to heal; even Paul suffered from an infirmity which the Lord did not choose to remove. These instances within the original membership where healing was not effected forced the afflicted individuals to rethink their conception of the Christian faith. And the Lord guided them mercifully as they listened to this interpretation of the cause of their continued suffering. The charismatic movement at work in the church was now bringing misunderstandings and bitterness. This bitterness, however, was sublimated, most frequently being expressed in terms of non-agreement or noncomprehension.

I know a person in the church who suffers from a severe speech impediment. Because of the speech defect, it was less embarrassing and easier for him to be silent among people or to write his thoughts down. Among his own family and some associates, however, he would speak frequently. Once, after a faith-healing service, he was overheard conversing in a room somewhat apart from the area of activity. This was immediately attributed by a charismatic to the healing element of the service. Actually no change in his condition or habits had occurred. I would maintain that there is on the part of some an almost desperate desire to prove the efficacy of faith-healing which removes critical review of the circumstances. It certainly does little to quiet the dissonant feelings of the more sceptical.

Thus, at this stage of the account we have a congregation with many old-time members adopting an indifferent attitude to the healing services of the church family but nevertheless disquieted at the general direction of the church life. At the same time there are a number of members, mostly but not exclusively from the ranks of the newly added, convinced of their faith, rejoicing in refound health, who have become quite adamant in their beliefs. Their group has its antithesis in the members who are now feeling guilty and perplexed as a result of not having been healed or finding their theological beliefs and the sincerity of their faith brought into question. Add an additional factor closely related to a strict interpretation of the Bible, which in its vulgar form is open to abuse in practice and understanding. Previously we noted the liberality of the congregation but now see an unfortunate side development. Tithing, as has been explained, is giving 10 percent of one's income or a set proportion of it. For church members it should be an expression of joy and thanksgiving, seen as the least we, who by the blood of Christ are saved, can offer. When, however, this tithing is understood to be solicited with the promise, "Give and the Lord will bless you" or, "Give and the Lord will give you more in return," it develops into a testing of God. Apparently this was the meaning some of the congregation placed on the concept. It was undoubtedly aided by the testimonies of those who stood up and related how sudden windfalls, perhaps new business opportunities, had come as a result both of their pledging and the guidance of the Holy Spirit. Others, who had perhaps given more but saw no such blessings befall them, became disillusioned and gave up. In recounting this segment of the total phenomenon, one elder, a dear friend with whom I love to disagree, pronounced the sage truth that God has already blessed us, and has been doing it for years; we can never repay him, fully or partially. The tithe is but a token.

The charismatic movement is, in the public mind, regularly identified with "speaking in tongues." This is too limited an interpretation, giving too much honor to but one of the gifts of the Holy Spirit. Yet it is considered one of the evidences of being "born again," almost the badge of recognition. To a limited degree this manifestation occurred during the worship service, and with foreseeable reactions. It was felt that such an interruption of the Sunday morning worship hour detracted from the solemnity and sacredness of the service and had no redeeming educational or uplifting purpose. This speaking in tongues appeared to be limited to newcomers who were attracted by the reputation of the charismatic events taking place. This greatly distressed the established congregation and also opened up another source of confusion very similar to that already mentioned in connection with faith-healing.

In this situation we can visualize the reaction of sincere believers who earnestly desire this gift but discover it is withheld from them. But those who experience the phenomenon take it as a mark of salvation from which they derive great comfort. It has been my experience that this can lead to an attitude of severe exclusiveness best explained in the implied statement, "If you don't believe as I do you are not a Christian." A neighboring church undergoing a somewhat similar experience discovered itself being drawn into factions by this attitude. In our situation the reaction of the majority was one of critical scepticism. The events following the public manifestation of glossolalia in the worship service no doubt confirmed the majority in their attitude. A reconstruction of the situation and the rationale for that attitude would be somewhat along the following lines.

The session must have come to the conclusion that when the authoritative interpretation of the infallible Word is disrupted, when the worship is interrupted by tongues, when any disruptive event occurs, this must certainly not be the work of the Spirit but of the Devil, or at least of evil spirits. (In truth, I believe the devil has a copy of everything holy and sacred which he uses to his own advantage and man's distress.) Some, then, who speak in tongues are of Christ and his Spirit but others are of the Devil and his followers. In any event, speaking in tongues and the interpretation were now removed from the Sunday morning worship hour. This was accomplished by bringing pressure to bear on those who interrupted the service, but without formal action being taken. That this gift continued to be manifested I have no reason to doubt, but it was removed from the view of the main body of the congregation.

Basically the congregation, notwithstanding the fact that it had been increased by the addition of members favorable to the spiritual movement, proved itself strong enough to resist a Pentecostal-type worship service. Apparently they were willing enough to tolerate nontraditional services at other than the regular worship hour, but were determined to preserve that hour. The cleavage is here apparent, exhibiting a division in the church life amounting to practically a two-faceted ministry with two worshipping styles. Tolerance of the other group was shown by the traditionally Presbyterian camp up to a point, and that point was what took place in the Sunday worship hour. And here the first reversal of the charismatic movement in the church is clearly seen.

While I have spoken of groups, there is no evidence of any formalized grouping having taken place. Theology was dividing people, but the opportunity for establishing hard-core factions did not materialize. That individuals were feeling gravely estranged the following will show.

One of my revered professors used to contend that the Holy Spirit blows where he wills even on the councils and synods of churches. Presently the higher bodies of the church organization come in for a great deal of criticism, sometimes justifiable. During the late sixties the United Presbyterian Church adopted a new Confession of Faith which placed a certain emphasis on the Christian's social obligations while upholding the traditional standards of faith.

The confession, prior to its adoption by the national body, the General Assembly, was given to the congregations for study and review. Suggested amendments were solicited. The verbal infallibility of the Bible was not maintained in this document and other criticisms could and were made against it. Given the situation prevailing at the church, which contained elements of critical suspicion of the denomination and uncertainty as to the developing direction of the local congregation, we see the confession as an added source of conflict. Since the pastor opposed the confession's adoption as an official confession of the church, conflict with the denomination was now assured. As we have already noted, the congregation had withdrawn from social activities. Now this confession could conceivably be seen as laying the ground work for an attack.

At the same time some members now felt they were not hearing the Presbyterian faith being preached from the pulpit. Quietly several of these disturbed souls approached the officers of the Presbytery, no doubt in the hope of having the situation alleviated. It cannot be ascertained whether their complaints against the spiritual movement were ever formalized; certainly there is no local record of them in the church files. My definite impression is that no action was taken by the Presbytery and consequently that the Presbytery failed in its obligation to follow through on the complaint.

The situation briefly could be described as a confused congregation with a spiritual movement in its midst, wrestling halfheartedly with a new confession, disquieted and disgruntled with its worship life, uncertain of its own denomination's intentions. The adoption of the Confession of Faith of 1967 terminated that situation. Many of the members describe themselves as having been unexcited over the Confession of Faith, but with its adoption the pastorate was terminated at the request of the pastor, who felt he could not subscribe to such a confession.

Looking back, one can discern a quite pronounced division between those who adopted the new movement and perhaps even wished to see the church become independent of its parent denomination and those who felt alienated but convinced that eventually there would be a return to the more normative theology. No statistical evaluation would assist this review, for while several members left at the end of the pastorate and followed the pastor, the social situation also caused a loss of membership from migration from inner city to suburbs.

The congregation which remained found itself, after the scars healed, enriched by the experience. It was a dedicated fellowship seeking to carry on Christ's mission faithfully in its own location. Often the problem has been how to preach the word, as pastor and members, in a new day and in changed circumstances; how to preach openly to brethren across racial and social lines rather than in tongues; and how to emphasize that "God so loved the world. . . ." I think this is indeed speaking in tongues!

Enough cannot be said of the dedication of the congregation and of the individuals who continue to serve so faithfully. Not a few who wholeheartedly followed the spiritual movement also remained faithful to the church and continued in leadership and worker roles. In a new ministry which emphasized the church's responsibility to the community this was no easy transition. They stuck to their faith and their church, which now consists of an almost new congregation.

Immediately after the Washington fires of 1968, I became pastor of the church. As some of the members had prophesied, I had to watch the all-white groups in the church die and members leave for one of at least three reasons: the desire to follow my predecessor, or to take up residence at a distance from the church, or the old catch-all, racial prejudice. Yet we have been building in faith. It has been necessary to adopt new methods of evangelism and discard some perfectly good old methods which do not work for us. An active youth program and what started as a young-adults organization have continued throughout the new pastorate, although the former has undergone several transformations. A spirit of sacrificial giving enables the congregation, in conjunction with a local service organization, to run an emergency food bank and to remain a self-supported inner-city church. A healthy deafness to militants and reactionaries, both black and white, within the church bureaucracy and without, has been a blessing. But above all the faith that in Christ we are one has been the real bulwark of the congregation. This has not become a social-action church but one which has as its first concern love of Christ and then love of fellow man. The congregation now has begun to grow again and continues in faith along a road far from easy . . . as the Spirit guides and harmonizes the believers.

The person, the work, and the gift of the Holy Spirit have not been negated nor in any way denied. Individuals are free to interpret this influence as they will. However the whole ministry is based on the centrality, the divinity, and the sufficiency of Christ Jesus alone.

Bibliography

Agrimson, J. Elmo, ed. *Gifts of the Spirit and the Body of Christ: Perspectives on the Charismatic Movement.* Minneapolis: Augsburg, 1974.

Bartleman, Frank. *What Really Happened at Azusa Street?* ed. John Walker. Los Angeles: Voice Christian Publications, 1962.

Bennett, Dennis J. *Nine O'Clock in the Morning.* Plainfield, N. J.: Logos, 1970.

Bittlinger, Arnold and Kilian McDonnell. *Baptism in the Holy Spirit as an Ecumenical Problem.* Notre Dame, Ind.: Charismatic Renewal Services, Inc., 1972.

Bittlinger, Arnold. *Gifts and Graces: A Commentary on I Corinthians 12-14.* Grand Rapids, Mich.: Eerdmans, 1967.

Bloch-Hoell, Nils. *The Pentecostal Movement.* London: Allen and Unwin, 1964.

Bruner, Frederick D. *A Theology of the Holy Spirit.* Grand Rapids, Mich.: Eerdmans, 1970.

Christenson, Laurence. *Speaking in Tongues.* Minneapolis: Bethany Fellowship, 1968.

Clark, Elmer T. *The Small Sects in America.* Nashville: Abingdon Press, 1949.

Clark, Stephen. *Baptized in the Spirit.* Pecos, N. M.: Dove Publications, 1970.

Cutten, George Barton. *Speaking with Tongues: Historically and Psychologically Considered.* New Haven, Conn.: Yale University Press, 1927.

Dunn, James D.G. *Baptism in the Holy Spirit.* Naperville, Ill.: Allenson, 1970.

du Plessis, David J. *The Spirit Bade Me Go.* Plainfield, N. J.: Logos, International, 1972.

Frank, Jerome D. *Persuasion and Healing.* Baltimore: The Johns Hopkins Press, 1961.

Frazier, E. Franklin. *The Negro Church in America.* New York: Schocken Books, 1963.

Hoekema, Anthony A. *Holy Spirit Baptism.* Grand Rapids, Mich.: Eerdmans, 1972.

Hoekema, Anthony A. *What About Tongue-Speaking?* Grand Rapids, Mich.: Eerdmans, 1966.

Hollenweger, Walter J. "Black Pentecostal Concept: Interpretations and Variations," *Concept,* Special Issue, No. 30 (June, 1970).

Hollenweger, Walter J. *The Pentecostals.* Minneapolis: Augsburg, 1972.

Hilgard, E. *Hypnotic Susceptibility.* New York: Harcourt, Brace & World, 1965.

Jones, James W. *Filled With New Wine.* New York: Harper & Row, 1974.

Jorstad, Erling, ed. *The Holy Spirit in Today's Church.* Nashville: Abingdon Press, 1973.

Jorstad, Erling. *Bold in the Spirit: Lutheran Charismatic Renewal in America.* Minneapolis: Augsburg, July, 1974.

Kelsey, Morton T. *Tongue-Speaking: An Experiment in Spiritual Experience.* New York: Doubleday & Co., 1964.

Kildahl, John P. *The Psychology of Speaking in Tongues.* New York: Harper & Row, 1972.

195

La Barre, Weston. *They Shall Take Up Serpents: Psychology of the Southern Snake-Handling Cult*. Minneapolis: University of Minnesota Press, 1962.

Laffal, Julius. *Pathological and Normal Language*. New York: Atherton Press, 1965.

Logan, Rayford. *The Betrayal of the Negro: From Rutherford B. Hayes to Woodrow Wilson*. New York: Collier Books, 1965.

McDonnell, Kilian. *Catholic Pentecostalism: Problems in Evaluation*. Pecos, N. M.: Dove Publications, 1970.

Mead, Margaret. "Holy Ghost People," *American Anthropologist*, LXX (June, 1968).

Nichol, John T. *The Pentecostals*. Plainfield, N. J.: Logos, 1970.

O'Connor, Edward. *The Pentecostal Movement in the Catholic Church*. South Bend, Ind.: Ave Maria Press, 1971.

Office of the General Assembly. *The Work of the Holy Spirit*. Philadelphia: United Presbyterian Church U.S.A., 1970.

Patterson, Joseph, German R. Ross, and Julia M. Atkins, eds. *History and Formative Years of the Church of God in Christ with Excerpts from the Life and Works of Its Founder, Bishop C.H. Mason*. Memphis: Church of God in Christ Publishing House, 1969.

Piaget, Jean. *The Language and Thought of the Child*. New York: Meridian Books, 1955.

Ranaghan, Kevin and Dorothy. *Catholic Pentecostals*. New York: Paulist Press, 1969.

Samarin, W.J. *Tongues of Men and Angels: The Religious Language of Pentecostalism*. New York: Macmillan Company, 1972.

Sargant, William. *Battle for the Mind*. Garden City, N. Y.: Doubleday & Company, 1956.

Scheiner, Seth M. "The Negro Church and the Northern City, 1890-1930," *Seven on Black*, eds. William G. Shade and Roy C. Herrenkohl. Philadelphia: J.P. Lippincott Company, 1969.

Sherrill, John L. *They Speak with Other Tongues*. New York: Grune & Stratton, 1970.

Sullivan, H.S. *The Interpersonal Theory of Psychiatry*. New York: W.W. Norton, 1953.

Swete, H.B. *The Holy Spirit in the New Testament*. London: Macmillan & Company, 1909.

Swete, H.B. *The Holy Spirit in the Ancient Church*. London: Macmillan & Company, 1912.

Tellegen, Auke, James M. Butcher, Nathan L. and Louise B. Gerrard. "Personality Characteristics of a Serpent-Handling Religious Cult," *MMPI—Research Developments and Clinical Applications*, ed. James M. Butcher. New York: McGraw-Hill, 1969.

Watkins-Jones, H. *The Holy Spirit in the Medieval Church*. London: Macmillan & Co., 1922.

Wolburg, L. and J.P. Kildahl. *The Dynamics of Personality*. New York: Grune & Stratton, 1970.